I0518113

Praise for Michael Engelhard

Engelhard is a splendid writer and captures the beauty of the Arctic and his day-to-day experiences with penetrating and moving prose.

— NATIONAL OUTDOOR BOOK AWARDS FOUNDATION

This is Alaska as only someone who knows it deeply can give us—a deliciously readable encounter with the place beyond the myths.

— BATSHEBA DEMUTH, author of *The Floating Coast*

Engelhard's writing has the sort of calm authority that reminds me often of Barry Lopez.

— DAVID KNOWLES, publisher of *EARTHLINES*

Engelhard is a worthy guide across thresholds that can provoke profound, irrevocable change.

— *FOREWORD REVIEWS*

As an anthropologist, Engelhard is accustomed to training his eye on the motivations and excitations of those around him. — *BOOKLIST*

Engelhard's work is at its finest when he shares not only his own experiences, but also the rich histories present in the land and its occupants, as well as his concern for its future.

— LARA MESSERSMITH-GLAVIN, author of *Spirit Things*

Praise for *No Place Like Nome*

Murder, mayhem, mystery, and of course gold—it's all here, but as Engelhard shows, the real gold lies in Nome's people, the culture, and the land. *No Place Like Nome* is a gritty, gorgeous dive into the heart and history of a town with an indomitable spirit.

— Don Rearden, author of *The Raven's Gift*

Delightful, informative, and crafted with precision and flourish, Engelhard's book brings Nome and the Bering Strait to life for readers, allowing them to truly dwell there for the breadth of its pages.

— Michelle Theall, editor of *Alaska* magazine

No Place Like Nome evokes the unique palette that joins Beringia's ancient past to characters as diverse as Kivetoruk Moses, Roald Amundsen, Sally Carrighar, and Edward S. Curtis, all of whom inscribed these streets and landscapes into our imagination.

— Igor Krupnik, Arctic Studies Center, Smithsonian Institution

Engelhard leads the reader to explore Indigenous cultural practices, historic episodes, quirky personalities, and dramatic elements of the landscape, while always connecting to the present through his experiences and current events.

— Angela Linn, UA Museum of the North

No Place Like Nome is as swashbuckling as the characters whose trails crossed in this notorious Beringian town. Local lore, language, high drama—and of course gold— march through these pages in breathless progression. Nome is no normal place, and this book captures its storied essence. I loved it for its information and irreverent style.

— WILLIAM FITZHUGH, co-author of
Crossroads of Continents

This impressively panoramic view of Nome and the Bering Strait provides a deep exploration of the region. Engelhard's lively writing and fresh insights pop off the page.

— IAN C. HARTMAN, author of *Black Lives in Alaska*

Engelhard guides you into realms both rich and strange. You'll learn about a material you can wear that's eight times warmer than sheep wool. You'll hear about a woman naturalist who constantly craved the company of lemmings. You'll find out what music will heal your soul and what plant will heal your various physical wounds. *No Place Like Nome* itself will heal your desire for a good read.

— LAWRENCE MILLMAN, author of
The Last Speaker of Bear

Elegantly written, balanced, and alluring. Engelhard doesn't shy away from controversy or painful topics, but doesn't become mired in them either, choosing instead to focus on the unexpected.

— STEPHEN R. BOWN, author of *Island of the Blue Foxes*

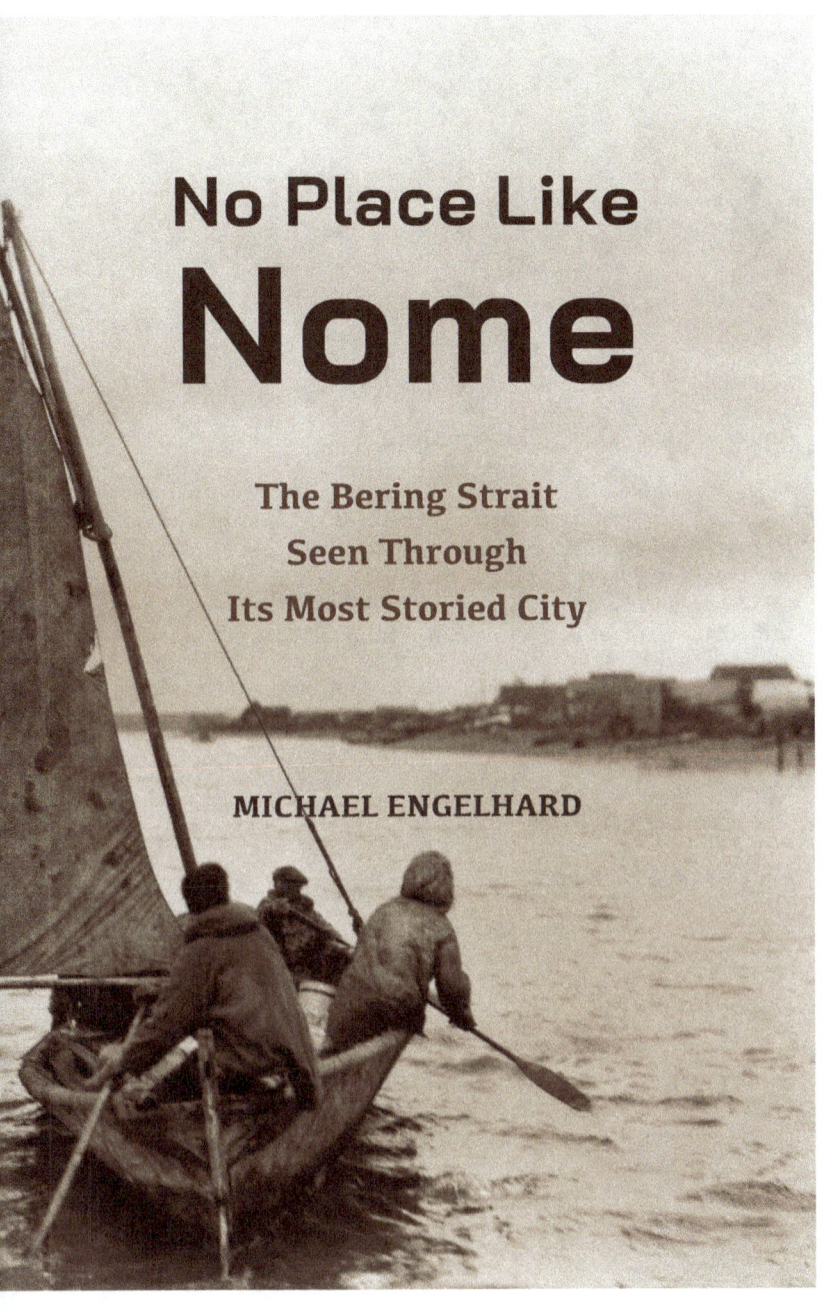

No Place Like
Nome

The Bering Strait
Seen Through
Its Most Storied City

MICHAEL ENGELHARD

CORAX
BOOKS

Published by Corax Books, September 2025.

Copyright © 2025 by Michael Engelhard

All rights reserved. No part of this publication may be reproduced, stored in a retrieval system or transmitted, in any form or by any means, electronic, mechanical, audio, photocopying, recording, or otherwise (except for copying permitted by Sections 107 and 108 of the US Copyright Law and except for book reviews for the public press), without the prior written permission of the publisher.

For permissions or review copies, contact: michaelengelhard.com

Printed in the United States of America

Editor: Doreen Martens
Design and Layout: Nadine Ludd

Author photo: Melissa Guy

Front cover: Carl Lomen (at left) in 1919, with one of his four brothers. Lomen Brothers / Alamy

Back cover: Bowhead whales near sea ice. Vicki Beaver, Alaska Fisheries Science Center, NOAA Fisheries

Library of Congress Control Number (LCCN): 2025900317
ISBN (paperback): 979-8-9899202-2-8
ISBN (e-book): 979-8-9899202-3-5

CONTENTS

Before it can ever be a repose for the senses, landscape is the work of the mind. Its scenery is built up as much from strata of memory as from layers of rock.

— SIMON SCHAMA, *Landscape and Memory*

It's no longer a river anymore in these days. So, it's just an old site—which becomes just a story.

— GIDEON KAHLOOK BARR SR., *Ublasaun*

In the north, the road does not generally belong to reverie. It belongs to industry… But the road in the north is anomalous, jerky. Small and thin. Vein-like, perhaps. Vital and inconsequential at once.

— CORINNA COOK, *Leavetakings*

To be able to see the spacious horizon in all directions is something that I well remember, and with nostalgia.

— JOSEPH ENGASONGWOK SENUNGETUK,
  Give or Take a Century

Author's Note: Deep-Time Horizons

"Finding out everything you can about the people whose land you live on and allying yourself with its rightful owners is vital," the radical thinker Derrick Jensen insists.

Nome, or "Anvil City," as it was initially named, was born when a century died, in the throes of two fevers that would alter lifeways. The physical sickness, measles, introduced by the miners, also, killed a quarter of the region's Inupiat.

Most histories of Nome start with the year 1898, as if a vacuum had existed there before. Admittedly, this results in part from a spottiness of the archaeological record for the span before first contact. But it owes more to the prevailing exclusion of Native points of view. As the former Nomeite and artist Joseph Senungetuk saw it, the era of non-indigenous occupancy in North America—and, extrapolated, the Johnny-come-latelies' knowledge of local oral traditions—equals "the first sixteen inches of a football field." By contrast, our ecological footprint on the land and our arrogance in managing it match the leftover ninety-nine yards plus change. Put differently: if the book in your hands were Alaska's whole human story, colonist history would amount to less than the Suggested Readings, roughly five-and-a-half pages. That is linear thinking, though, imposed through boarding schools and extractive industries, foreign to cyclical minds. Alaska changed hands recently—a paltry five generations ago—passed from one world power to another for cash. As in small, so in large, from an Amerindian perspective, anybody who came after 1492 or 1741 (when Georg Wilhelm Steller, under Captain–Commander Vitus Bering, set foot on Kayak Island), or who is descended from those who came and stayed, qualifies as an uninvited guest.

Two hundred Kaweramiut ("People of Kawerak") Inupiat had already claimed the sweep of hills, tundra, and beaches at the bottom edge of the peninsula shaped like an arrowhead aiming west, at Chukotka. Predating first contact with Russian explorers, families of the Thule culture in the sixteenth century had inhabited houses they half-sunk into the earth near present-day Nome's modest harbor. Proof of year-round residence comes in the form of spear points, harpoon heads, fishing gear, a pottery cup, halfmoon ulu knives, sled pieces, and an incised slender figurine, mixed with seal, whale, and caribou bones that this Snake River sandspit site yielded.

A row of thirteen limestone hollows riddles a bluff at the top of the Seward Peninsula at Trail Creek. Two of these contained more than 300 stone tools and charcoal, plus 25,000 bone shards, mostly of caribou, along with horse and bison, some 9,000 years old. DNA from the tooth of a toddler resting in one of those jagged squeezes marked her as an Ancient Beringian. Hers are the oldest human remains from the Arctic found to date. Putting data points to Senungetuk's metaphorical assertion, archaeologists think that these "bear-holes," in which two Inupiat from Deering who escaped a blizzard in 1928 found arrowheads, served hunters as short-term shelters, meat lockers, or caribou lookouts off-and-on from 10,000 years ago to 1760 CE. (According to a bush pilot, the two storm-hounded Native miners first tossed dynamite into the cave, flushing not one bear but three bears from it.)

Farther inland and to the east of the half-isle, a scatter of 267 obsidian and chert tools outlined an ancient campsite in the twenty-six pleated square miles of the Nogahabara Dunes. The archaeologists who studied Nogahabara's projectile points were impressed with the near-mint condition and craftsmanship of some; other points were broken or had been worked to various degrees. Several showed transport wear, signs that they had been "carried for a substantial distance." The grouping may have been a mobile band's toolkit knapped from a nearby source pinned down by chemical analysis. Perhaps hunters who briefly stopped to dress game, cook a meal, and repair weapons while bantering or swapping stories stashed this wealth of volcanic, scalpel-sharp black glass there for later retrieval. The same dunes host Baikal sedge and a gemlike tiger beetle, relics of similar antiquity from the Bering Land Bridge, seen almost nowhere else. This site, thought to have been active sometime between 10,740 and 11,850 years ago, sits smack-dab on the path migrants with Northeast-Asian roots would have taken as they plunged deeper into the unknown.

All this is my roundabout way of acknowledging, humbly, gratefully, that forever unsettled I live in the homelands of strangers—of Beringians and their rightful heirs—in Fairbanks now as I once did in Nome. Senungetuk, the first Inupiaq to author a full-length book, commented on the transience of transplants in a habitat other than their original one: "Although some have violated the warnings of the Ancient Ones, and have indeed ventured beyond the 'Tree Line,' sooner or later they return to their land and their homes." His is the slant of a tundra people wary of woods. Flipped on its head, viewed from a boreal angle, the statement rings true for me as for most Naluagmiut ("Bleached-Sealskin People") dwelling south of the matchstick forest's ragged fringe. Except that, having spent more than half of my life on this stolen continent, I no longer know where my homeland lies.

A linguistic note is in order here. While the colonial usage has rendered "Eskimo" offensive in Greenland and Canada and for some United States indigenous segments, Alaska's Inupiaq speakers, especially of the older generation, continue to embrace the term. Most do not identify as Inuit, and it still crops up in names of events and organizations like the Alaska Eskimo Whaling Commission and the World Eskimo–Indian Olympics as well as in federal statutes and offices. Fully aware of the word's baggage and context, I keep using it as a handy umbrella that covers diverse yet related groups where I can't or won't differentiate. Whenever possible, I've applied the proper ethnonym—the group's name for itself—just as I've sought to include autochthonous voices.

Within the Eskimo language family, "Yup'ik" refers to southwest Alaska's people between Norton Sound and Bristol Bay and on Nunivak Island, offshore the Yukon–Kuskokwim Delta; and "Yupik" to those on St. Lawrence Island and on the southern tip of the Chukotka Peninsula around Provideniya. Inupiaq can be heard in villages from Norton Sound's Unalakleet to Kaktovik on the Beaufort Sea coast near Canada's Yukon border.

Rachel Craig from Kotzebue drew attention to a grave, gnawing problem with ethnographic literature, pointing out that "white people have written a lot … but in their own understanding." I do not presume to speak for indigenous peoples (or women or Americans of any stripe for that matter), but merely about them. And I would like to apologize in advance for the audacity of hammering fine-grained, rich, four-dimensional lives into meagre paragraphs.

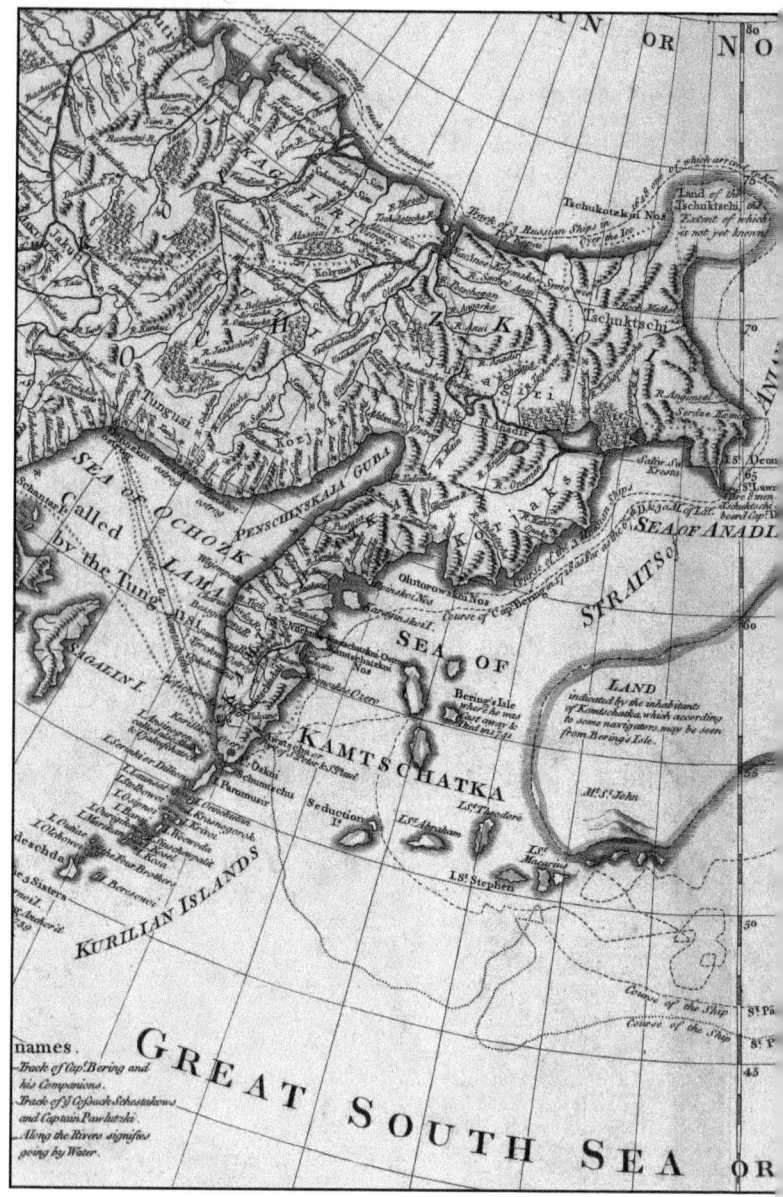

Map 1

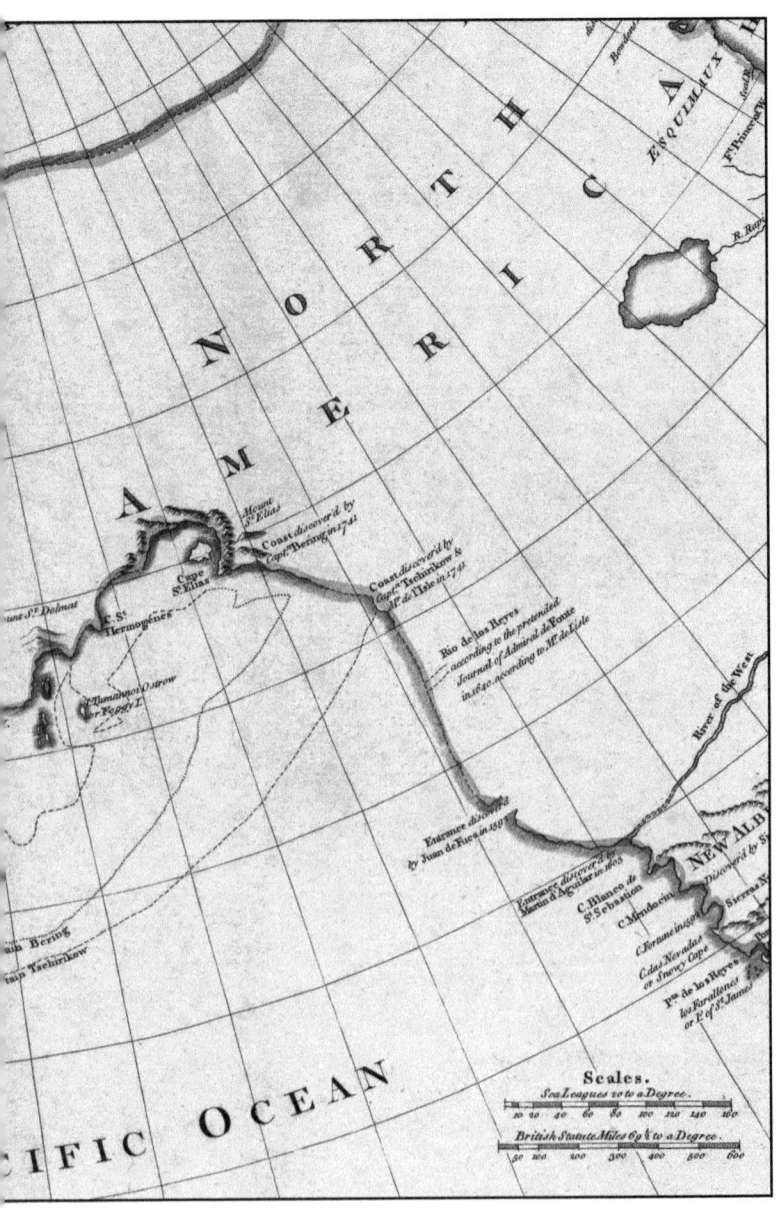

Russian Map of Siberia and Alaska, 1754

Map 2

Native View of the Bering Strait, 1860s to 1870s

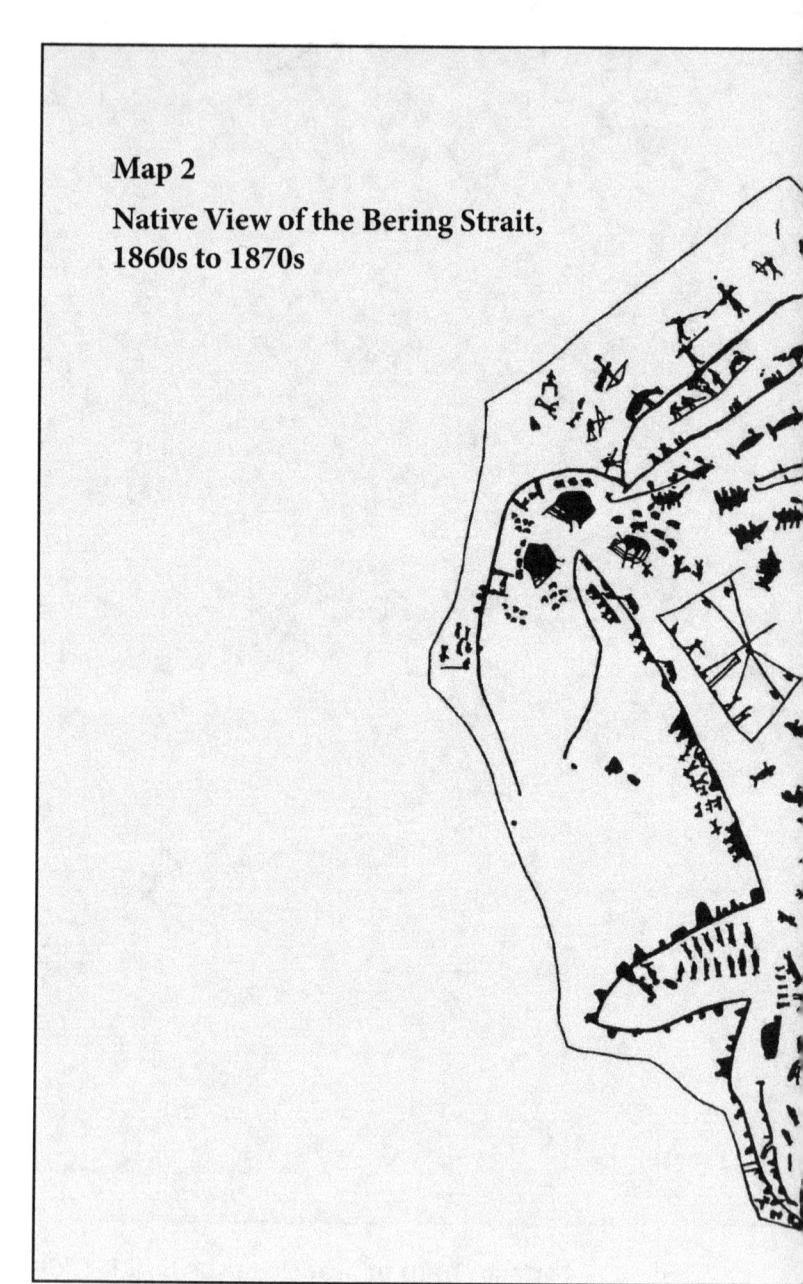

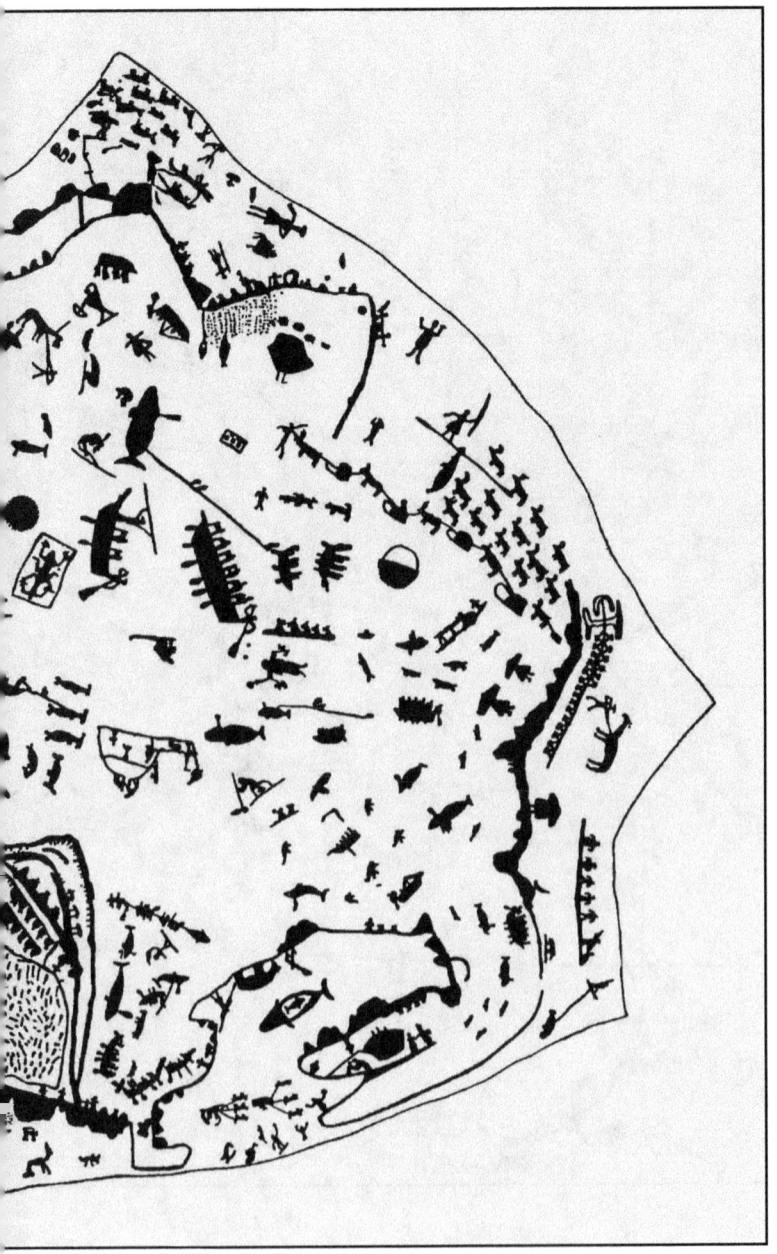

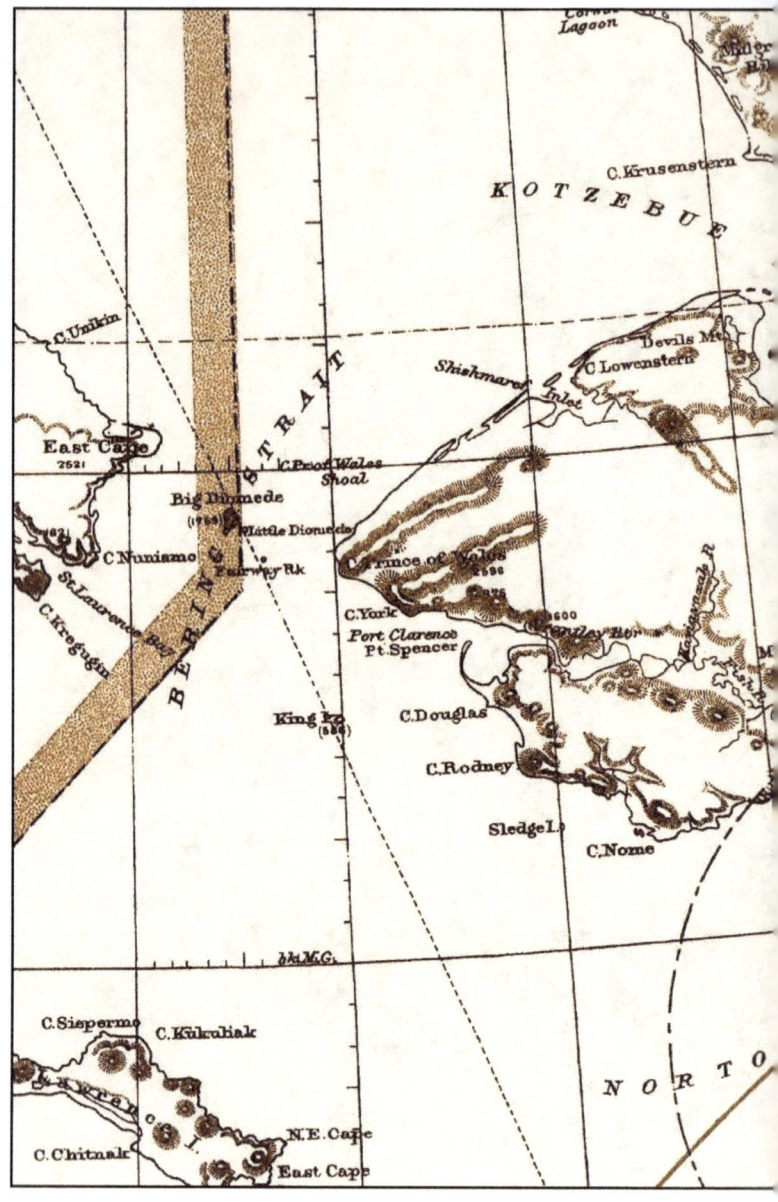

Map 3

US Map of the Seward Peninsula, 1898

Introduction:
Blustery Hub for Two Continents

Despite being a scant 125 years old, Nome is one of the most storied places I ever have had the pleasure of calling "home." Stories hide within stories there, nested like matryoshka dolls. These pages are but the tip of the iceberg. Imagine the shimmering, spinning, crystalline whole, the massive wedge partaking in disparate worlds. Few environments that are not wildlands have inspired me so as a writer, though the passing of years may have tinted memories sepia, as it tends to for people with a romantic streak. "Recollection is the only paradise from which we cannot be turned out," the failed prospector Rex Beach wrote in *The Iron Trail: An Alaskan Romance*.

In truth, Nome's contrasts at once can jar one and stimulate thought. There is racism, poverty, femicide, domestic and substance abuse. There is laughter, beauty, resilience, and vibrancy, too. The nature writer Sally Carrighar, who rented and then bought a miner's mansion at the East End of town (where the King Islanders settled after their relocation), noticed a "curiously long-lasting attraction" that to me seems independent of a person's length of residence in this city.

The fact that this is the first of my books with an urban nucleus should speak volumes. For any student of cultures and history, neither Anadyr on the Asian side, nor Kotzebue or Point Hope to the north, nor Unalakleet to the south can match the riches of Nome. A burgh with a recent population of under 4,000, Nome is marbled with toil, heartbreak, failure, folly, misalliance, misunderstanding, and accomplishment. Much of that stems from the extreme conditions under which life is and always has been lived there. Carrighar recoiled at "the world's worst weather," ten blizzards striking within six weeks, each chasing the tail of the previous one to the point where she felt they were contiguous. Six planes attempting to get through the "snow-blows" crash-landed, and an elder who slipped on an icy path near the town's center froze to death before he could be discovered. A storm in 1901 entombed houses so deep that owners trying to enter had to overnight in one of the saloons—I am sure many old yarns were unspooled and new ones spun there while waiting. Another Big One, in 1913, "ripped up the cemetery and swept away some coffins with bodies, scattering them over the plains in the vicinity." Beer barrels bobbed in the middle of Front Street like so many booze buoys; a piano washed up at the cape thirteen miles to the east; and *Karluk*, having weighed anchor in August for her swan-song voyage, groaned in an ice-vise, headed for the East Siberian Sea, where, under auroras like lucent breaths on the cosmic windowpane, almost half of her crew perished. The pack could squeeze hard enough to buckle iron plates reinforcing a ship's engine-room deck.

I myself got a taste of such mayhem. During my three-year stint in Nome, 2011's "blizzicane" spewed sea foam onto

Front Street and shook Icy View subdivision homes elevated above permafrost on the heights north of town, making the water in our toilet bowl hiccup. It drove thirty-foot waves inland in an 8.6-foot surge. After two days of that, you want to punch walls and scream or curl up in a sensory deprivation chamber. If an inclement climate builds character, as some people say, then Nome teems with gumptious sages.

That 2011 storm rivaled the howler of 1974, the strongest in Nome's annals, which overwhelmed the riprap sea wall of quarried stone with a thirteen-foot rise bearing driftwood, flooding low-lying areas. A contender had hit in September 1900, at the peak of the gold rush, unhousing 1,000 miners. Dislodging her anchor, it wrecked the mammoth barge *Skookum*, "staunchest of all the storm-tossed fleet," sending her on a "journey towards the beach and destruction"; 10,000 tons of coal, a winter's supply for the town, spilled from her broken holds. People stripped *Skookum* of wood for fuel instead. The launch *America*, trying to aid the stricken ship, went down with her captain and her engineer. Three *umiak* skin boats carrying more than 100 King Islanders shared that vessel's fate. Winds pushing shoreward could also heave ice into forty-foot tsunamis, thunderous ride-ups or pile-ups that crushed Inupiaq crews and dwellings.

With winter sea ice now forming later and going out sooner, an unruly ocean unlidded will wreak more serious havoc still in the years ahead. If you envision the Seward Peninsula as the nose of the irate-looking bearded-troll profile that western Alaska suggests, Nome lies where the nostrils would be. It's a farmer's blow away from sliding into the sea. Wind may do the job yet.

Wind decided at least three Iditarod Trail sled dog races, forcing some mushers to seek cover or bail. Others persevered, one in a ground blizzard so severe that he could not *see* the ground.

Winds of fortune for the explorers equally often were winds of ill fortune. They seized Vitus Bering's *St. Peter* near the south entrance to the strait named after him. "Our ship was like a piece of dead wood," First Officer Sven Waxell wrote. "We had to drift hither and thither at the whim of the wind and waves." By November, the scorbutic crew had surrendered, languishing in the tempests' furor. No one was left to steer *St. Peter* while "a day seldom passed without our having to throw the corpse of one of our men overboard." Winds west of present-day Wainwright barred Captain Cook's farthest-north probing at the other end, on his last voyage, just 400 miles north of Nome. It drove ice "compact as a Wall ... ten or twelve feet high at least" down upon HMS *Resolution,* which would have shoved her ashore. Low on provisions, Cook's sailors killed "sea horses, huddled, one over the other, like swine, and roaring and braying very loud, so that in the night or in foggy weather, they gave us notice of the vicinity of the ice before we could see it."

Leaning into gusts on a Nome hillside, when the air assumes a bodily presence, defies you to picture a calm. If the wind ever stopped, you'd do a face plant. It's a bossy reminder of forces beyond our control, a humbling that some folks welcome. A Lower Yukon Eskimo myth claims that in the primordial long ago, winds never stirred. They waited, corralled by the wall at "the edge of day, where the sky comes down to the earth," behind apertures shuttered with gut-skin covers. An animated boy doll thought "It is very quiet in here. I think a little wind will make it better." He released winds by loosening all the covers. When Doll cut the edges of the lid in the northwest, a blast laced with snow and ice rushed out—*pfffft*—and he almost froze to death.

Winds have been scouring the country ever since. Once, a headwind slightly less substantial than a river made it almost impossible for me to return from a Glacier Creek bicycle ride. (To boot, I had dislocated my shoulder again, slipping while descending on steep shale at my turnaround point.) Winds sculpting and texturing snow aided Eskimo wayfarers of old in their navigation, enabling them to keep rather than lose their bearings. The Inupiaq language has eight wind terms corresponding to compass directions, with winds from the ocean bearing different weather than winds from the land. Especially brusque western Alaska weather events in the early 1900s may have inspired a Yup'ik set of masks that embody the cardinal winds. One at the Heard Museum has a black-tube mouth. Being assailed in atmospheric tantrums can feel like entrapment inside a wind tunnel. The horses I've worked with grew spooked in windy conditions, and human bodies likewise ramp up the adrenalin for a flight or fight response when it blows. A gusty day in bear country, with noise-cancelling leaf rustling and alders and willows swaying, will set your teeth on edge.

But, hey, a timely whiffle keeps the mosquitoes at bay!

As already mentioned, Nome even boasts a whiteout raging at eye level. When the wind really got going, Joseph Senungetuk remembered, "the whole foot or so of blowing snow atop the [sea] ice, around the pressure ridges, would begin an eerie snake dance of white. During stronger winds, this layer would lift, to become five feet of blinding, crisp, fast-moving snow." You can see how this would mess with a person's wayfinding and state of mind. Spindrift on the bare mountain flanks in these parts fuses into slab fit for igloo walls. During the 1925 Serum Run that saved lives with diphtheria antitoxins—a grueling 674 miles from Nenana to Nome without breaking a single vial—wind chill shrunk the mercury column to the minus-eighty-five-degree mark.

Shortages still cripple the town when pack ice or a stray extratropical typhoon lock down freight and fuel barges. (The same means of transport conveys cars, construction materials, and machinery.) It's a dynamic environment, a place where storms taking bites one hundred feet deep breach or bury roads and reconfigure whole coastlines, where a chopper once whisked miners off a floe adrift and about to splinter into gigantic shards, a lethal jigsaw puzzle. In such circumstances, with midwinter days hanging on for a skinflint four hours, there is simply much time for storytelling driven by visiting, which, granted, was more common before the age of TV. Lastly: being cut off from Alaska's road system has spawned a touch of island mentality, and congruent anecdotes, in a state that itself could be considered remote. With 230 miles divided between three scenic gravel drives, Anglos who plant their spent Christmas trees on the sea ice for a "Nome National Forest" set out on one just because they pine for scraggly spruce in its natural niche, spaced like whiskers on a warthog's chin.

Nome in its heyday enticed misfits, dreamers, the colorful, fabulists. Its parade of gallants and rogues displayed derring-do worthy of Tombstone or Dawson. But Nome as much breeds as it draws a different sort of person. In 1911, a music teacher, exercising skills he had gained from piano repairs, cobbled together Alaska's first aircraft there, a 500-pound biplane with a thirty-two-foot wingspan and a propeller behind the pilot. It was a mobile of muslin and white spruce, a spindly, incomplete greenhouse on skids. *Tingmayuk* ("Small Bird") never took wing at the well-attended launch but instead scootched a few feet across the snow. A pioneer Photoshopper manipulating an image of "The Professor's" attempt blurred the horizon and tundra to achieve the illusion of flight. "If Peterson can't fly he can play the fiddle," *The Nome Nugget* defended the aviator-inventor.

Equally immune to some harsh realities, kids in swim trunks excitedly point out a sculpin limp on the beach, their lips purple, their teeth clacking like castanets. Others frisk in the swells, sleek seals reveling among bergy bits, or, daring the sea, ride BMX bikes through horse-mane surf. A fundamentalist Christian at the grocery store mistakes a least weasel for a rat; the same woman thinks "Earthquake!" when her bed rocks in the early morning hours, to learn that it's the handyman leveling the house, jacking up one corner; and a teen from a Pepto Bismol-colored house, with teal hair, a scoop, and a trash bag, will apologize for dog turds dropped in your front yard. Ever pragmatic Nomeites swap white golf balls for orange ones and tees with shot glasses or shotgun shells after laying out scraps of green carpet near each coffee-can hole at the Bering Sea Ice Classic. With their fairway now unreliable, they may well concoct an aquatic version. People buy a couch sight unseen here. The same people flock to *On the Ice*—the film with an Inupiaq in a lead role who later was sentenced for attempted murder involving a Kobuk River shooting spree and escape by inflatable raft—but if you were to remove the formerly segregated Nome Dream Theater's back wall, the seascape view would replicate that on the screen.

In the past, non-glamorously, Nome was "the jumping-off place" or "the outfitting point," a port of call for maritime expeditions and the trailhead of one livestock drive that equaled the Old West's in epic scope. Before regular air traffic bound Nomeites to the outside world, the first summer boat mooring offshore was the year's highlight. It was "in fact the beginning of the year," Edward S. Curtis's daughter Beth thought, who steamed in on one.

Despite its apparent seclusion, Nome remains a rivet joining hemispheres. This capital of Beringia, the largely vanished land mass almost the size of Alaska that comprised the mammoth steppe, sits on crossroads that hitch Asia to North America, Russia to the United States, the Bering Sea to the Chukchi Sea, the Pacific to the Arctic Ocean, and the Subarctic to the Arctic. Here, a Wild East met the terminal-stage Wild West for years after the historian Frederick Jackson Turner had declared the nation's frontier closed. In many ways, Nome typifies the nation's psyche in a boom-and-bust nutshell still.

"It is as if the two continents had been hacked apart at this point to create an unnatural division where nature had intended none," the historian William Hunt wrote apropos of the Bering Strait. A milder climate had been the axe blade, raising sea levels at the end of the Pleistocene.

With bowhead whales ploughing the strait and Siberian birds blasted off course, the region's connective character finds its grandest terrestrial faunal expression in the overlapping of ursine ranges, with Nome as the polar bear's southernmost haunt on the US mainland and grizzlies the home team there. The far-roaming, amphibious bears of the narrow sea—which spend more time on land nowadays, grounded by global heating—belong to a single (the Chukchi Sea) sub-population, as do its bowheads. Nomeites recall only two sightings of those white ghosts on plate-size paws for the past two decades, while out in the strait, around King Island, in winters with plenty of sea ice, they were rampant. One of the two visitors nosed through surf breaking on Nome's beach to inspect a miner's tent camp below a huge Stars and Stripes. This male was *not* a celebrant of the Midnight Sun Festival's annual Polar Bear Swim, though he had the girth of some. A Texas birder first spotted the other bear days before the summer solstice. Missing its ride on outgoing pack ice had stranded it. According to the birder, the bear "didn't look like he was in the right place" and "appeared to be confused." He gnawed on an orange-tipped wood post by the road and, finding it wanting, broke it before padding back to his marine-mammal environment. It's different in Wales, on the cape 109 miles to the north that snags floes at the passage's pinch point. There, despite school staff whapping the stalker with shovels, a starved polar bear mauled to death a young mother and her infant son leaving during a snowstorm.

With the bear's shifting hunting grounds seaming two fraying continents, Nome is the crucial stitch—and the sinew of her people the thread. Before the Cold War's "Ice Curtain" guillotined international dealings, King Island, St. Lawrence Island, and the Diomedes had been stepping stones. The fragment of a bronze buckle on a leather scrap from Cape Espenberg resembled horse-harness trappings wrought during the first six centuries BCE in north-central China, Marco Polo's "Cathay." Radiocarbon dates showed the leather to be 500 to 800 years old. Blue Venetian glass beads traveled on a Siberian spur of the Silk Road into the western Brooks Range, likely by way of an ancient trade fair in nearby Kotzebue Sound. How many hands must have cupped these tokens of pre-Columbian commerce on their 10,000-mile journey! How many miraculous rumors must have been swapped as these sky bits circulated over that distance! When *Resolution* popped up above Norton Sound's horizon in the late summer of 1778, a strange cloud or a tundra swan stretching its snowy wings, Cook noted that the Inupiat already had "no dislike of tobacco." It was held "in great repute," the Russian circumnavigator Otto von Kotzebue elaborated in 1816. "They chew, snuff, and smoke it, and even swallow the smoke." Kotzebue's expedition artist Louis Choris observed that they hesitated to part with their weapons, but disrobed to exchange clothes for tobacco, which was "what they liked best." Toddlers indulged in the habit, puffing and chewing like old tars. US Navy lieutenant George Stoney wrote that "It is customary for the mother to take her babe from the breast and put her pipe or quid of tobacco in its mouth." *Umiak* crews hoisting fox pelts on a pole while approaching schooners and brigs signaled their zest for trade.

Despite the pull of rare commodities and many sketches of Bering Strait Natives that the explorers left, accounts of first contact with white men are as rare as white reindeer. Inupiat underwhelmed by the newcomers' ships described "big old square ones." The world always had been larger than what met the eye and hitherto unknown phenomena been absorbed by an adaptive philosophy. What was a wool-clad paleface with a sour aura compared to a polar bear supine, wiggling eight legs, luring seal hunters to their deaths? Or compared to lice the size of lemmings, feasting on giants?

People in Golovnin Bay *smelled* their first ship before it anchored there—a reeking whaler perhaps? And an Inuk on the Kuzitrin River, checking his ptarmigan snares, saw strange footprints in the snow, and then, looking up, a man with eyes the color of blueberries a few weeks from ripe. That stranger gave him needles and a knife as gifts and in turn was warned off the lava beds, where he might fall into "bubble holes" and die.

The craving for foreign wares grew exponentially, regardless of the foreigners' charisma or lack thereof. A woman eyeing Captian Kotzebue's uniform buttons sent her two children to bite them off. More harmful whiskey and rum came with the whalers. Confederate sailors from the raider *Shenandoah*, boarding the New Bedford ship *Abigail* "lying in the ice" in the spring of 1865, seven weeks after the Civil War's official end, seized more than fifty barrels of liquor and plenty of wine and champagne, all meant for barter with Bering Strait Natives. In a mercantile trickle-down, *umiak* captains from both Alaska and Siberia purchased whiskey wholesale in casks and profited by refilling smaller quantities into flasks sewn from the intestines of bearded seals. Iron kettles, hatchets, and lances, brick tea, tobacco, and guns arrived via trade, as did Chukotka reindeer hides. Conversely, inhabitants of the American side ventured as far as Kolyma, the river delta on the Sea of Okhotsk, a future site of gulags. Walrus-skin boats, some of them two-masted, sixty feet long, propelled by sails, carried the merchandise.

If only objects could speak. The Penn Museum collection holds a cylindrical bamboo box collected in 1905 at Cape Prince of Wales. Stoppered at both ends with Alaskan wood and incised with Eskimo-style designs, it is "doubtless of Malayan origin, probably Philippine." (Bamboo fragments *do* ride the broad backs of currents into the Bering Sea and even up to Point Barrow on their own.) Another antique, the drill-bit tusk of a narwhal from Baffin Bay or the Beaufort Sea, sailed the opposite way aboard a whaler. The Samoan salt "who first came into possession of this horn of the unicorn of the sea and saw at once how well fitted it was to the exercise of his handicraft" carved it into a club "in his own country['s] fashion."

Coining the catchiest phrase for the Northwest Passage I've ever heard, a TV character in a series about Sir John Franklin's doomed voyage, referring to the British Admiralty secretary, called it Sir John Barrow's "chilly shortcut to China." With that island maze no longer so chilly but ice-free for large parts of the year, with cruise ships disgorging tourists, and Lower 48 miners sluicing her beaches, Nome and its satellites again feel the thrill of connectivity. A deepwater-port project worth

$663 million attests to the reborn geopolitical orientation. Since the Soviet Union's demise, exchanges across the strait have resumed. In 2013, traditional dancers from Chukotka competed against six Alaskan village teams in a three-day event at Qatŋut, a regionally famous Kotzebue trade fair. You could not see Russia from our house, not even from the Icy View one. But you *can* see Siberia from Cape Prince of Wales, the mainland Americas' westernmost point. For roughly half of the year, the station chief of the Tin City Air Force facility there enjoys vistas of mountain ranges backing Lavrentiya.

In short, except for World War II and the Cold War interlude—when Nome functioned as an alarm post, the nation's eyes and ears on its defensive perimeter—the narrows were never a barrier but rather a channel for goods and ideas. Mountain ranges divide while oceans connect, littoral dwellers in the age of sail realized. Joseph Strauss, the Chief Engineer of the Golden Gate Bridge, certainly thought so. In his undergraduate thesis, in 1892, he proposed a Bering Strait rail bridge, which the Russian government deemed too costly and dangerous. Unfazed, he designed 400 other spans. More recent Beringian connectors were planned as tunnels, but none materialized.

Equivalent to the mingling of peoples, the region was a "melting pot of sled dog breeds," since man's best friend heels wherever man goes. A 1940s archeological dig of Ipiutak (Thule) sites on a Point Hope gravel finger prodding the Chukchi Sea brought to light dog bones from several burials.

In one grave, a dog skeleton about 1,500 years old rested next to those of an adult human and infant. Scientists identified Point Hope canine remains as being related more closely to Siberian than to local Alaskan breeds.

Traffic freely flowed toward Nome from the east as well. The Danish explorer Knud Rasmussen stopped by on "The Great Sled Journey," the Fifth Thule Expedition—an 18,000-mile trip from Greenland to Siberia aimed at recording Inuit intellectual culture: legends and songs. Greenlandic kayak builders and filmmakers lately have given presentations in Nome. Their closeness to the Inupiat is that of one spread-out people who speak dozens of dialects of a shared tongue, whose ancestors, tracking the peregrinations of bowhead whales, settled harsh shores 4,000 miles apart within a few centuries when cathedrals in Europe were spiring skyward.

Nome street names and buildings that have weathered frequent fires and time's ravages emit echoes of a frontier legacy. After we moved downtown from Icy View, my wife, Melissa, and I lived on Lomen Avenue, a block to the west of the former Discovery Saloon, Nome's oldest surviving place of business. We married at the courthouse, under the black stare of a tusked walrus-skull wall mount, having rounded up a second witness at the post office, downstairs. He declined a free meal for that service, saying he only wanted to do us a civic favor. This was the same post office where, in a photo from 1905, a queue exclusively male had stretched from the entrance all the way across Front Street. The day of our witness hunt was the day before Germany snatched their fourth soccer World Cup from Argentina. I watched matches at a pizzeria with the motto "You buy, we fly" that delivered pies also to Bering Strait islands. A German film crew in town for a documentary about modern placer miners bought a round for the house when the full-time whistle blew. I almost tipped over in my chair as substitute Mario Götze chested down a Hail-Mary pass in extra time and drop-kicked the long longed-for winning goal. (My wife teases that I remember our anniversary date only because of that.)

The Discovery Saloon, with its false front, one of the few houses left from the gold rush, survived as a private residence. The pot-holed dirt road it faces commemorates a particularly ambitious dynasty, spores that the winds of opportunity blew into this capitalist petri dish, a family who became its wealthiest and had fingers in many a pie: shrewd hawkers of reindeer meat, Santa, and his sleigh. In 1903, Carl Lomen and his father, Judge Gudbrand J. Lomen of St. Paul, Minnesota, relocated to the Seward Peninsula's Sin City after a working vacation there. Many lawyers had tilled those legal fields, and for years: in 1900, 127 practiced in Nome. Carl's mother, four brothers, and one sister soon followed, lodging at the Discovery. Lomen senior had hoped to profit from settling claim-jumping disputes but ended up forging a multi-tentacled corporation.

In 1908, the brothers bought a photo studio on the ground floor of the Hotel Sheldon, as well as equipment and glass plate negatives from other photographers, the latter of which they sold under their name—an accepted custom in those days. Though Harry ran the studio, all of the brothers took photographs. Situated on Nome's main artery, Front Street, they promised "Kodak Finishing of the Better Kind." They quickly mastered the art, keeping fingers and cameras functional at sub-zero temperatures. Chasing elusive angles, brother Alfred, the most prolific of them, and a player in Nome's basketball team, once rowed to a ten-by-six ice platform and set up his tripod. Amazed passengers aboard S.S. *Victoria* snapped pictures of the picture-maker. Alfred also managed *The Nome Daily Gold Digger*, one of several local newspapers. A born promoter, Carl, employing Inupiaq seamstresses, outfitted Roald Amundsen with reindeer-skin mukluks and sleeping bags from their herding and meatpacking operation. The studio produced a signed portrait of the explorer that served as a model for the bronze bust that now greets tourists who saunter down Front Street.

Lomen creations helped to sell meat, along with the fiction that herding benefitted all Alaskans equally. In these photographs, young Inupiat straddle reindeer imported from Chukotka as a livelihood, and herds flood the tundra in a tide of furry backs. There are wolf-headed dancers, man-beasts sprung from a creation myth. There are broad faces haloed by fur ruffs, and a beauty whose cascade of raven hair capes her upper torso. Some photos featured bare-chested Siberian Yupik girls from across the sound and one a mother, nursing two infants. Both kinds of images, the indiscreetly exploitative and the idealized, fed an exoticism stoked by polar exploration, by East Coast "natural history" exhibits, and by expositions such as the 1904 St. Louis World's Fair. While these shots preserve ethnographic details, many are studio portraits of Inupiat in their Sunday-best traditional garb, staged in the style of Lomen's contemporary, the luminary and one-time Nome visitor Edward S. Curtis.

The September 1934 conflagration that razed most of the business district, despite houses being dynamited to prevent it from spreading, destroyed the studio and 25,000-30,000 negatives, which finished the enterprise. Many of the roughly 3,000 salvaged reside in the Library of Congress archives—the memory of the depicted, like their descendants, abides. So does the settlement facing seaward, a sprawl of dirt roads, dun sands, emptiness, tundra, and whistling winds, a coastal Eldorado its Inupiaq founders named Sitnasuak. No paved vias or aqueducts spoke from Nome into the enfolding hills. Still, in this neck of no woods, all paths or wakes—be they straight or meandering—before long lead to it.

A reader on Amazon panned one of my books as "embellished rambling." I cannot think of a better summary of the wandering, pondering essayist's work, this "variegated vagabondizing," to borrow from Mark Twain. The essays here assembled shine a light on select facets of Nome's past and present, while others have been excluded. This in no way reflects their importance in local lore or the larger context but merely my preferences. I felt, for instance, that with much already written about the *Karluk* crew's thirty-six-month ordeal or about Ada Blackjack and the "Canuck occupation of Wrangel Island" (officially, the Canadian Arctic Expedition) I had no new angle on those topics. Ditto for the Iditarod, which has lost a bit of luster anyway: its sponsors are corporate or backing out over allegations of animal cruelty; the race start this year has been moved to Fairbanks, north for the fourth time, since Southcentral Alaska snow is in short supply again; and most Nome mushers no longer exercise teams on its trail for fear of getting hit by a snowmachine. So, here, you'll find Bobo the street brawler, and Katmai the goggled pack husky, not Balto the Serum Run's star, "scrub dog" to snobbish critics. You will look in vain for the four-time race winner Susan Butcher or the former opera singer Emily Riedel, in her skivvies, diving into the drink for *Bering Sea Gold*. Get acquainted instead with Frances Ella Fitz, a mushing Manhattanite who struck it rich before she opened the first Arizona dude ranch, The Garden of Allah.

"When does the past become the past?" John Banville asks in his memoir *Time Pieces*. "How much time must elapse before what merely happened begins to give off the mysterious, numinous glow that is the mark of true pastness?" For me, the zone in which that glow dims—at least in regard to this region and for no reason I can discern—is the fallout of World War II, the repercussive era preceding my birth. "If I've lived through it, it cannot be history," I wrongly think, milestones like the *Apollo 11* Moon landing or the Berlin Wall's dismantling notwithstanding. The distant past offsets the novelist Lydia Millet's "familiar flatness of the present," the "pale repetition of our days." Banville, though speaking of his youth, hints at a possible explanation: "The present is where we live, while the past is where we dream." Never mind that the glorified years in the rearview mirror, too, held plenty of ennui and drudgery.

I am offering much material of less than earthshaking significance simply to fill in the colors of the personal, the idiosyncratic, or the purely eccentric that too rarely enliven anthropological and historical reconstructions. Those details, for someone who has known Nome intimately if fleetingly, from the vantage of muskoxen on its bare-shoulder ridges to the Board of Trade Saloon's twilight innards, tell a story of this home by the sea that heroic headlines and academic tracts fail to tell.

It is as vital to link the past with the present. The two are not sovereign countries; we have one foot in each. History first and foremost is storytelling, as the two nouns' shared root shows. In Emerson's phrasing, "All history becomes subjective ... there is properly no history, only biography." The fable of the elephant and the blind men gets it wrong. A bigger understanding *does* hide in the sum of smaller ones. Only by comparing and synthesizing individual experiences can we hope to grasp the humongous, intangible whole in a way that enriches our own years. Perhaps it's a preoccupation of late middle age, this passion for bygone things—warts and all—for personal names and for narratives, rising from a need to see how my existence braids into currents at large, how to value, as the writer Jack Loeffler put it, "our brief link with Eternity." Can we hold micro and macro perspectives at once, yet another historian mused, "to connect the rivulets of everyday human experience with the grand flow of history?"

Ethnology and the field of history likewise are twins. One examines the mores of contemporaries, the other those of precursors. Ethnohistory is where both disciplines meet. Embracing its goals, I have sought to achieve in one handy collection, for this city and region and as nonfiction, what William T. Vollmann did in his Seven Dreams series of novels about culture contact in North America.

Unlike another foil, Bathsheba Demuth's luminous *The Floating Coast*, which traced the energy flow into and out of the strait tied to various enterprises, this book favors a prismatic, eclectic, microcosmic, anecdotal approach. I am interested more in the sparks unique agents emit as they brush against their surroundings, be those surroundings social or natural. This mirrors my belief that individuals mold human societies as much as political and economic systems and environmental factors do. For me, deeds and lives played out in the orbit of a singular settlement most bewitchingly illustrate patterns. Let this be my time-warp spyglass, then, to Demuth's radio-telescope.

I. THE PLACE

NOME, ALASKA, 1900.

City of Dreams

The odds are good that a visitor to Nome—landed as a cruise ship passenger or spectator of the Iditarod finish—will pause before an antique roulette wheel enshrined at the Carrie M. McClain Memorial Museum. A label below the hairline-cracked, painted disc says it came from George Louis "Tex" Rickard's saloon, the Northern, once located just up the street.

Celebrities from Wyatt Earp to Jack London, pulp fiction writer Rex Beach, and President Herbert Hoover supposedly touched this relic of boomtown entrepreneurship. That has been hard to prove. A son of the couple who gave it to the museum remembers playing with it as a child in his parents' attic. How it got there from the Northern and how it got to the Northern remain mysteries.

Rickard had befriended Jack London during the Klondike gold rush and opened the first Northern, in Dawson. A gambler to the hilt, he lost his share in it. Conceivably, the roulette wheel then traveled with Rickard from Dawson to Nome. He convinced his pal Wyatt, who briefly managed a canteen in Saint Michael, at the Yukon River mouth, to help him in mining Nome's miners. The starry-eyed visitor imagines the town's rowdier, glory days. "For there's never a law of God or man/Runs north of Fifty-Three." Jack London used Rudyard Kipling's lines as an epigraph to a tale set in the city where no tree could be found for a lynching.

Nome, incorporated in 1901, during the summer of 1900 swelled into the territory's largest settlement and the world's busiest seaport without a harbor. About 15,000 gold hunters alighted in June, weary of the Klondike, Seattle, or San Francisco. More left Adelaide, Australia, on the steamer *Inca* two years later. Droves of mariners jumped ship to join the fray.

Nordmän woefully late for the Klondike in 1898 had unleashed all this wanton craving: the Swedish tailor Erik Lindblom leapfrogged north as a deckhand on a whaler; Jafet Lindeberg from Norway wrangled free passage pretending to be an expert reindeer herder; only John Byrnteson, the third of these "Three Lucky Swedes," had wrested a living from the ground professionally, mining iron and coal.

A battleship-gray plug of marble and schist perched up high like a busted Atlantic Wall bunker lent the settlement its initial name: Anvil City. Flecked with lichen, it crowns a summit above the creek where the trio of diggers struck paydirt. Anvil Creek's entire bed had been worked over at least once within a year. A mapmaker's scribbled *Cape (Name?)*, misread, may have morphed into the headland and town's current designation.

From the perspective of arrivals anchored in Norton Sound, the foreshore's low ridges lay littered with icebergs.

Camps sprawled across thirty miles of coastline, from Cape Rodney to Cape Nome. Up close, those dissolved into a canvas-tent warren. The scene resembled a page from one of those *I Spy* busy-picture books, with the search object being sanity. Men piggybacked women to shore, queens vastly outnumbered in the Anglo anthill. Mountains of freight clogged the beach, a gray-sand strip sixty feet wide: grain, hay, general merchandise, sewing machines, mining equipment, and provisions ... . Luxuries heaped up amid driftwood: pianos, fancy mirrors, casks of bourbon and brandy, and eggs, selling for fifteen dollars a case—this where stevedores slaved for $1.50 an hour. Nome's only milk cow kicked the bucket in the following spring. But what did it matter, if $1,200 to $3,000 could be washed from a single pan? One foresightful miner arrived with two valises, one filled with fresh fruit and the other with vegetables. When he paid his boatman with an onion, that fellow ate it like an apple. The editors of the St. Michael *Aurora Borealis* gazette, equally pressed by the times, defaulted to barter, offering "Ten subscriptions for one porter-house steak."

Longshoremen simply dumped freight next to the sea's wrack line. Humanity and its artifacts choked the beach to such a degree that a New York typist-stenographer with her spaniel in tow saw "one man pay another ten dollars simply to move his small boat a little nearer to the water. So the other would have room to pitch his tent." This Frances Ella "Fizzy" Fitz later owned a log cabin in nearby Council, where the labor shortage forced her to excavate a cold-storage cellar for it with naught but a dustpan, a trowel, and a tin spoon.

Absent natural shelter or sanitation, mayhem reigned, with tarps flapping and dog packs marauding between fly-buzzed offal and broken boxes. The city eventually commissioned waterfront water-closets on pilings the tides flushed.

Greenhorns broiled in the sun or, shivering under blankets, hugged hostile ground. "A veritable Egyptian plague" of mosquitoes descended. Some "beach rats," not eating regularly, knocked up huts with packing crates or slept in boats flipped onto their sides. A team of huskies hauled a wheeled water cask, as if powering Bacchus's chariot. Typhoid got a Newcastle-upon-Tyne coal miner in his beach abode. He left behind a watch, knife, compass, and rifle as his sole possessions. The chief of police pulled a letter from the miner's pocket. Phema, a sweetheart in England, had begged her man not to go to Alaska but to come home.

Rome wasn't built in a day, but Nome almost was. Lumber had to be freighted in, as the driftwood was of poor quality. An embalmer and undertaker announced his hope to put up a morgue as soon as supplies arrived. The Yukon River steamboat *City of Chicago* became a hotel and beer garden, and *Quickstep*, reached via gangplank, a restaurant and hotel. "Jackass machinery" comprised all manner of dredges and pumps, and windmills "in charge of modern Don Quixotes." A *Wild, Wild West* Steampunk forerunner, designed to ease into the shallows on barrel wheels to gouge the seafloor, was so heavy it never moved. An even grander harebrained scheme was to build a casino—theater, saloon, hotel and dance pavilions—on the ice a marine-league from shore, to evade gambling laws. The town teemed with lawyers and laborers, horse-tending hostlers and quacks, card sharks and clerks, madams, storekeepers, laundresses, land speculators and dance hall girls. Nome sprawled "all length and no breadth," two blocks wide and five miles long. Boardwalks covered Steadman Avenue only. Front Street, a dust bowl in the summer, here and there bottlenecked to fifteen feet. A "slough of despond" in the fall, it swallowed wagons up to their axles and mules to their bellies. Traversing the two-foot-deep mud, one wag joked, "the pedestrian was at times uncertain whether he would arrive at his destination or suddenly find himself in China." For another fortune-seeker, town "really was part of the beach." Mobs roiled. Foghorns moaned. Saws ripped, combers and hammers thumped. Mongrels snarled over scraps. Men haggled and argued and fought. Mules bawled in their traces. At night, from crude dance halls, "the scraping of a fiddle rose above the noisy clattering of heavy boots that sounded like a chariot race in an empty garret." Nome struck newcomers as "a perfect Babel of noise."

The veteran prospector E.C. Trelawney-Ansell thought cheaper, easier access to Nome—merely stepping out of a lighter ten days after boarding a steamer in Seattle—lured more shifty-eyed schemers than had the arduous Klondike:

Nome was different, it was a place where the creeks and the town itself filled with thousands of cheechakos who had never known the hardship of the trail and few if any other hardships. Worse still, the camp and surrounding country was filled with gamblers, cutthroats and murderers of the worst kind.

Nearly all the promising claims had been jumped at least twice by July 1899, and multiple claimants contested others. The Three Swedes were accused of being aliens and thus having staked the best grounds illegally. Two actually were naturalized citizens.

In November, a headless body washed ashore. A Cape York recorder suffered when his cabin and books burned; the fact that one miner had secured over 140 claims there could have been a clue. A Cripple River recorder refused to surrender his books, holed up in a house converted into "an arsenal." He swore the re-election ousting him had been rigged, that more ballots had been counted than persons present in the room, and that some lived outside the district or had not lived at Cripple thirty days—the more things change, the more they stay the same. In December, a man was killed on his sled, with his two partners, guns and provisions missing mysteriously, since they shared three prospect pits and a fine house, a tower made mainly of sod. A missionary noted seven funerals in ten days, all violent deaths: four murders and three suicides.

Petty criminals prospered as well. Joseph Carroll, a fleet

mail carrier and expert trailsman, absconded with three dogs and the wrong sled. He'd been in a bad frame of mind for a day or two, it was said. Thieves wheelbarrowed coal away, and, from a permafrost cache, snagged twenty sacks of flour and seventeen dressed chickens saved for Thanksgiving and Christmas.

Firewood got so scarce during the first winter that bear-proof Inupiaq burial platforms high up on poles were pilfered. Brazen burglars slashed tent sides, pumping in chloroform to rob marks the moment those fainted. Other assailants sandbagged their victims, knocking them out with a pouch full of beach. In later years, two Nome men were shanghaied as crew by "a band of fierce walrus hunters, taken from their beds and forced to drink drugs which made resistance on their part useless."

Rex Beach, having encountered Nome's blaggards, fictionalized some in *The Spoilers*. (It saw five screen adaptations. The wartime one starred John Wayne and Marlene Dietrich, with a cameo by Robert Service, playing himself.) "Yellow Kid," operating a gold scale, smoothing his hair often, harvesting ounces of "trading dust" after each shift from his head brilliantined with syrup, perhaps was invented. But real weighmen grew long fingernails to snag a share, which they secretly wiped on a damp sponge below the counter. Unlike those fleecers, Nellie Humphrey, an Australian who had made a fortune as a milliner "gowning Dawson's belles," became a trusted weigher of gold for the prospectors in Nome. She carried a

.44-caliber Colt in her belt, "to stop any monkey business." Beach's real-life foils included an embezzling postmaster, a tax assessor nabbed for shady financial deals, and a crook federal judge. "Proper encouragement" protection monies changed hands where bar owners ruled the city council. Drinks pushed across the wood in some establishments were "spread out a little," watered down. "Town dust" gold used in ordinary exchanges could be laced with sand, or brass or iron filings. For the poet Thomas Hood, gold—honest or false, driving all—was "Heavy to get, and light to hold; Stolen, borrowed, squandered, doled."

And squander they did. Saloons in which gamblers "bucked the tiger" mushroomed seemingly overnight, forty-two by one count, more than sixty by another, among them Earp's Dexter, Rickard's Northern, Charles Cobbs's Horseshoe, William Robertson's Eldorado, and, one of Nome's finest, The Only Second Class Saloon in Alaska, as a sign proclaimed. In its first iteration after the 1905 fire, "The Old Reliable" Second Class looked like a showbox constructed from planks. Dick Dawson had owned it with partners—plush Brussels carpets, electric lights, Eastern Beer Only, the extravagance of a sewer, and all. Dawson felt that every saloon-man but him bragged about running a first-class establishment; hence the tongue-in-cheek advertising of his.

The Nome Gold Digger, one of four local papers, covered epic gaming sprees, noting that keno caught on at the Hunter "like an epidemic of the measles" or that an Eldorado craps session run haywire forced the dealer to upend his cash drawer on the table to prove the bank had really been busted.

The clink of coin wasn't always so crass. The first baby born amidst it, to an ex-whaler and a sister of the reindeer herder Sinrock Mary in the Eskimo camp on the Snake River spit, was christened Nome, and the proud father reserved a claim for him. A fox-robe fundraising raffle, a free Thanksgiving meal at the Northern, a club supporting Scandinavians, miners' grassroots meetings, the odd Congregational service, and Literary Society debates and recitals sounded social grace notes. A Christmas tree that "the thirteen white children at Nome enjoyed had to be brought by dog team a hundred miles. It was decorated with walrus ivory toys and with others made of driftwood and the furs found in the country."

Mail, if sporadic, was a lifeline to the larger world. "Those of us who had reached that bleak, exposed north-western coast and wintered there did not get any mail for six months," remembered Samuel Hall Young, the "Mushing Parson" and friend of John Muir. He penned this "fifteen hundred miles from a post-office."

Frontier mailmen were a hardy breed, "men with the bark on," like the cowhands that Frederick Remington idolized. Eli Smith on a wager in 1905 mushed from Nome to Washington D.C. to lobby for Alaska railroads and roads and dined at the White House with Teddy Roosevelt. A Klondike wolf Smith had rescued as a pup ran with the team. The 8,000-mile roundtrip was accomplished partly by ship and wheeled sled, with the wolf's nose finding the way during storms.

Another stout carrier, the "Flying Dutchman," Carl von Knobelsdorff, en route to San Francisco, dropped off mail for miners still stuck in Dawson or Skagway. The previous fall, he'd skated on dulled whipsaw blades hundreds of miles between Kobuk River camps, delivering newspapers and letters for one dollar each. Rumors and gossip he carried for free. One of his stops was Reilly Wreck, where the steamer *John Reilly* had struck a gravel bar and lay stranded for the winter. Miners not quite living "the life of Reilly" perished from "black leg" (scurvy) or "bloody flux" (dysentery) and overwork, drowned—becoming "floaters"—or went missing. The bearded Germanic Hermes, dressed in knee-high, checkered socks, wool cap, sweater and mitts, a pack with sleeping roll on his back, pistol and hunting knife on his belt, swung a metal-tipped pole for propulsion and balance and to probe weakness in the ice. His fellow stampeder Joseph Grinnell, an ornithologist who'd met John Muir on a cruise and would help establish Yosemite National Park, called the sailing mailman a "rustler" with "more grit than all the rest of the men on the Kowak [Kobuk]." After giving some lectures in San Francisco, Knobelsdorff, poling with his staff, glided off into the white noise of history.

This newest migration, word of which Knobelsdorff had helped spread, swamped the "Poor Man's Diggings," because on the public beaches no man—or woman—had to stake or register claims. No ground had to be thawed out, either. "Besides the rich ruby [garnet] sand," the news trumpeted, "there is coarse gold, it may be in large amounts." Latecomers marveled at damsels in flowerpot bonnets and ankle-length skirts over petticoat layers feeding surf rockers and "Long Tom" sluices with shovels of muck and pails of water dipped straight from the incoming waves. "For many miles along the beach double ranks of men were rocking, almost shoulder to shoulder ... passing jokes or singing as they worked," a US Department of Labor agent reported.

Together with hopes soon to be mangled for many, Klondikers brought their lingo from "John Bull's territory," a code tinged by earthy gallows humor that flummoxed cheechako neophytes. Coffee was "belly-wash" for rinsing down "Alaska strawberries" or "whistleberries" (beans), "salt horse" (bacon), and much more rarely "hen fruit" (eggs); it was preferable to "Adam's ale" (water) and "desecrated vegetables": a pun on the sometimes less than palatable dried variety. "*Skookum*," an adjective for hardworking folks from the Pacific Northwest's Native Chinook trade jargon, meant "big," "strong," "brave," "excellent," or "impressive." A malamute dog could be *skookum*; so could a drink ("hooch"), or a creek, or a feller. And jail, "*skookum* house," certainly was. Miners, for once forgoing "chin music" (grousing), if they were not too "done up" from a day's work, joined in erecting a neighbor's cabin in a "building bee" to be followed by "jollification," perhaps with wild fiddling and a "hop." Partners splitting up over a claim "got a divorce." And, where gold-digging and gambling ruled, someone who had "cashed in" had pulled up his stakes and left for the pearly gates.

Instead of streets paved with gold, five-year-old Klondy Nelson, joining her father (a Klondiker) on Ophir Creek, saw "an ugly blanket of soft-coal smoke hanging low over everything." Homesick miners there paid a herder to play Santa for Klondy and gave her nuggets as presents, crumbs from Lady Luck's table.

True whoppers lay hidden in them thar hills. Until 1989, a slug from Anvil Creek's Number 5 Bench weighing as much as a gallon of paint held the title of largest lunker unearthed in Alaska. The district also coughed up the sixth-, seventh-, ninth-, and tenth-ranked ones. Strictly speaking, "nugget" refers only to stream-smoothed bits, Ben & Jerry's Super Fudge Chunk goodies engrained in drab placer deposits—sand, silt, or gravel. Erosion in league with weathering of a motherlode often shot through with quartz—a vein sometimes formerly molten—creates these geologic Easter eggs, which account for less than two percent of all the gold mined. A one-ounce nubbin remains rarer than a five-carat (0.035-ounce)diamond the size of a potato beetle.

The placer miners amalgamated fine gold with mercury, and large-scale smelting in the wake of the steam dredges left a legacy, in windborne dust, of the substance that made people "mad as a hatter."

By century's turn, the Bering Strait fields already had

yielded $3.5 million, and the next two decades netted a further $80 million. Settling for motes of that wealth, the future Hollywood actress Marjorie Rambeau, dressed like a boy, sold donuts, busked with a banjo, and swept Front Street dancehall floors, reputedly earning up to seventy-five dollars a day from gold dust that drizzled from pokes when tipsy miners paid for refills.

The glitter Marjorie dust-panned hid grimmer realities. Behind false-front boxes lay dozens of prostitutes' cribs fenced off in the "Stockade" with their own phone and messengers. Women billed as "actresses" or "vaudeville entertainers" worked at saloons where their popularity boosted lucrative sidelines. "There were more of these in Nome than in any mining camp I was ever in," Trelawney-Ansell recalled. "Nothing in the worst days of Montmartre in Paris, or on State Street, Chicago, ever paralleled the shows given here." Cigar stores too could serve as a front for ladies of the night.

A few escaped this dour meat market. "Charlie the Bear made off with Halibut-Face Mary. A stinker named Misery Chris eloped with Toodles, and the King of Denmark stood up before the preacher with Deepwater Dorah," wrote Klondy's future husband Frank Dufresne. As town got more civilized, the retirees' primrose past was forgotten or politely ignored, since "in almost every case the old dance-hall habitués became the strictest sort of wives."

Nome's bibulous nature endured. A woman working there in the '70s was told not to wear good mukluks into the bars, the floors of which were awash in beer. Three stores in the four-block downtown stretch sell liquor today and a laundromat near a Bible bookstore "suds." Legally "bone dry" in 1918, Nome remained a moonshining hotbed despite the Women's Christian Temperance Union's best effort.

Entertainment, as in most roughshod settlements, tended toward bawdiness and athletics. Freestyle matches of boxing, a disreputable sport then still banned in most states, followed the stage shows in the town's theaters on Saturday nights. Spectators showered the winner with coins, his only purse. Future prizefighters of fame bruised their knuckles in Nome. Sometimes, a pugilist took on an audience challenger.

Indoor marathons were the rage, too, held at Eagle Hall, Nome's largest building at the time. In 1907, the unlikely victor of two runs within one week was Jujiro Wada, the son of a samurai. A crack musher, Wada had entered the U.S. as a stowaway and hustled a living as a cook, prospector, and a sealer and shore whaler in the Beaufort Sea. "He was in on most of the big stampedes and many of the less important ones," a gold-rush historian wrote. The footraces were gambling events with prizes measured in thousands of dollars. A head shorter than his competition, without preparatory training, Wada won $500 in the first and $2,800 in the second race. As the *Dawson Daily News* relayed, "While on the run he ate a little raw egg and some tomato, drank a little mineral water, and that was all." For the last two laps of 1,600 that made up the fifty-mile distance, Wada, whom miners in Fairbanks had threatened with lynching four years earlier, carried an American flag in the charged hothouse-barroom atmosphere. One story had a prostitute bet $5,000 at five-to-one odds on the quicksilver Japanese and use her winnings to leave for a respectable life Outside.

Alexander "Scotty" Allan, the champion musher of several All Alaska Sweepstakes, which started and finished in Nome, placed second in that hamster roundabout. Like some of today's Iditarod stars, Allan observed the diets of his competitors' dogs, gave up smoking, and practiced going without sleep. His first leader, Dubby, a Mackenzie River husky, came from the Hudson's Bay Company kennels.

"Japanese Mary" was less fortunate than Allan or Wada or the "soiled doves" (in the parlance of the day) who successfully flew the coop. Ever the sporting woman, she wagered $1,000 on her compatriot in that indoor-track, winter marathon and grew her winnings by grubstaking prospectors. Alas, she was found strangled with a towel and shoelace, all her money and a gold-nugget necklace with a cross gone from her hutch. Demimonde dames could be tough as jerky, though. They drugged and rolled Johns or rigged scales weighing payments for services rendered. Daisy Straws, "of evil repute," in the street brained a man with a hammer, for reasons unknown, but a soldier broke up the fight. In extremis, morphine or opium made life bearable—or ended it.

Nome's grand jury recommended that to curb vice, women should be barred from saloons and that those without visible means of support should be watched and, if lacking decorum, prosecuted. Raiding the red-light district, the Law threatened prostitutes with arrest unless they paid ten-dollar "fines" that funded the police and fire department. Patrols from nearby Fort Davis enforced compliance with public health regulations. A "pest house" for medical cases quarantined with smallpox had sprung up a mile and a half away. The federal government, having set an exclamation point to its Indian Wars with the Wounded Knee massacre, did not dispense charity. One critic complained that, while the municipality would bury an "indigent Eskimo" at its cost, the fort's quartermaster must refuse a starving one sustenance or charge himself for the food doled out.

The way for unruly troopers on leave to the "brig" was short, as it was for the town's citizens. Built around 1901, the Fort Davis guardhouse sat on Front Street. It later became a saloon and then the seat of *The Nome Nugget*, Alaska's oldest existing newspaper today and the only survivor of Nome's six gazettes. The Army also expelled men without lodging or means to procure it before winter's onset. Assisting, the Revenue Cutter *Bear* on its last sailing in the fall expedited the broke and known troublemakers to Seattle. Captain Michael A. "Hell-Roaring Mike" Healy had helmed her until 1895. An excellent ice pilot and the first African-American to command a US government vessel, Healy had grown into a law-enforcement legend on his 20,000-mile beat. His policing spanned from Point Barrow to San Francisco. USRC *Bear*, acquiring its own, Native nickname, "Healy's Fire Canoe" (for its erupting smokestack), rose to the rank of most famous ship in Coast Guard history. Retired in 1904, Healy died a year later, perhaps bored to death.

Returnees on the schooner *Hera*, at sea for almost a month before docking in Seattle, were treated like dogs. Two passengers on one run succumbed to exposure and starvation. A third, famished and crazed, was bunked on the dining room table "until meal time when he was placed somewhere else."

Only on this Barbary Coast of the North could a man like Captain Alex MacLean have become sheriff. Jack London's model for the "Sea Wolf" Wolf Larsen—a man with "eyes that masked the soul with a thousand guises"—was allegedly wanted in the US, Russia, and Canada, and likely in England, Australia, and Japan, for pearl theft, fur-seal poaching, murder, and piracy. In the Klondike, he had challenged a gambling "yellow-bellied son of a sea cook" to a point-blank-range duel, only to pummel and throw his opponent out of the saloon. Two prospectors with whom he had partnered on the Yukon disappeared. "They just got sick and died," the Cape Breton brawler averred when pressed. MacLean, whom one journalist described as "absolutely reckless and fully determined," tried to ram and sink a Russian patrol ship in the Bering Sea, risking his crew's life and his own vessel. He was jailed several months for that. During his brief Nome tenure, inexplicably, "A deep and beautiful calm descended on the city." As in many frontier fables, the facts mattered less than the stories' gist, their enshrinement of virility.

A man with an even brassier reputation, Wyatt Earp was fifty-two when he disembarked in Nome. Though his walrus moustache showed streaks of silver, he'd not reformed into a proper senior citizen. The aging gunslinger traveled with his common-law wife, Josephine "Sadie" Sarah Marcus Earp, a former dancer and "good-time girl," still a beauty at thirty-seven. Her gambling habit ran rampant in Nome until Wyatt cut off her funds and asked fellow barmen to do the same. An octagonal bone chip, if authentic, suggests that he signed some of the Dexter's custom-made gambling chits, which he handed to promising customers as a calling card while he roamed town looking for Sadie or on business. These could be redeemed for a drink. Other establishments used trade tokens for liquor or dances with girls. In a pinch, male partners sufficed.

In 1897, the couple had heeded gold's call. Two years later, Earp and Charles Ellsworth Hoxie had built the Dexter, Nome's first two-story wooden showpiece. Among the town's largest, poshest saloons, it sported a dozen clubrooms upstairs. Under twelve-foot-high ceilings, miners went broke playing faro, monte, blackjack, or billiards. Across from the Dexter, Rickard at the Northern banked on a "scientific mixologist" tending bar below paintings of nudes, but foremost on roulette and bare-knuckle prizefights. (He would go on to become a Barnum-like Madison Square Garden boxing promoter, staging Jack Dempsey in the first match to attract a million-dollar crowd.)

On slow days, Earp walked the cratered beach, plinking whiskey bottles he threw in the air. Once, after a drink or two too many, he fancied himself "a bad man from Arizona and was going to pull some rough stuff," according to B.D. Blakeslee, a civil engineer mapping the region. Marshal Albert Lowe simply slapped the face of the erstwhile terror of cowhands and took his hog leg. He asked Earp to go home, to bed, or he would run him in.

In 1901, the year before the Fairbanks gold strike, the Earps returned to California $80,000 richer. Locomobile's "steam chaise" car at the time cost $600. The year after, they moved to Nevada, where more brawls, another bonanza, and yet another den of iniquity beckoned. By 1915, Earp had drifted into Hollywood, trailing Jack London, whom he knew up north, having wintered at Rampart on the Yukon River when London left the Klondike luckless and wan but brimming with stories. One day, both were dining with one-time cowboy, sailor, and movie actor-turned-film-director Raoul Walsh. Before long, the world's highest-paid entertainer and future star of *The Gold Rush* strolled over. "You're the bloke from Arizona, aren't you?" Charlie Chaplin said to Tombstone's ex-deputy marshal with evident awe. "Tamed the baddies, huh?" He then looked at London and nodded. "I know you, too. You almost made me go to Alaska and dig for gold."

The "Giants" at Work.

Miocene Ditch Co.'s Operations on Glacier Creek, Alaska, Aug. 7th 1910.

Where Giants Once Walked

White Mountain, an Inupiaq village two snowmachine hours from Nome, bustles during the Iditarod as it becomes a checkpoint for racers and their teams. In 1992, a local woman returned there from a fishing trip with a fossilized, blue-black arc strapped to her four-wheeler's back, a "big old log-looking thing," as the husband recalled this tusk. Villagers who had fetched permafrost chunks from that riverbend in the past to make ice cream with had noticed the stink of rot in that muck. They had also found mammoth teeth and guessed that it must have been a mudhole, some northern kind of La Brea pit in which animals bogged down and succumbed. More than two decades later, only ten feet from the site of the mother's discovery, her son, who had caught just a single salmon that day, pried another tusk from the river gunk. It had the length of two men and, his bathroom scale indicated, weighed roughly as much. At up to $75 per pound, the young finder-keeper thought, his twelve-footer would yield a downpayment for a starter home in Nome. Absorbing minerals, tusks underground assume different colors, from powdery blue to golden-beige to maroon. Polished fragments can shine like gemstones.

Another, seven-foot blueish tusk weighing more than a hundred pounds was thought to be worth $20,000 to $70,000.

Adding to the chafing of ice, waves, mining dredges, and floods, melting permafrost now releases animal bodies. The rapidly growing mega-slump of the Batagaika crater in Northeastern Siberia, among other fossil materials, gave the world its best-preserved mammoth yet—a calf fifty millennia old, deflated but without visible damage.

Perhaps surprising to Southerners, such finds are no rarity in what remains, albeit transformed, wetter and brushier now, of the Pleistocene mammoth steppe. The first mammoths may have crossed more than 300,000 to 400,000 years before the continent's first circus elephant did. They, not Don Young or Ted Stevens (insert name of your favorite senior politician here) are Alaska's official state fossil.

Mammoth parts saw the light of day more often in our state's northern half partly because more placer mining occurred there. Numerous mammoth bones and tusks were exposed during the Klondike and subsequent gold rushes. Canadian and American scientists led expeditions into the Yukon Territory to search for a mammoth or mastodon, skeletal or mummified, to haul back to a museum. Marsh fleawort or "mastodon flower" often grows in sites from which bones have been excavated, and some people believed that they sprang from seeds preserved in a mastodon's stomach.

One stampeder supposedly put up a cabin with the

prized bones. Humankind's oldest built homes, assembled from them, arose in the Dnipro River valley, Ukraine, and have been dated to 25,000 years ago. Twenty thousand years earlier, Neanderthals in that region laid a house foundation of mammoth bones, some of which they had decorated. Early human hunters also derived energy in the treeless steppe by burning the bones as fuel. So, mammoths warmed them in three different ways.

Large-scale hydraulic sluicing near Nome—imagine water-jet cannons—firehosed unexpected treasure from the ground. A Mammoth Gulch gold mine operated in the Cripple River headwaters, twelve miles northwest of Nome, in the wrinkled Seward Peninsula highlands. It's a prospector's name, displayed on the 1904 "Map of Cape Nome Precinct," a map that limits itself to the topography's drainages, which delineated the best chances of getting rich. The rest lies bland, unmarked, unnamed, unworthy of the extractive attention: "Walrussia," as Secretary of State William H. Seward's purchase had been mocked. In 1905, Andrew J. Stone, disproving detractors by surveying for a gold mining company in Nome, gave an inscribed tusk to Lincoln Ellsworth, which may have influenced the future congressional gold medal recipient to become a polar explorer. (We shall meet him later, in the company of one of polar exploration's greatest.) Growth spurts like tree rings, visible in the cross section at the weathered root of this tusk, which today rests in an Ohio museum, helped scientists to determine the animal's age. Ancient craftsmen, after incising fossilized tusks with flint burins, peeled lengths of "bark" off them, which they modified further. They may have softened the material with urine beforehand, as their Siberian counterparts did.

Enterprising Inupiat sold mammoth ivory to Nome carvers, collectors, and curio stores. Michael "Big Mike" Francis Kazingnuk, the author of a handwritten *Bering Sea and Arctic Coast Eskimo History*, returned from a 1910 Norton Bay trip with "four coal sacks full of petrified mammoth tooths for $300.00 and two six-feet-long tusks, four four-feet-long tusks and some scraps of all-black ivory, two sacks full [of which] we sold for $200.00," a small fortune in those days.

The Czech-born collector for the future American Museum of Natural History, Aleš Hrdlička—"Hard Liquor," we called him as students—wrote that Bering Strait Eskimos "assiduously excavate the old sites," providing fossil ivory "to be worked up into beads, pendants, and other objects of semi-jewelry that find ready sale among the whites … The more striking the coloration of the ivory, the more desirable it is for the beads, etc." Those Eskimos did not at all hesitate to dig up the old sites, noted the man in charge of the Smithsonian's "Racial Brain Collection," the man who took two human skeletons and a skull from Cape Nome's historic Nook village, the man whom President Franklin D. Roosevelt handpicked to head a postwar resettlement scheme for Europe's uprooted Jews. (The "less developed skulls" of the Japanese, Hrdlička advised FDR, were a sign of their warlike nature and lower level of evolutionary development.)

At present, carved mammoth ivory, the real deal, sometimes as inlays in walrus "ivory," is sold at a store for Inupiaq art on Nome's Front Street. Beach erosion on the Bering Strait islands does the work of mainland rivers or miners. The back office of the Bering Land Bridge Visitor Center in town on occasion houses a tusk. A ranger there told a mammoth fan who was eager to spot a tusk in situ to walk the streambeds right after breakup in the spring and to "Look along the line where the ice has stripped away the banks." Sooner or later, he promised, "you'll see a bone or a tusk sticking out."

Beware, though, of removing such slivers of a bold bygone world from public lands, or Native corporation lands, or from private lands without the owner's permission. An outfitter for whom I once worked was fined and had her permit suspended when a client, with her acquiescence, kept a tusk they picked up in the Alaska Petroleum Reserve on the North Slope. She got nailed because an undercover wildlife agent had booked a seat on that same rafting trip. The feds had been tipped off by her advertising thinly disguised paleontology plundering on her website.

I well understand the urge to want to own a piece of that past, a prestigious token, like tribal masks, of lifeways beyond our full grasp. While the lost civilization of Atlantis leaves me cold, the fantastic beasts of Beringia make me dream about time travel, the kind that transcends historical delving. If that ever became a reality, theirs is the era I'd choose to visit above all others. The nature writer as well as the anthropologist in me tingles at the chance of witnessing a biological Eden right before the fall.

Furball Frankenstein mice with golden-brown hair—like something a cat coughed up—have been engineered by isolating the woolly mammoth gene responsible for that trait. But for now, the giants stay gone, no more to be seen in their full shaggy glory, movie CGI, lifeless museum displays, and future gene-splicing stunts excepted. Even with these ersatz elephantids, facets that captivate me remain obscured. What did mammoths smell like? How did they react to humans approaching? Did they tutor their young? Did they share attributes with their distant African kin, which detect rain thrumming the ground 150 miles away, forming mental maps, following matriarchs, mourning their dead, or communicating through infrasound, sensing vibrations through the pads of their cushioned feet? What use did they make of their dental endowment? Wear patterns, prominent near the tips, suggest that mammoths wielded their parenthetical prongs in jousting and fending off predators, and as snowplows and ice scrapers, to clear buried forage. Their metabolism was geared toward letting them burn fat more efficiently in their chilly habitat.

Isotope analyses of thin slices from a bull mammoth tusk in the University of Alaska Museum of the North's collection allow us a glimpse of one individual's wandering. He spent the first years of his life in the lower Yukon River basin. As a juvenile, expanding his range, he roamed interior lowlands from the Alaska Range to the Brooks Range, with seasonal treks to the northern Seward Peninsula. Death found him at the age of twenty-eight, on the Arctic Coastal Plain, where he starved in late winter or spring. Did warm bodies surround him in comfort as he drew his last breath?

Showy incisors saved neither him nor his conspecifics.

So how did those finally exit their icy stage?

In 1999, hunters on St. Paul Island—at seventy square miles the biggest of the Pribilof cluster's spent volcanoes—stumbled upon a sensation: a forty-foot-deep lava tube beneath tundra, housing a charnel hoard. During a 2003 expedition to Qagnax Cave, named after the Unangan (formerly: "Aleut") word for "bone," University of Alaska Anchorage scientists sorted its faunal debris. Among more than 1,750 fragments, most from foxes the pit had devoured, lay five woolly mammoth shards plus two teeth. Mammoths made up one third of Alaska's paleo-mammal biomass, so that alone hardly warranted much excitement. But dates obtained by various methods at different labs did. A University of Alaska investigating geologist "couldn't believe it at first." Radiocarbon decay measures showed that this animal breathed roughly 5,700 years ago, 4,000 after its last known relative paced our continent.

The heights of the Pribilofs once overlooked Beringia,

a land bridge extension of the mammoth steppe the size of Alaska plus Alabama. As the glacial epoch's largest biome, these rolling grasslands linked Spain and northern Canada via Siberia. Late-Pleistocene icecaps storing additional snow had lowered ocean levels by 160 feet. Having crossed newly bared Bering Strait seafloor, hunters of East Asian descent with their dogs and families about 13,500 BP ("before the present") scouted Alaska's interior and the Yukon, opportunistically spearing or scavenging strawberry-blond or chestnut-brown colossi, each of which hoovered the equivalent of four alfalfa bales daily. Rising seas around 11,000 BP swamped America's threshold again. Subsequent migrants, Unangan and Eskimo ancestors, stepped into the New World from skin boats. Wildlife moving upward from flood zones got marooned in highland refugia.

Shipboard sonar and seafloor-sediment coring recently outlined swamps, floodplains, and snaking streams that dominated the land bridge, unlike on the typical mammoth steppe. This terrain, "buggy bogs" instead of "great grazing," formed a barrier for animals like woolly rhinos, which never reached North America. For the same reason, short-faced bears and camels of the now extinct *Camelops* genus did not colonize Asia. The marshes could not deter moose, with likely origins in Central Asia, and bison from the southern part of that continent, migrating twice. Neither did they stop mammoths; those tromped toward new horizons along drier ridges and across tablelands.

An isotope analysis of bones from Anzick Boy, a nursing Clovis infant in southern Montana, revealed that his mother's diet 12,800 years ago had consisted almost entirely of mega-fauna meat (elk, bison, camel, and horse), with 40 percent derived from mammoths. The University of Alaska Fairbanks (UAF) archaeologist Ben Potter credits this high-protein fare with fueling the Clovis push into South America—within mere centuries, foreshadowing the blubber-eating Thule whalers' rush to Greenland—as well as with contributing to the blinking out of ice-age species. Mammoth was a Pleistocene power breakfast, the ultimate paleo-diet, on which you could jog all day.

Bugling still shattered the silence on Siberia's Wrangel Island in 4,300 BP, centuries after the completion of Giza's Great Pyramid. Insular woollies could be 10 percent smaller—fairly common in deprived, confined populations—but they were no dwarf race like California's Channel Islands mammoth; in height, they rivaled African elephants. Mainland mammoths forged on until circa 10,000 BP. Wetter, warmer years turned steppe into forest and tundra, with the behemoths' decline reinforcing the trend. Saplings no longer trampled became woods less reflective than prairies. Snow, like a down comforter, no longer compacted, screened soil from cooling winds. To a degree, mammoths created and maintained the steppe that fed them.

Inevitably, Alaska's state fossil keeps making the news. Bioengineers want to resurrect it as a niche-filler in rewilded experimental settings or "Pleistocene parks." Inland rivers and coastal storms frequently unveil sudden organic outcrops, the toupée-tufted, dome-headed grazers' remains. Shishmaref duck hunters in 2018 pulled out a twelve-foot, 177-pound, shiny, teak-colored tusk, a sweeping twist of a C whose tip poked from a cutbank. Already in 1816, Kotzebue, on his Pacific loop, found "a very fine tooth" near today's town bearing his name. So did Frederick William Beechey in 1826. Or rather, he discovered two, in a cliff of frozen mud. As the captain of HMS *Blossom*, he named Elephant Point, whose trunk noses into Eschscholtz Bay at the head of Kotzebue Sound, for this find. A curator thought that, with a length of more than ten feet, the larger tusk must have belonged to an animal fifteen or sixteen feet high.

Wilhelm Gottlieb Tilesius von Tilenau, using as his blueprint the skeleton of an Indian elephant in Peter the Great's Kunstkamera museum in St. Petersburg, reassembled the bones of a mammoth discovered in 1799 in northeastern Siberia. Tilesius had worked as a ship's surgeon, marine biologist, and expedition artist on *Nadezhda* during Adam Johann von Krusenstern's 1803 to 1806 circumnavigation of the globe, the first in the Russian annals. His was only the second attempt ever to put back together an extinct species, the first for a mammoth. This German physician, draftsman, naturalist, and appointee to Moscow University was kin in spirit and talent, if not fame, to Georg Wilhelm Steller, the first European to set foot on Alaskan soil, and to Alexander von Humboldt, "The Last Man Who Knew Everything." (This was a time when Germans traversing the world still knew which things truly mattered: sea cows and jays, the pull of sea ice and the fervor of active volcanoes, the hallowed bond between the living world and the inorganic environment.) Humboldt had a Pacific Ocean current named after him, Tilesius a plain yet powerful plant that will be discussed later in these pages.

Tilesius had replaced the bones of a missing foreleg with plaster-of-Paris replicas of the extant, subcontinental ones. His etching of the puzzling whole impresses one with its veracity, except that, since he had switched the tusks, the Bruegelian dentition flared rather than almost touched at the tips. A merchant's earlier reconstruction based on the nearly intact carcass, drawn before the ice around it had completely melted—a skin-and-flesh hillock clinging to bone, which polar bears, wolves, wolverines, foxes, and Evenki feeding their dogs had not yet mutilated—lacked the trunk but depicted "mammoth horns … of extraordinary size and beauty," which were later sawed off and sold. In this raw envisioning, the tusks curved downward, like fishhooks or fangs, on a beast in the shape of a hoofed boar. The original still had had both eyes preserved, with the pupil of one distinct; the brain, a prune in the cranium; the leathery soles on two feet; and dark-gray skin tufted with hair, including a male's luxurious neck mane. The skin was so heavy that ten helpers "found great difficulty in transporting it to the shore"—the shore, sixty feet away, being that of the Arctic Ocean.

Johann Friedrich Adam, the botanist who had retrieved the flesh ruin, also had dug up the ground in search of more bones and collected more hair—nearly forty pounds of it—trod into the earth by scavenging bears. Some of it, underwool, was "of the colour of the camel, an inch and a half long, very thick-set and curled in locks." Different pelage, from the mane, was flame-red, with black bristly guard hair much thicker than horse hair, measuring up to a foot and a half. The rusty hue of preserved hair samples may be due to their burial or leaching out of pigment. Genetic analysis limited the actual fur colors to a range of dark brown to black and pale ginger to blond, like the coats of Arctic bears. DNA for the first time had unlocked details of an extinct species' appearance. Behavior could be next.

Be that as it may, Adam had considered the Lena River leftovers not slim pickings but ample recompense "for the fatigues and dangers of the journey, and the considerable expenses of the enterprize."

From that century's end on, prospectors throughout the Yukon and Alaska unearthed timber–like femurs; ivories spelling the status and health of bulls and cows; and washboard-ridged molars abraded by gritty food. In 1948, Effie, a rare, 20,000-year-old mummified calf, eroded from Fairbanks Creek's bluffs. Nineteenth-century rumors of her kin's survival began with a zoologist aboard USRC *Corwin*, to whom Cape Prince of Wales Inupiat offered bones and tusks in trade. Bering Strait Eskimos long familiar with embedded pachyderm parts, which they carved into tools, took them as proof of mythical creatures tunneling underground that died when they surfaced, inhaling. The shape the inquiring collector sketched on the ship's deck embodied the enigma whose continued existence they might then have affirmed. The present and past, like the Far East and Far West, meet in surprising, quixotic ways. Tales coursing among lower Yukon River residents tell of people feeding mastodon flesh from the riverbanks to their dog teams. And it feels as if Inupiaq legends carry a faint echo of those lumbering jumbos:

> Long ago, the land had animals that are no longer present. They were large and dangerous ...

Edward Sanford Harrison, another failed miner, who had secured "pick-and-shovel wages" at one of Nome's gazettes, reported that Inupiaq mammoth sketches had been "transmitted from generation to generation, from one of their ancestors who saw the animal." If they had, their creators would have drawn those in wet sand or snow, not on paper.

Outlier species, from dodos to humongous tortoises, often lingered—or arose—in predator-free island havens until sailors, settlers, or ecological shifts doomed them. The question of what finished St. Paul's holdouts has vexed paleontologists. They've considered "overkill," the idea that early humans hunted wildlife to extinction—70 percent of North America's megafauna simply disappeared around the time of their arrival. However, except for stray Unangan kayakers, Russian sealers in the 1780s were the first people to land on St. Paul.

UAF researchers probing the mystery in 2013 cored lake sediments on this Beringian remnant. The layers betrayed poor water quality during the period when the tuskers vanished; algae and aquatic insects embalmed in the muck profiled the region's dwindling ice-age lakes. Nitrogen isotopes contained in an organism's diet leave unique, local signatures in its skeleton. These underscored creeping aridity before the St. Paul bruisers' end. Lack of fresh water, according to the aptly named Matthew Wooller of UAF's Water and Environmental Research Center, was "the smoking gun" of causes that coalesced into a dire situation. When melting ice caps shrank the island to its present dimensions, its four-legged tanks ran out of fuel.

This study, some of the most in-depth sleuthing yet to pinpoint a case of prehistoric extinction, is another reminder of the balancing act small population face, of their vulnerability to changed circumstances. Compared to the St. Paul scenario, droughts and sea level rises we cause will seemingly strike overnight. *Mammuthus primigenius* (the "Original" or "Firstborn" Mammoth), one of the last of at least six mammoth lineages, failed to adapt to the threat through millennia. *Homo* not-quite-so *sapiens* and fellow creatures now, at best, have decades to do so.

Treasure Island

Recreationists in Nome, if they climb Anvil Mountain's reworked limestone crown on a clear day, may notice a bulge offshore twenty-four miles to the west. Its unassuming, volcanic square mile suggests an Arctic ziggurat or an aircraft carrier turned turtle. Small, crystalline snowmelt reservoirs like gemstones set in rocky pits dot its tundra top. Mirages sometimes distort it into a blue berg afloat on quicksilver wavering. Debris from a Ryan Air flight litters its eastern slope. On maps, it reminds you of a crude arrowhead. Photos rarely do it justice, and you can't measure the wealth of this outcrop in coin.

In 1778, Captain Cook, on his terminal journey, finding a ten-foot sled with baleen lashings and bone runners "neatly put together" near decayed, semisubterranean houses, named Sledge Island. He "saw neither shrub nor tree either upon the island or upon the continent." One of Catherine the Great's explorers later claimed the Eskimos called it Ayak, Inupiaq for "spear" or "whaling harpoon." About fifty Ayakmiut hunted seals but also walrus migrating through the straits before they abandoned home around the 1899 gold rush. Seas could get so rough that, to launch, two hunters would heave a kayak with a third seated in the cockpit into the water. If he went topsy-turvy in the surf, he righted himself with a paddle stroke and upper-body twist, the renown Eskimo Roll.

The last person born on the island remembered nothing about her home because she'd left as a baby. Ayakmiut kept visiting until the Spanish flu's ravages stranded them on the continent. In 2011, the Smithsonian repatriated grave goods and nineteen skeletons it had taken from Sledge Island. Nome's Eskimo community welcomed these dead, which now rest at Cape Nome near an unmarked wooden cross.

Five prospectors almost lost their lives on Sledge Island in 1899. Late in the season, they ran into mush ice in their dory and barely managed to land, nearly exhausted and as numb as the rocks on shore. Peculiar tracks led one of their party to a man inside a sod house, a castaway who had holed up there for three days without food and a fire. He had cut the sleeves off his coat and wrapped them around his feet to keep them from freezing—hence the unusual tracks. The starving man, "blue with cold," joined the miners at their camp, but the ice worsened, with currents dragging floes so rapidly that "it seemed like foolhardiness to attempt the crossing." Nevertheless, on the morning of the twelfth day, when the conveyor belt slowed a bit, they set out, inexperienced in sea-ice travel, unlike the Inupiat. At times, in the channel, they had to get on an ice cake and ferry themselves over to another like gondoliers, wielding a long pole. They reached firmer, anchored ice and finally, nine miles from the island, after hours of draining work, shore. When they did, the rotten field they had traversed broke loose and joined the mass sailing eastward.

In one of the region's bizarre footnotes, Kāpena George Gilley, the only known Native Hawaiian (or "Kānaka Maoli") whaling captain in the Bering Strait, died during the gold rush, twenty miles east of Sledge Island. Nome-bound after a trading mission to Siberia, he had sat on his schooner's railing for a last view of the receding mainland when the wind suddenly shifted and swung the boom around, knocking Gilley off his balance. His crew watched him drown but was able to retrieve the body. Like the sinuous name of the Hulahula River on Alaska's North Slope, Gilley's fate here serves as a reminder of wider North Pacific connections. Hawaiians had a reputation of being fearless on the water: "They will chase a whale when they know they are in the greatest danger and think it is the greatest fun," one captain told a reporter. If a boat towed by a harpooned whale capsized during the rush of a "Nantucket sleigh ride," "it makes no difference to them for they can swim like fishes."

Gilley's life also reminds us that those transoceanic connections could be fractious. While his ship lay becalmed somewhere between East Cape and Cape Prince of Wales in the summer of 1877, a dozen Inupiat who had boarded to barter for liquor were murdered when tempers flared, with the knotty rum-running captain himself shooting one in the face before throwing him overboard. Still, on a later voyage, with the sea overhunted and starvation rampant, he "killed two schooner loads of walruses and carried them along the settlements and gave to the natives." And this sea dog, whose forty-year career included a turn as first mate under William "Black Ahab" Shorey—the Pacific's only African whaling captain (from Barbados)—sometimes hired Yup'ik and Inupiaq hands.

Sledge Island was the nexus of further losses. A tug steaming to Teller six days into World War II caught fire, forcing both hands to jump overboard. Equally unlucky, in the winter of '42, MV *Crown City*, supplying Nome with coal, gas, food, clothes, bulldozers, airplane components, and Quonsets, foundered in its rock-and-ice cordon. Coastal foragers salvaged machine parts and a deck load of lumber for tools and building material. Her smokestack rose from the surface until, jarred loose months later, she submarined.

Thousands of island births balance the litany of death and distress. Surf laces bleached, slanted southwestern cliffs of the Alaska Maritime Wildlife Refuge, a metropolis aswirl with auklets, kittiwakes, mini-penguin murres, puffins, and cormorants, jostling, raising chicks in burrows and cracks or on ledges when not fishing in discordant frenzy. Neither foxes nor King Islanders, who formerly summered on the mainland and egged here, dented these populations.

In the 1950s, an ornithologist in the footprints of Knud Rasmussen observed thirty-five species on, in the waters around, and above the island within one week. Pelagic cormorants avoiding the foxes lived in great concentrations packed tightly "along the rim of the rocky precipices just below the grassy slopes," with nests often no more than a foot apart. Large tabletop boulders near the water's edge became "loafing platforms" for hundreds of birds. A pair of dotterels—buff-breasted, white-browed Asiatic plovers—approached without fear, which was their undoing. (They were "obtained" as specimens.) Yellow wagtails on this northern Galápagos could be caught by hand. Egging for the Ayakmiut was a giddy, adrenaline-fueled Easter egg hunt writ large.

Point Hope Inupiat at Cape Thompson scooped turquoise murre eggs with black Jackson Pollock dribbles and orange yolks from rock shelves. They used hoop nets on poles like long lacrosse sticks. Gatherers spidering on slick walls slipped eggs into the neck holes of parkas belted at the waist while a partner belayed them from the top with a walrus-skin rope. A third man kept a boat at the cliff base in case the climber tumbled. Packs could be lowered and, emptied, sent up again. By custom, families claimed special roosts. They boiled and then stored eggs in sealskin pokes sloshing with seal oil, for the unavoidable lean days. Only one egg from a clutch of two was taken; a hen whose single egg was removed would not replace it. Some pickers lifting the coveted snacks explained their need to the occupant and asked the bird's permission.

Ayak's most exceptional treasure, however, lay hidden, forgotten, as such things often do.

A teacher and his class from the Inupiaq village Sinuk in 1912 sailed across for an end-of-term picnic. Students scaled the top to scan for walrus, over boulders whose lichens crinkled underfoot and that frost had riven. Descending, Johnnie Tumichuk noticed a pole wedged between those rocks. Shifting some, he recognized it as a boat crook for repelling ice and retrieving harpoon lines.

More laboring opened a cave mouth.

Inside waited a workingman Aladdin's hoard: a dozen chert- as well as obsidian-tipped lances; scrapers; chipped-stone amulets; bentwood buckets with walrus-ivory handles and whale figurines; a chest holding bear claws, an eagle's foot; and a bowhead-effigy container, carved from a walrus mandible, holding several whetstones. Two chains, each carved from a single unbroken tusk, ending in flukes, hung from a harpoon rest for a skin-boat. Their craftsmanship far surpassed that of the sled Cook had stumbled upon. Each link represented a whale that captain had killed. Spare slate lance blades lay sheathed in a box shaped like a polar bear head. The box was meant to bestow that predator's prowess upon the weapons inside. Projectiles stored in a third, whale-lookalike box, cushioned by dry grass, preserved the edges of projectiles stored inside, but also, the hunters thought, allowed the points to become magically acquainted with their intended prey—before, hopefully, striking it. Among birds stuffed into the cave was the skin of a raven, the first creature to feed on a dead whale; Point Hope whaling-boat captains wore raven-skin headbands.

The slate may well have come from Glacier Creek, in

the Kigluaik Mountains (the early prospectors' "Sawtooth Mountains"), from the slippery slopes that made my shoulder pop out. Local lore holds that it was so sharp that men had to wear mittens to pull pieces from the ground and that it cut the webs of geese that nested up there. An Inupiaq legend tells of a giant who sank enemy *umiaks*—boats sewn from walrus skin—by hurling sharp stones he had gathered and piled near the shore. William Oquilluk, who gathered the ancient Kaweramiut tales, said his grandfather would not take him to where they got those sharp rocks for ulus and other knives, because it was "pretty high up and it is a dangerous place to climb."

Before metal became widely available, curved slate blades were inserted in wood or ivory handles to make the iconic ulu women's knives now sold as tourist souvenirs. Slate is an unusual material for projectile points. A metamorphic rock composed of shale-type sedimentary stone and quartz, it cleaves nicely into sheets but is softer than flintstone or chert and more easily damaged, shattering upon impact. However, quickly and effortlessly shaped into spear and harpoon heads, with edges whetted on other stone rather than flaked, it is perfect for piercing the thick blubber coat of marine mammals. Slate points in North America are extremely rare, except at coastal archaeological sites like Ayak.

Survival in the perimeter of the Bering Strait was also a matter of aesthetics. Beautifully fashioned hunting implements pleased the whale's spirit, which in Northwest Alaska was thought to be female: giving herself, nurturing, nourishing. People believed that she offered her life, her blubber and meat, to a prepared and respectful crew. A wooden crest from the cache features a relief carving of a bowhead hung inside the bow of an *umiak* as a whale attractant. The whaling captain's wife remained still and calm in her house during the hunt, to keep the prey from getting spooked. When a bowhead was landed, she gave it a freshwater drink from one of the ornate buckets. Bowhead Woman, having spent all her life swimming through salty water, would have been thirsty and deserved the welcome of a guest. People discussed the caught whale's nature during the ensuing banquet and praised the quality of its meat in the hope that another whale honored so would surrender itself in the future.

The captain of an *umiak*, the *umialik*, formally opened the whaling season by taking his charms and hunting paraphernalia—like those on Sledge Island—from a chest in his cache.

Preparing for a hunt, the crew first danced and feasted and then fasted and "sweat-danced" for twenty-four hours in the sod-house *qargi*. There, the men also carved special paddles, different from those used in trade or war. They painted them with figures of red alder pigment, and added tufts of reindeer hair. To this day, Inupiaq whalers sometimes repurpose a paddle as a simple but effective kind of sonar. With the blade in the ocean and the grip pressed against the echo chamber of their skull, they detect game moving underwater, through the wood's vibration. They can distinguish bowheads from bearded seals—a question of volume—as if they were reading tracks in the snow. During the launching of an *umiak* in May, when bowheads ploughed northward through the strait, the *umialik*'s wife sprinkled ashes made from the shavings of new paddles along the boat's path on the shorefast ice, to keep evil spirits at bay. After the launch, the *umialik* blessed his boat and crew with a beachgrass whisk and seawater. "Power songs" calmed the weather, improved the harpoon's aim, and mesmerized whales. Each whale landed, feeding a village for months, was manna from the deep coaxed ashore. The meat kept well in cellars dug into permafrost; it still does, if no longer reliably. The twenty-inch blubber coat fueled stone cooking-lamps that also heated pit houses that from the outside resembled green hillocks.

With the bias of the times, White observers skewed the Inupiat's restraint in the hunt into counterproductive superstition:

Their superstitions prevent them from catching large numbers of whales. Whales run in schools, and when the natives have captured one, the man who has harpooned him must be blindfolded for a certain length of time, and the boat in which the capture was affected must be taken ashore and put out of use for a certain time. In short, whaling operations must be suspended for a brief period so that the Eskimo can perform his superstitious ceremonies, and by the time he is ready to resume whaling, the school of whales have gone by and are out of reach.

The man who lacked insight into these conservation practices, Edward S. Harrison, was generally astute, fairly openminded, believing that a perceived lack of the Inupiat's faith in any higher power or the hereafter was a "result of hasty observations"; and that "if this region should be converted into a tropical climate, the melting of the ice would result in the encroachment of the ocean so that where now is tundra there would be mud-flats covered with water at high tide."

The missionary teacher Susan R. Bernardi documented the old-style pursuit at Wales around 1905 in *Story of a Whale Hunt* gift albums, down to dogs gobbling up scraps from the marine motherlode. Her photographs were among the earliest that showed traditional Inupiaq whaling, highlighting rituals and ceremonies. Wales, in the folklorist Susan Fair's words, was "one of the largest and most powerful centers of Inupiaq whaling."

As an amateur ethnographer, Bernardi moonlighted as a field collector of artifacts and a part-time grave robber.

The scenes she preserved contrasted starkly with Victorian commercial, assembly-line slaughter. Planted on a whaler's grave, the mast of an *umiak* broken by a whale's thrashing tail reminded people of the physical dangers involved, which compounded spiritual ones. Her pictures of butchering and the hunt speak of the intimate bodily contact between cetaceans and humans, of up-close and personal meetings with a fellow mammal who, with her dying breath, showered you with her blood. You don't really know a whale until you've had your face right in the warm, salty breath of a misting one, a modern Native artist once told a friend.

Whales that fed people also housed them. Thule predecessors of the Inupiat favored bowhead bones as a construction material. Curved twelve-foot jaws formed the rafters, shored up by ribs, roofed with driftwood, skins or sod, depending on the season and available resources. Architectural details meshed with symbolic meanings. At Barrow, sets of upright mandibles planted into the earth formed entryways—the home whale swallowed humans to disgorge them again, as if in birth. In Wales, the round ends of whale vertebrae paved portions of entryways, and ribs arched above the *qargi*. The blubber lamp at a house's center was the hot, flaming heart of the whale, its guttering life. The current settlement of Point Hope, myth has it, grew from a harpooned whale, and all whales since then have been birthed from the jawbone tunnels of ancestral houses—suggestive of rites of passage—to lobtail back into the sea. In a variation on the theme, men in seal-gut suits during the butchering "stepped up on the backbone," as Bernardi described it, and "into the body of the whale." In one photo by her, a Wales man stands chest-deep in a half-submerged whale carcass on the shore.

Jonah's abode, by comparison, was an Airbnb.

Inupiat like the upper Noatak's Nuataagmiut, floating down the braids of Brooks Range rivers to Kotzebue Sound's annual summer fair at Sisualik ("Where There Are White Whales"), hunted belugas, as coastal predecessors had done at least since 3000 BP. Until the late nineteenth century, these bands may have engaged in large-scale hunts similar to the caribou drives they were familiar with, those roundups in which bunches of animals funneled into a body of water or corral were dispatched. Another Seward Peninsula cave, which a permafrost scientist discovered in 2010 in Lost Jim Lava Flow, held seventeenth-century implements associated with such a hunt. Among them were two kayak paddles with blades shaped like a willow leaf, and a lance tipped with slate lashed to the shaft with braided sinew. The caribou, punched by drivers like a herd of antlered longhorns, would have avoided the sharp terrain boobytrapped with volcanic vents and tubes and surged instead toward Kaweramiut hunters waiting on Imuruk Lake. For the drive's oceanic version, a line of about twenty-five kayaks and *umiaks* parked along the water's edge. Children carrying sticks kept noisy village dogs away. Whitecaps could make it difficult to spot telltale dorsal ridges wheeling out at sea. But as soon as the bay was unmistakably "filled with the white backs and spouts," the flotilla was launched under the leadership of a headman chosen for the occasion. A respected senior hunter at each end of the drive line maintained its integrity. Pods of whales were shepherded into the shallows or onto the shoals, to be lanced or harpooned. A skilled hunter in pursuit could surf behind a *sisuaq* as if bound to that target by animal magnetism, saving his strength, letting one arm of a whale's V wake propel his kayak along. A sealskin float tied to the harpoon line kept the carcass afloat. Meat and *muktuk*—chewy skin with a pink blubber mantle—traveled upriver to fuel winter activities and the flame of survival in the boreal zone. Oily meat "full of nutriment" not only fed people but also the region's malemute dogs.

Beluga numbers have plummeted, though. With climate breakdown, noisy ship traffic, and mercury that accrues in human tissues as well, dozens or even fewer miniature Moby-Dicks now visit the sound in the spring. Like orcas, populations of these squeaking, blunt-headed "canaries of the sea" with eyes like jet beads build distinct cultures, transmitted orally and behaviorally. While this may be news to biologists, it is not to the locals. Any resemblances with the Inupiat are not a fluke, tradition bearers would say. In indigenous northerners' tales, all animals in a distant mythical time lived in societies mirroring those of humans, a different sort of "people," with the boundaries between them and us two-legged ones porous. Shapeshifting was common, facilitating unions between two kinds not too different overall.

Offering glimpses of an all-encompassing worldview and economy, the Sledge Island whaling assemblage remains the only extant pre-contact captain's outfit, an heirloom owned by a shaman who'd vanished mysteriously. Many had sought it. Johnnie's teacher acquired the find, which today, no longer scattered throughout the University of Pennsylvania collections, resides at the Penn Museum, whole but warehoused.

A shaman or *angatkuq* named Punginguhk—he may even have owned the Sledge Island cache—for years had troubled whalers who waited in sheltered bays of the Bering Strait for the ice to clear out before they headed farther north into the Beaufort Sea. In a legendary faceoff in 1896, at Port Clarence, one hundred miles north of Nome, officers of USRC *Bear* on her annual policing tour to Point Barrow finally clapped him in leg irons belowdecks on the cutter. Punginguhk escaped and challenged the captain to a duel of magic. "You cut off my head first, then I will cut off yours," were the words supposedly uttered. The captain refused, whereupon the *angatkuq* ran around the deck, carrying his own head like a bowling ball, before making the captain's knife chase its owner into his stateroom. The captain freed the *angatkuq* and sent him ashore, whether sick of the hassle or impressed with supreme showmanship we shall never know.

Some Inupiat sold furs, "whalebone" (baleen—horny lamellae hanging comb-like from the upper jaws of filter feeders), and ivory and worked shore-based hunts or on ships. Some scavenged wood and iron from wrecks. But despite Eskimos finding scraps and employment through Yankee whalers, competition and ill will between the two groups festered. One notorious whaler traded for a year's worth of furs, blubber, and seal oil from St. Lawrence, leaving the islanders to starve. When missionaries two years later visited Kukuliak, scattered skeletons greeted them. Ninety percent of its population had died. During the 1918 to 1920 flu pandemic, physicians could not prescribe medicine mixed with alcohol and complained that patients perished because of the prohibition.

Even alive, many Bering Strait Eskimos were shadows of their former selves. Anchored for four days at the mouth of the Sinuk River in 1791, Captain Joseph Billings' secretary and interpreter Martin Sauer—both Englishmen served in the Tsarina's fleet—had painted a different picture. He thought the locals "well limbed, rather tall"; "handsome and healthy"; with "fine open countenances." Crowding the ship, the Inupiat had sought to trade for the Europeans' iron, metal buttons, knives, and blue glass beads.

Mere decades later, the subsistence hunters felt, rightly so, that the sea was being depleted. By 1852, 220 ships were scouring the Bering Strait region, killing more than 2,600 bowheads, the commercially most valuable of all whales. The tongue by itself yielded twenty-five barrels of oil. The steam-whaler *Alexander* docked at San Francisco with one season's cargo of 20,000 tons of baleen. Bundled, standing upright to dry in the Arctic Oil Works yard there, this loot looked like a palm plantation. Busks cut from the thin, long, fringed bone plates through which bowheads sieve zooplankton—krill and other crustaceans that feed them—stiffened corsets, hoop skirts, parasols, umbrellas, coach whips, riding crops, and hat brims. In a single voyage, the brigantine *Mary D. Hume* alone rendered thirty-seven whales, worth $400,000. A 380,000-ton mountain of fat from about 18,600 bowheads, its own treasure island thinly sliced into "bible leaves," between 1848 and 1914 went into cast-iron or copper shipboard trypots, huge vats heated by burning blubber chunks. The toil made underground mining seem like fun. Imagine a slaughterhouse, smoke-cloaked or slick as a skating rink, its greasy floor pitching. "We have to work like horses and live like pigs," one green hand wrote in his diary. On one six-year whaling voyage, the longest on record, sailors succumbed to madness, scurvy, and clinking cold. Their bodies were stored frozen until spring, when they could be buried. That first oil boom, lighting eastern homes, streets, and factories, greased the wheels of the pre-World War I US economy in the Gilded Age of unscrupulous capitalism.

Attitudes toward whales that had manifested in the Sledge Island artifacts more or less still prevailed when the Greenpeace skipper Paul Watson anchored his *Sea Shepherd* at Nome. On the way to confront Soviet factory whalers in Chukotka, he first had to face the anger of the Inupiat, who considered themselves cetacean caretakers also. Volunteers from the *Sea Shepherd* crew bought tees at the Native corporation store that cheekily read *Save the Whales, Eat an Eskimo.* Happiness on Alaska's west coast is a chin glazed with oil. The whale "feeds our spirit," the Inupiat say.

In Sledge Island's most recent newsworthy event, a charter plane homebound from a Russian Far East church mission in 1993 plowed into three-foot swells when both engines stalled. Seven people clambered from the sinking fuselage. Clinging to empty gas cans, they expected to live twenty minutes at best in the icy chop.

Hearing the charter's *Mayday!*, Anchorage air traffic control alerted a Bering Air pilot in the area who thought he'd spotted a whale's fluke, though "It could have been the tail of a plane." Circling, he then saw drifters below. Two helicopters arrived from Nome forty minutes after impact, with body bags instead of rescue gear. Surprised helpers leaning from the birds hovering low pulled in castaways, one or two simultaneously, and shuttled them to Sledge Island. The last stayed immersed for over an hour. One woman, her coat soaked, was too heavy to be boarded. Her unfazed savior head-scissored her between his legs while the aircraft ascended. Shortly before landing, she plunged from his grip, once again into misery.

All returned safely. The pilots and freestyle wrestler– guardian angel were officially honored; they'd tended to the sole Bering Sea plane crash on record with any survivors.

This former Beringian height keeps on giving. Lionized on TV, *Bering Sea Gold* Argonauts crew pontoon barges that snarf gold sands from the seafloor adjacent to Ayak. But its real riches lie in its layered stories. And Alaska is blessed: scores of Sledge Islands dapple its maps.

Nomehenge

Anvil Mountain, five miles north of Nome, offers a great vantage on muskoxen or, in July and December, sunsets and sunrises merely three hours apart. A schist-above-marble outcrop crowning the 1,200-foot peak inspired Nome's original name: Anvil City. On its southern toe, the Norwegian-American Leonard Seppala, known for his feats in the Serum Run, precursor of the Iditarod, made a 103-foot ski jump. Alaska's first ski club practiced there after 1901. Later, four Mordor-type towers near the Anvil spied on the dark fiend to our west in vigilance born of the Pearl Harbor debacle.

The monuments—diesel-powered "tropospheric scatter antennas"—belonged to the Cold War's White Alice Communications System (WACS), a forward defense against Russian nuclear and conventional strikes. This web, like a spider's, spun between the Aleutians, the North Slope's Barter Island, and the Canadian border, would spread any news of intrusion. It linked the Distant Early Warning System (DEW-line) to Air Force bases and strategic command centers. Seventy-one compounds throughout Alaska, nerved with miles of wiring and cable aimed at preventing Armageddon.

Western Electric built Nome's five-story-tall structures, an alien defiance of tundra hill profiles, concave like skateboard ramps, in 1957. As in other locations, one "feedhorn" per "movie-screen" antenna sprayed an ultra-high-frequency radio signal onto the parabolic surface, which then beamed it toward the horizon. Wave fractions bounced off the troposphere five miles above, kept from dissipating. More ordinary, short-range microwave towers augmented some sites. In this doomsday bucket brigade, "Nomehenge" received messages from Saint Lawrence Island's Northeast Cape, 126 miles away, and relayed them 136 miles to the eastern Seward Peninsula's Granite Mountain. Its crews lodged in Nome, but WACS outposts elsewhere had windowless cube annexes with dormitories and kitchens, laundries, walk-in freezers, and dining rooms. Designed to withstand nuclear blasts, they were as self-sufficient as lighthouses or aircraft carriers. Most installations straddled mountains far from civilization. "Siting and testing parties got there by dogsled, by tractor, by helicopter and by shoe leather," Western Electric reported, and "On numerous occasions, the men were forced to surrender before the onslaught of cold, wind and snow and were immobilized for days, even weeks."

The WACS code name could not have alluded to Jefferson Airplane's much later song "White Rabbit," which glorified *Alice in Wonderland* psychedelics. According to one tradition, Nome's "Alice" was an acronym for Alaska Integrated Communications Enterprise. But military code names had to consist of two words. "White" was chosen as apt for long

Alaskan winters. Alice White, however, had been a silent-film actress, so the two words were transposed.

The new transmission technology enhanced and stretched telecommunication services. Before WACS, only one phone call at a time could travel between Fairbanks and Nome. Northern lights "static storms" had disturbed World War II–era high-frequency (HF) radio communications. Until the mid-1970s, TV broadcasts were daily flown up from Seattle. If Seattle was fogged in, the previous day's evening news was repeated.

Launched in 1957, the Soviet *Sputnik* was the first nail in WACS's coffin. Alascom leased WACS eventually, but with satellites now on security and communications duty, by the late 1970s most of the system would be deactivated. Sheathing on the back of Anvil Mountain's giant ears contained lead paint and asbestos, and the Air Force, during Operation Clean Sweep, shipped over eight million pounds of contaminated top soil for treatment to Oregon—but choosy berry-pickers still won't harvest near the antennas.

Nome's Anglo military legacy is as old as the bridgehead city itself. Fort Davis, four miles from downtown along today's Nome-Council Road, lies wedged between the Nome River and beach near an estuary that the Inupiat, ardent eggers, value for its abundance of geese, cranes, gulls, loons, and shorebirds and for chum, pink, and coho salmon ascending the stream, where they mingle with burbot and Dolly Varden, an oceangoing troutlike char. Subsistence camps now take their rightful place at the Nome River mouth, as they did before the US Army moved in, though the shore is eroding and salmon runs have dried up. Construction on Fort Davis began in the spring of 1900. In June, companies of the 7th US Infantry took possession of the new post. The rows of two-story gabled barracks in what was then "Uncle Sam's farthest northern Army station" were abandoned in 1921 and dismantled after the boom had petered out. A Montana mining newspaper reported Nomeites protesting the closure of a fort "closer to overseas foreign shores than any other American mainland Army post." What an embarrassment it would have been "if a sloop load of hostile bolsheviki should sail across from the Eastern Siberian shores."

In its heyday in 1904, the post comprised an icehouse, stables, a bakery, grainery, coal house, oil house, gymnasium, hospital, magazine, bathhouse, pumphouse, shooting range, wagon shed, and its own cemetery. Housing infantry companies of up to 130 enlisted men and their officers, it was a frontier society unto itself, though not self-supporting: Sinrock Mary specifically relocated her reindeer herd south to supply the post. Soldiers on skis with overlong poles hunted, drilled, and policed their unruly realm to prevent claim-jumping, and recreated on ice skates as well. They maintained and extended the Fairbanks-to-Nome telegraph line to Port Safety, loading 150-pound rolls of galvanized iron wire onto packhorses and stringing it between poles they cut from the wilderness. An undersea cable from Port Safety linked up with the Military District of Alaska headquarters, Fort St. Michael. In a task not quite as risky or toilsome, "a posse of two soldiers" deputized to the marshal guarded bullion at one of the three banks.

Two soldiers prospecting near the edge of the tundra had discovered the beach sands that became known as the "Poor Man's Diggings." The place was promptly named "Soldiers' Gulch." The Nome-Sinuk Mining Company, which had staked the richest part of those shallow placers, asked the commanding officer, Lieutenant Cragie, to arrest 365 miners it accused of trespassing. He marched them "in a body" to town, where they were "confined in a frail building under guard." The men were discharged when the mining company refused to pay for their upkeep.

At and around the fort, veterans of the Spanish-American War, far from Cuba's hothouse climate, hauled ice for drinking water on horse-drawn sleds, cuddled polar bear cubs, shot swans for supper, shoveled snow wearing goggles, and poked fun at the sweepstakes with a musher in a clown getup. They ice-fished for herring, gave concerts, panned gold, camped in bell-shaped canvas tents, and paraded through town on the Fourth of July. Snow sometimes buried the roofed porches of Officer's Row. Races on skis issued by the quartermaster formed a part of field days, plank-hopping maneuvers meant to improve the troops' fitness. Contestants were forbidden to use more than one pole.

A squadron of four De Havilland biplanes commanded by a Captain St. Clair Streett left New York's Mitchell Field one July two decades later. The first Alaska air expedition, it touched down on the Fort Davis parade grounds before returning to Long Island in August. Commercial air transportation in the region developed soon after. The old Frontier was finished. A new era of flying machines dawned.

Hosting more pilots from afar, Nome became a springboard for materiel deployed on brutal Eastern Front battlefields during World War II. It served as a final refueling stop for almost 8,000 airplanes sent to the Soviets on the Alaska-Siberia Route (totaling 7,900 miles) during the war, as part of the Lend-Lease Act of 1941. Soviet pilots, many of them women, took over the planes in Fairbanks from their Air Transport Command WASP (Women Air Service Pilots) counterparts, who had ferried the planes from the factories, using the newly built ALCAN Highway as a compass bearing for the last leg of a journey the whole of which was accomplished in days, rather than the weeks or months that the more dangerous sea routes required. At Ladd Field in Fairbanks, the Soviets inspected the planes and painted red stars over the white ones on the wings and fuselages.

Soviet airmen stationed in Nome and Fairbanks saw their posting as "rest from combat." They "gypsy-danced," or armwrestled and drank with the Americans, toasting Stalin and Roosevelt, doused in perfume as an antiperspirant.

In the spring of 1944, a civilian Fairchild Pilgrim 100 A

hit trees and crashed on a mountain slope after takeoff from Nome in whiteout conditions. The crash claimed the lives of three crewmembers and three passengers. Nome's civilian airport shared use of the runway with Marks Army Airfield at the site of today's airport. Liberator B-24s, B-18s, and P-39 Airacobras (the Soviets' *Kobrushka*—"Little Cobra") stationed there guarded the northwest coast against Japanese attacks anticipated after the June 1942 Dutch Harbor bombing in the Aleutians. Reports of an enemy invasion fleet in the Bering Sea in the same month had triggered a massive troop buildup. In the unceasing midsummer daylight, pilots on 179 flights had rushed 2,272 men, twenty anti-aircraft guns, and tons of matériel to the nearly deserted mining camp, all within less than thirty-six hours. Army staff dubbed this, the first mass airlift in American military history, "Operation Bingo." It proved to be excellent training for the 1948 Berlin Blockade. (Deprived Germans nicknamed the transport planes bearing provisions the "Raisin Bombers.")

Two months before Bingo, Col. James "Jimmy" Doolittle had made history with the first-ever bombing run on Japan, a raid in revenge of Pearl Harbor that equally rattled the empire's psyche. His B-25s daringly launched from the 500-foot deck of the carrier USS *Hornet* without fighter escorts. The pilots of all but one of the planes, after hitting their target, ditched at sea, bailed out, or crashed in an occupied part of China. Doolittle had parachuted into a rice paddy, expecting to be court-martialed. His pluck has been credited to rough-and-tumble formative years (from 1900 to 1908) as a seven-year-old paperboy in the "Poor Man's Gold Rush" in Nome, where his father prospected and carpentered and his mother sewed for extra income. Irked by his long curls and cherub face, taller boys bullied him. Lithe but wiry and scrappy, Jimmy earned a reputation as a pugilist. He returned penniless to Los Angeles, as a stowaway on a freighter, from a later visit to his dad, who remained in Nome. "Nome Town Boy Makes Good," *The Nome Nugget* punned after his World War II Medal-of-Honor mission. The Japanese retaliating in the Aleutian chain suspected that Doolittle had struck from air bases there instead of a mobile runway.

Another icon of western Alaska during the war and in the early postwar years had earned his sobriquet by matching the gusto of a village chief in a raw whale-blubber eat-all-you-can.

In 1941, Major Marvin R. "Muktuk" Marston, stationed in Anchorage and visiting St. Lawrence Island with a comedian on a morale-boosting tour to military posts, noted that all the white men, except for a schoolteacher, had left and that the 700 Yupik villagers in Gambell and Savoonga felt nervous about hostile Japanese. They sensed that "strange and threatening events were impending," Alaska's wartime territorial governor Ernest Gruening wrote. A crew from a Japanese vessel had recently come ashore and spent several days on the island on undisclosed business. After the Dutch Harbor attack, the US Army greenlighted Marston's idea for a reserve troop of Eskimo Scouts. Enter the Alaska Territorial Guard (ATG).

No stranger to Nome's beaches, Marston had briefly worked there in 1906, at the age of fifteen, as a longshoreman. He'd returned to high school in Seattle before joining the Washington National Guard. Back in Alaska again, he helped volunteers to "trade a spear for a rifle," in one modern journalist's patronizing and incorrect view (given that rifles had arrived even before the whalers). Armored against the cold in fur—garrison cap to toe to fingertip; "Mukluk" as much as "Muktuk" Marston; clean-cut like a mid-career Sean Connery—traveled by dogsled across Alaska, recruiting more than 6,300 women and men from 107 communities who knew how to fight and survive in the stern terrain and climate. They were Tlingit, Unangan, Tsimshian, Haida and Athabaskan, but particularly, Yup'ik and Inupiat. Fondly remembered by many Inupiat, Marston would roll out a reindeer skin and bed down on the floor of any host's house. The ashes of the man commemorated posthumously as the honorary musher of the 1988 Iditarod were scattered on a midget island in Norton Sound. The guerilla army that he had conceived was to scope out mountain passes and river fords, place food caches, capture invaders, report enemy aircraft, shoot down incendiary balloon bombs that sailed in on the jet stream, and to assist in the evacuation of civilians. The ATG parka-sleeve badge, worn with pride, stood for "Alaska's Tough Guy," one guard member told a young daughter.

The same fear of invasion that swept through the Bering Strait had energized Barrow (now: Utqiaġvik) on the Beaufort

Sea coast. Inupiat there blacked out light seeping from cracks in their homes with reindeer skins. With Irene Itta's husband stationed in Nome, and the Territorial Guard requesting help from the Barrow Mothers Club, she stood guard during twelve-hour shifts on a tower, armed with a loaded pistol and spare bullets, while breastfeeding her baby. "We hear seven Japanese planes are coming to bomb, but they freeze and have to turn back," she remembered. Another Inupiaq woman, a mushing postmistress from an incorporated mining camp at the Seward Peninsula's neck, scored forty-nine out of fifty possible bull's-eyes during her Territorial Guard shooting practice. She bagged eight ptarmigans with three shots to feed Marston and a companion on one occasion. Women in Kotzebue made up a quarter of the force. One in Koyuk held the rank of sergeant, her gender disguised in the records by Marston. Young Guard members in Nome, when not drilling with wooden rifles, carried ammo or messages. Some Inupiat, bridging centuries during breaks in their military routine, went from firing machine guns back to carving harpoons—the whales would not cease their voyaging simply because of the quarrels of men.

Under the "Ice Curtain's" shadow of distrust and vigilance, brazen plans had been drawn up to deploy atomic weapons on western Alaska's soil, right under the enemy's nose. Already in 1949, a US "Sniffer" plane, a converted Superfortress outfitted with air sampling filters and patrolling between

Alaska and Japan, had detected debris from the first Russian nuclear test, years earlier than anticipated.

In 1958, one year before statehood and one year after Western Electric built Nome's antennas, the Atomic Energy Commission hatched a scheme that makes the White Alice landscaping look like child's play in the sandbox. It proposed the excavation of a coal-shipping harbor at Cape Thompson, 250 miles to the north, with a near-surface chain of six hydrogen bombs. Beating some post–World War II swords into plowshares, some spears into pruning hooks, government engineers considered the remolding of "a slightly flawed planet." The economic and military benefits of this Project Chariot—a port designed to faze the Soviets—were dubious.

Radioactive matter was sprinkled around Cape Thompson to measure how it moved about in runoff and groundwater. Ecological and technical concerns ultimately doomed the Ploughshare program. Funding evaporated; plans to pulverize caribou pastures fizzled. Chariot closed shop in 1962, the year Rachel Carson's *Silent Spring* revealed the creep of toxins up food chains. Reindeer herders by 1970 were well aware of the radiation load accumulating in slow-growing lichen from the fallout of US and Soviet nuclear testing.

Nothing could have clashed harder with attitudes toward the land and its creatures that the locals embraced. They voiced them in a story about the founding of Kauwerak, a Kuzitrin River village at the peninsula's center:

The old men told the people they must not disturb the ground around the place where they were going to build the houses. They told the people to go some distance from the village place and get the earth and sod to cover the parts of the houses that stood up above the ground. They told them to pack the earth to the village site on their backs or to work together in pairs to haul the sod in skins. This was so the ground around the village would not be broken up.

That's the sort of green NIMBY I can get behind.

Let us not, however, mistake the Inupiat for nose-rubbing, sod-hugging (for lack of trees) peaceniks. One-dimensional, idealized portraits deny them their full humanity. The threat of transcontinental violence underlay the Bering Strait region like plate tectonics about to rend bedrock—then, as it does again now. But traditional warfare as a rule was small-scale episodic raiding, not ideological all-out campaigning bent on occupation, subjugation, or ethnic annihilation.

Blood feuds or the lust for furs launched Chukchi incursions on the American coast by baidarka (the Siberian *umiak*) or by sleds, acts of revenge for fellow tribesmen killed in trade encounters in which tempers flared and mutual exchange and bargaining went awry. In the rare reverse direction, Ninikmuit from Cape Prince of Wales foremost earned battle laurels in Siberia. Ethnographic informants have glossed the Inupiaq verb *anuyak*, "to make war between nations," as "to seek vengeance." The "nations" could be other Eskimo societies or Athabaskan Indians also. Alliances were forged and broken in this Far-East rendition of *War and Peace.* Diomede Islanders "leagued with the [Yupik] Eskimo of the Siberian shore against the combined forces of those on King island and the American shore from the head of Kotzebue sound to Cape Prince of Wales and Port Clarence," but "at one time the inhabitants of the lesser Diomede island became angry with those of the greater Diomede island and united with the people of Cape Prince of Wales against them." It all reminds me a bit of Europe during the Napoleonic or Thirty Years' wars.

Captives, especially younger women and children, lived in servitude and could be sold, in one case for an iron spear and the hides of two white young reindeer. Alaskans killed hunters blown off course, stranded on their shores. Keeping male prisoners was too risky. The odd man might be spared to spread word of defeat, instilling fear in the enemy.

Conflict was sometimes settled in individual combat, with the duelists fighting it out on a stretched walrus skin staked with bone shards—pointy at both ends—and greased with lard. These wrestling bouts often resulted in death.

Attacks by a dozen or up to a hundred men happened at dawn, with warriors slipping unnoticed past sentries into a hostile camp. Pitched battles were brief, normally. Still, one between Wales and Teller contingents and Siberians near Teller lasted two days. With the invaders vanquished, the neighboring bands began to trade; one assumes the dead men's possessions changed hands. The fighting could turn no-holds-barred. A Russian source mentions Qawiaraq (Kaweramiut) women hiding in caves in the Imuruk Basin, throwing stones from steep cliffs onto the baidarkas who "even dove down and ripped their bottoms; the severed heads of the Siberians were left at the place of victory." The Siberians had sacked several villages.

For a Chukchi, victory warranted a tattoo, a dot on the back of a wrist. Veterans boasted constellations of those, since Chukotka's herders never submitted to Russian Tsarist rule enforced by the Cossacks. Inupiat parties wore slat cuirasses of animal ribs lashed together like xylophone bars, maneuvered in lines, loosed arrow volleys, considered wind directions, even erected earthworks and stockades. A favorite Yupik tactic the naturalist Edward William Nelson described "was to lie in ambush near a village until night and then to creep up and close the passageway to the kashim [qasgiq / qargi], thus confining the men within, and afterward shooting them with arrows through the smoke hole in the roof." Nelson also relates the fate of an enemy so hedge hogged with arrows that they prevented the corpse from touching the ground. In one instance, a fort of poles and skin boat covers protected women and children. Warriors on occasion secured the approaches with camouflaged pitfalls armed with spikes. In a commonly reported ruse, stone structures dressed as warriors suggested bigger than actual numbers of defenders. A "whole cloud of arrows" in 1820 welcomed Lt. Gleb Semenovich Shishmarev, who had come to explore in the ship *Good Intent*. His crew faced warriors not fooled by such propaganda, "armed from head to foot with spears, bows, and long rifles." The ethnohistorian Ernest S. "Tiger" Burch, Jr., whom I briefly knew as a student, called the Inupiat's "a sophisticated kind of warfare that rarely has been described for hunting peoples anywhere."

The basic Chukchi weaponry consisted of bows made from birch and larch wood, tipped with bone, canines, or flintstone, the bowstrings of sealskin strips or tendons. Arrowheads smeared with poison from the roots of certain buttercup species—an early form of chemical warfare—killed a wounded victim within a day if not "immediately sucked out." Slingshots too bridged the distance, while knives, clubs, and lances did damage up close. Early explorers remarked upon the fine shape in which the locals kept their arsenal. Body armor was cobbled together from tough walrus skin more than an inch thick, with telescoping bands, a hoop skirt of defense reaching from waist to ankle. Alternatives used breastplates of walrus-ivory, driftwood, or of steel obtained in trade. Helmets, shin and wrist guards as well as neck protectors and bendable elbow joints completed many an outfit. Protective suits were bulky and heavy, like knightly armor or lobsters' shells, and Chukchi braves considered wearing one the mark of a coward. The unencumbered, ungirdled, sometimes unclad, excelled at dodging missiles instead or at parrying them with the butt of a spear or at striking and breaking them with their shafts as they flew past, toward comrades. Headed straight for you, such arm rockets were hard to detect, like the round that gets you, which is the one you never hear. The extremely limber combatant caught spears with his hands to fling them back.

Some of the incoming death without doubt arrived in the form of five-foot whippy darts launched with an atlatl (an Aztec word; *nuqaq* in Yup'ik). These thin, grooved throwing boards with a bone spur at the end extended the arm's length by about twenty inches and provided an extra joint, thereby boosting a notched, fletched dart's speed, power, and reach. Its maximum range is the length of a football field—doubling the world record of the admittedly heavier javelin—with a kill zone of up to 130 feet. A recent archaeology paper doubts the atlatl dart's penetration power. It surmises instead that charging mammoths died by impalement on planted pikes tipped with stone points, with a force much greater than a thrown spear could deliver—the Inupiat hunted bears with that method. But a friend who recreates ancestral technologies assures me that early hunters acting in concert were perfectly capable of turning their target into an eight-ton dead hedgehog, a windfall like a whale, enough meat for a small band to feast on for weeks. Darts had to hit soft parts where they could embed deeply enough to reach vital organs, tests on elephant carcasses showed. Ditto for humans.

In flight, the flexible cane snakes through the air,

accelerating while building up energy, drawing on wave dynamics, a breaker pounding fleshy shores. Atlatl darts pierced the chainmail, leather, and cotton armor many Spanish conquistadors wore. This is a state-of-the-art technology at least 17,500 years old, a Stone Age bazooka for knocking out hirsute tanks. Carrying it across the Bering Strait, Siberian hunters also deployed it against mammoths, horses, camels, and ground sloths so big that they swallowed whole avocados. Stretching one's neck out from academic armor, one could even surmise that this missile system contributed to the mass destruction of megafauna unused to human hunting: those species never knew what had hit them. My money would have been on the tanklike, Beetle-size glyptodonts, armadillos on steroids, some of which swung a spiky-mace tail—humans on the pampas may have crawled under the carapaces of butchered ones for make-do shelter—but those were herbivores slow and probably no Einsteins.

Elsewhere in North America, the bow and arrow, faster to reload and easier to aim, replaced atlatls around 3000 BCE; the archery combo packed a wallop as well. A famous bowman in the battles on the Yukon once nailed an enemy to a house wall with an arrow like a bug pinned to cardboard.

Atlatls remained popular in the Arctic, western Alaska, on Kodiak Island, and in Prince William Sound and the Aleutians even after guns had been introduced. The Snake River site at the Nome harbor sketched in my author's note contained a rare, well-preserved, pre-contact specimen. A hunter in a kayak stalking sea-otter, walrus, seal or beluga could loft a dart seated, almost soundlessly. Raw materials for a set—driftwood, flintstone or ivory, sinew, ptarmigan or cormorant tailfeathers—were free for the taking, available locally. Hunters in the Yukon–Kuskokwim Delta retain throwing boards, albeit from aluminum skiffs. "Everyone carries one in his boat," Jimmy Okitkun from Kotlik told a journalist. "It's still the best way to kill a seal around here. We're not bringing them back—we never stopped using them." Buoyant themselves, with a bladder float attached darts remain effective in low salinity, in which rifle-shot seals quickly sink beyond retrieval. On the downside, especially on land, with the hunter taking a running start, another enthusiast grants, the atlatl's "extravagant throwing action" leads to more wild shots and can startle prey.

To prepare for war, all able-bodied Eskimo boys and men kept fit through drills and vigorous exercise. Target practice involved a game at the *qargi* in which darts were cast at a board with a bullseye painted on it. "Every warrior undergoes hard training, and spends all his leisure in various exercises," the Russian revolutionary, writer, and ethnographer Vladimir Bogoraz recorded in 1909. "The hero must run for long distances, drawing a heavily loaded sledge. He carries stone and timber, jumps up in the air, but above all, he fences with his long spear."

A far cry, this, from the regimen of the crews who manned

Nome's Cold War installations, though some may have had a dartboard, or a hoop bolted to an unadorned wall.

In one of those eerie resonances that give writers goosebumps, in 1945, natural low-grade uranium had been detected on Ear Mountain near Serpentine Hot Springs, one of the peninsula's highest peaks. The prospectors' report—surprise—mentions that region's "almost continuous dull weather and frequent driving rains."

Iŋiġaġik, the "Ears," has cultural significance, no surprise there. Snowmachiners riding from Shishmaref to the springs still navigate by this landmark. For centuries, the mountain they nicknamed "Grandpa" also forecast fog and foul weather for seal hunters out on the sea ice. Wearing a cloud cap or seemingly changing in size, it issued a warning to leave the shorefast shelf or point the boats homeward before a storm broke or the wind changed direction. Listening to your elders bettered the odds of survival.

After the shuttering of the Anvil Mountain White Alice station, the eleven acres it occupied were to revert to Nome's Sitnasuak Native Corporation, which, concerned about liability, planned to demolish the landmark. The city in recompense traded Sitnasuak a more valuable plot in town. It voted to preserve the beloved symbol. Thus, when fog banks block the coast and low tundra around town, the White Alice transmitters still welcome Bering Strait crabbers five miles offshore like beacons above. In the winter, they orient pilots, snowmachine riders, and a few hardy hikers. With all other scatter antennas dismantled, "the last ones standing" emblazon hometown pride on small-batch T-shirts. At some point, the druidic assemblage was considered for a listing on the National Register of Historic Places.

On a crisp cerulean Christmas-Day afternoon, I climb Anvil Mountain, accompanied by my wife, to burn off the feast's calories and mental glut. Our mukluks barely indent snow that the northerlies packed into slab. She has micro-spikes strapped to the soles of her boots. For me, it will be a challenge to descend without slipping and falling. In places, our steps ring hollow, like walking on summer's tomb.

Eight muskies at the crest paw the crust for lichens and encased grasses, moving shadows that seem to absorb light, umber boulders whose breaths plume in the air. They look like they sprang from the Anvil, chips from the old metamorphic block. The breeze numbs my cheekbones. It rimes eyelashes and my beaver-skin hat, the same way hoar has feathered weather gauges on scalloped drifts close to the curved "Billboards" proclaiming hostility. The Cold War was always a tad colder here in Nome than in DC.

Last rays gild distant Sledge Island and Eisenhower's billowing sails, meant to thwart noxious darts. Brightness recharges them for a few moments, signal fires on a forlorn cape. The hills quickly will dim, swelling dusty blue below a lilac horizon.

"Will your shields bedarken me?" the Inupiaq poet Joan

Naviyuk Kane asks in "White Alice Changes Hands." On this fourth eve after the solstice, they do the opposite, cupping an apricot glow while Earth boomerangs, drawing closer to the sun again.

"Working To Beat The Devil" JE

Northland Shangri-las

There are spas where history lingers like a consumptive ghost. Pilgrim Hot Springs, sixty washboard miles north of Nome, is one of those. In the early 1900s, during the gold rush, it was a resort for socialites and for miners with sore backs, complete with a dance hall, a roadhouse, and of course, a saloon. The roadhouse and saloon burned in 1908, and the property (in an act of penance?) went to the Jesuit Father Bellarmine Lafortune. Seizing his luck, Lafortune turned it into an orphanage. Famished children found a home of sorts at Pilgrim Hot Springs. The Spanish flu epidemic of 1918 struck Native Alaskan communities especially hard, leaving behind an army of dependents housed in the Catholic mission that "Little Father" Lafortune had established. Though there had been outbreaks before, "The real bad times did not come until the miners came to look for gold," an Inupiaq history states. The hot springs kept indoor plumbing from freezing and the ground thawed early, and with summer daylight around the clock, food was grown there successfully. Vegetable gardens yielded boxes of cabbages, turnips, potatoes, and greens; fresh, antiscorbutic victuals that were always in short supply. A mining town of about sixty sprang up close by that had a post office and stayed active from 1923 to 1941. It connected to Nome through the Kougarok Railroad. Leonard Seppala, who gained fame as a winter Olympics athlete and the musher pivotal in the Serum Run, drove a "pupmobile" on those tracks: teams of up to eight dogs hitched to a small railroad cart. One practical Sourdough ploughed his acres with sled dogs. Locals rode a railbike or the train, the Americas' farthest western and northern railroad, for sightseeing or hunting, or for fishing in Salmon Lake, much as they go there today by car.

Life at Kruzgamepa, as the springs also were known, "offered a pleasant relaxation from the business cares and social duties of Nome," Esther Birdsall Darling wrote in her huskie biography *Baldy of Nome.*

How different the Native experience had been.

In a group photo from 1922 staged near the springs, the faces of four Ursuline Sisters of Our Lady of Lourdes (the "black-and-white people" to the Inupiat, for their bicolored habit, not their dogmatism) framed by white wimples and scalloped coifs, shine like shells in a sea of children with tanned countenances. The descendant of one Inupiaq orphan relates how, "When they were picked up, they didn't speak any English at all. They were forced to learn English." Girls sewed mukluks and cooked while boys worked the fields. For one Fourth of July celebration, "a real, live" Uncle Sam rode on a four-wheeled cart decorated with bunting and pulled by some boys. This was Maggie Jack, a girl from Diomede Island "who did not look an inch like Uncle Sam," but spectators commended her effort, as she was the only one who had volunteered. The parade also featured two elephants: four boys under two blankets, though one lacked a tail. A pesticide sprayer used in the mission gardens served as the trunk of one of the beasts, which doused bystanders. Races were held indoors sometimes, to escape the mosquitoes. In the year after the historical photo was taken, a Jesuit priest froze to death on the banks of the Pilgrim River in an attempt to deliver a box of oranges to the orphans for Christmas. By 1941, with firewood in the area now scarce, the number of orphans declining, and the buildings in need of repair, the mission shut down.

I confess I never made it to Pilgrim Hot Springs, that oasis in the flats between the Kigluaiks and Hen and Chickens Mountain (a hill, really, crowned by animalistic tors) just as I never climbed Singatook Mountain, a "weather maker" with a gorgeous summit ridge on the Teller Highway (a fancy designation for a seventy-two-mile dirt road). Melissa did visit with friends one day in early June, after work. The road was so rutted that they parked and walked the final two miles. She had heard about children buried in the field. The place felt haunted to her, with a forlorn tricycle ditched in the grass. The grayed, two-story clapboard building, its front partly wood-shingled, a cross crowning its belfry, had been boarded up. The Kigluaik mountains—"the Kigs" to Nomeites—stood flecked with snow, the few poplars still bare. The sky, overcast.

The springs, channeled into a tub built from wood slats ringed by a deck, were too hot for my wife to soak in. They have been measured at 178 degrees. The laconic name, Uunaqtuq, if you speak Qawiaraq (the local Inupiaq dialect), should be warning enough: "It is hot." At the even more remote Selawik Hot Springs, east of Kotzebue Sound, where separate bathhouses accommodate Inupiat and their Athabaskan Indian neighbors, people warn you to exit quickly to keep from getting cooked if you see small hot-air bubbles rising in the water. Melissa and her friends left Pilgrim Hot Springs after midnight and arrived back in Nome in the morning twilight.

I *did* get a chance to indulge in another Seward Peninsula natural hot tub, and as part of my job no less. It was a fly-in trip with two clients I guided, to Serpentine in the Bering Land Bridge National Preserve. Unlike fountains of youth in Katmai and the Aleutians—North Pacific links in the famed Ring of Fire—Serpentine is an extension of the Interior Alaskan Hot Springs Belt. Its sources lie within or along the margins of granitic plutons—gigantic bodies of magma that slowly pushed through fissures and ballooned like aneurysms before cooling near the crust's surface at the same time the gold-bearing veins precipitated from mineralized, scalding-hot water risen in cracks; exposed, these elephantine outcrops become visible as tors. Radioactive decay of uranium and thorium in the rocks and the deep circulation of groundwater drive the heating, to 212 degrees at Serpentine.

That is our, science-based, story. The Kaweramiut have their own take on how Serpentine, Pilgrim, and other regional hot spots came into being.

In their account, Ekeuhnick, a larger-than-life figure credited with the origins of certain technologies—the first boat, fire, etc.—one day felt the ground underfoot shaking, followed by a deafening rumble. When he turned, he saw a great mountain about to blow up, with a red tongue of fire licking up from the smoke and glowing embers advancing down its slopes. Many kinds of birds and animals fled the confusion, creating a cacophony that drowned out that of the mountain. Ekeuhnick jumped onto the back of a panicky bear and held on tight to its neck ruff. When he was reunited with the people of his settlement, they all heard a "terrible bellow" accompanying "a great spear of fire" lancing upward from the mountaintop, and "red-orange color rolling all the way down" to the bottom. Ekeuhnick had foretold all this. Days after the eruption, the landscape lay dead: "black rock, like water frozen, everywhere."

Once again, modern science corroborates Native oral testimony. A mere 1,605 years ago, the earth indeed split wide open, giving birth to the Lost Jim Lava Flow in the Imuruk Basin, the peninsula's fiery souterrain, oozing and spreading from a cone now cooled, barren for the time being. Few of Earth's active volcanic regions are cold enough to support permafrost, and this field of ropy pahoehoe lava holds clues for volcano-ice interactions on Mars. Twenty thousand years earlier, eruptions thick with steam had quarried the largest known maars on Earth near Deering—Devil Mountain Lakes, five shallow craters now drowned—when lava tunneled through frozen ground. Otto von Kotzebue named the adjacent small shield volcano Teufelsberg, projecting Manichaean views onto the sundered landscape.

When I arrived at Serpentine with my clients, centuries after the cataclysm, the Park Service, charged with maintaining its facilities, occupied half the bunkhouse, working on them. The crew was fixing the bathhouse, but the pipe that should have siphoned cold creek water into the tub didn't pipe. It dribbled. The hot water spigot, however, worked fine. The only way to make the temperature bearable was to haul five-gallon buckets—about twenty—from the creek. I couldn't just wait for the hot tub to cool, because it leaked faster through cracks between the floorboards than it mellowed with cold influx from the pipe. My clients were shy, and after laboring with my coolant like Mickey, the sorcerer's apprentice in Disney's *Fantasia*, I had the bathhouse to myself. Arms wearied by heavy buckets turned into Jell-O in Serpentine's silky embrace. The warmth spawned dim memories of the womb.

Stark granite tors and bald hills and steam curling from the stream beyond the fogged windowpanes harked back to a bygone, primordial world. I half expected mammoths to come rumbling through. As it happens, archaeologists have found fluted stone spear tips in the Clovis style on one of the hills crowding around. They've also troweled up charcoal 12,000 years old, possibly from the fires Pleistocene hunters built while camped there.

The Inupiat of Shishmaref, on the coast, maintain close ties to Serpentine Hot Springs. They call their Blue Lagoon Iyat, "Cooking Pot," or "A Site for Cooking." This is a shamanistic training ground, a numinous boot camp; in the old days non-shamans shunned it until called upon. According to one legend, the mushrooming tors, jointed, suggestive of remnants of the Great Wall of Cuzco, are Deering women who got petrified as punishment when they approached the forbidden location. The setting, to borrow from Kierkegaard, "looks like a legend made visible" but with Inupiaq figures in place of Lot's anonymous wife. You can easily pick out another figure, The Drummer, seated, beating the skin of his wood-hoop *qilaun*—perhaps it was he who cast that spell. In the quiet, if you stay long enough, the air around him throbs. Each of these stone sentinels is said to exude specific healing powers. People in Shishmaref also told a visiting anthropologist that each tor near the springs had a name and related story, though they could not provide either. Perhaps, that lore has been lost. Or, old taboos still hold sway.

When Shishmaref residents plucked spear points or similar ancient artifacts from their eroding beaches, spirits that dwelt at the springs whisked the unsuspecting back here via out-of-body flight, or underground, for some harsh lessons. The initiates would enter Iyat, pulsing gateway to parallel planes of existence, diving through permafrost into the nether realm. Attesting to the numen of archetypal topographies, other cultures as well saw landscapes that swallowed humans—"shifting landscapes of wet and dry, hanging mists, bubbling marsh gases," in the broad brush strokes of one environmental historian—as conduits to elusive dimensions. In places like Serpentine's heath we still "commune with the more-than-human forces." We muted their voices when we walled off and roofed sacred space at springs, hilltops, groves, alcoves, and singular trees for shrines, temples, mosques, cloisters, and churches.

Shamanism is no longer practiced in Northwest Alaska, officially. But through its Tribal Doctor Program, the Maniilaq Association, a regional nonprofit, has arranged visits to Serpentine Hot Springs more recently for Inupiaq healers who, arriving by small plane instead of trance flight, uphold this curing tradition. Despite its remoteness, the rabbit-hole plunge pool is the preserve's most visited site.

Inupiat have taken the waters at thermal springs for generations. Mineralized baths promised relief for hip and back pain, for headaches, arthritis, skin rashes, and other ailments long before there were HMOs. Herbs for curing stomach problems, ulcers, and sores could be harvested year-round on snow-free ground close by. Tempering the body, people drank from the springs and consumed medicinal plants beforehand. Some collected spring water and herbal home remedies. Their pull made people travel hundreds of miles to frequent this spot. One elder recalled how in 1935, during the twilight days of western Alaska's reindeer-herding industry, a man brought his sick cousin from Cape Espenberg to Serpentine. The cousin rode bundled up in a sled hitched to four reindeer, on a journey that lasted a week. The patient and his driver stayed for a month, until they ran out of food.

Hot springs provided mental as well as physical breaks. "It was way more complicated than they are doing now, just focusing on the physical body," an Inupiaq man raised near Serpentine reminisced about the rites of immersion. Feeling the world's gravity reduced, literally, or entirely lifted from them, people connected with their better selves and family, with their culture and the land. Such springs demarcated a neutral, even a sacred, zone; conflict was not tolerated.

Those in the know not only consider the past at these springs, but also peek into their future. A mukluk's leather ties dipped into the seething water augur either a long life or impending death for the wearer. If your laces curl up, make sure your will is in order. Serpentine was, and still is, a precarious portal. Avoid visits while menstruating or with your mind or emotions on edge, elders advise—just when you need a soothing soak most. They caution against going alone or staying too long. A careless person may not make it back as him- or herself.

II. PERSONALITIES

The Lemming Lady

Rodents nesting inside one's home would prompt most people to set traps or to call pest control. For the Midwestern naturalist Sally Carrighar, during one season in Nome, they presented a chance to hone her literary and observational skills. Lemmings teem on the pages of her *Icebound Summer*, rubbing shoulders with walruses, arctic foxes, and whales. She wove them into the narrative as a theme, partly because she saw their short lives as symbolic of that season's brevity in the North. They also pop up in *Wild Voice of the North*, her memoir of living with Bobo the "boss dog," a blue-eyed gift, part wolf, part Siberian husky.

Bobo became a celebrity through a 1953 portrait in the *Saturday Evening Post Magazine* penned by his new owner, who once ate hamburger while she fed him prime moose steak. His rise to the top of Nome's fierce canine society held echoes of Buck in Jack London's *Call of the Wild*. Unlike Buck, who in print forever "sings a song of the younger world, which is the song of the pack," Bobo declined in his twilight years; but even then, Carrighar writes, "enfeebling age could not rob him of his dignity and sense of authority."

An undervalued Rachel Carson, Carrighar evoked animal lives in the way of a page-turner, melding scientific scrutiny—insights gleaned through the then still young discipline of ethology—with empathy. She was, in the words of one critic, an "animal anthropologist": a "visitor seeking admittance into the animals' community." Her lemming descriptions glow with intimacy, the knowledge that rubs off between housemates. Often, "they would stop in a kind of rapt pause, with their heads tilted pertly as if they were weighing delicious choices." They slept "curled over like infant porcupines, with their fur pushed out and their small button noses cushioned upon their chests."

The year before, in 1950, in Unalakleet, she had searched in vain for the prolific critters. Her butterfly net at the burrows dug up stayed empty. Not even the local Inupiaq kids, "whose interest in everything about animals is always intense and spontaneous," found any for her. The Coast Guard ferried Carrighar to St. Lawrence Island, but none could be captured there either, as if they had dissolved into thin air. Upon landing, she was told that the hordes reported were "mice"—tundra voles, in fact. Her Norton Sound stay, she had realized, coincided with one of the famed lemming population crashes that happen about every thirty years.

Everything out there eats lemmings, from eagles to grizzlies to weasels, gulls, arctic foxes, and wolves. Canadian Inuit caught and ate lemmings on occasion, but Carrighar mentions a bush pilot stuck on the North Slope who subsisted on them for three weeks before he was rescued. The fruitfulness of other-than-human predators' recurringly matches that of their rodent prey when those "breed at an abnormal rate." Conversely, when lemmings die off, fewer cubs, whelps, and chicks survive. Snowy owls irrupt as far south as the Carolinas after their Arctic morsels have dwindled. Female lemmings drop up to eleven pups at three- to four-week intervals. It's one of nature's win-win situations. Unless you're the one starving or eaten.

Since the sixteenth century, accounts of the creatures falling from heaven during storms before dying off suddenly had been circulating throughout the northern hemisphere from Norway to the Western Arctic. An Inuit name for the collared lemming, *kilangmiutak*, describes "one who comes from the sky." Active year-round, lemmings mostly stay out of sight, tunneling snow, digging into permafrost, scurrying through the low vegetation. When they overrun their habitat, they apparently manifest out of nowhere.

Another myth persists, about lemmings committing mass suicide in the open sea. The 1958 award-winning classic Disney documentary *White Wilderness*, which showcased such scenes, resorted to sleight of eye. It used editing, tight camera angles, lemmings running on a snow-covered turntable, and those herded off a cliff to suggest a tawny, bob-tailed flood, seemingly earless, with a death wish. In fact, lemmings, which can reproduce when they're a month old, migrate in mass to forage at the peak of population spurts. Carrighar, in her mind-in-a-foreign-body style, rendered that frenzy thus: "There were too many lemmings—that was the core of their difficulty… Being sensitive little beasts, they became overstimulated by superfluous numbers of their own kind. They had tried to escape, but with pitiable irony, all tried to escape together." In addition, she would learn that lemmings swim rather well. They waxed frantic near the time of each full moon, and Carrighar put them in a tub partly filled with water, to calm them. She thought lunar phases might explain their urges to migrate.

She'd finally managed to study her subjects up close and personal, though in much smaller numbers, after obtaining five specimens from children in Barrow, where she flew in on a charter plane that afterward wrecked, stranding her in town. One of the "tiny marmots" that she guarded against Bobo later birthed two litters. A sixth had been turned loose, as it was so combative that it endangered the others. She reasoned that relocating lemmings from Alaska—"away from their own kinds of food, water, hours of daylight, barometric pressure, weather, relation to the Magnetic Pole"—would imperil them or skew her results. Perhaps she quailed at yanking them from their environment, recalling her own birth by forceps, which had disfigured and traumatized her: she had suffered nerve damage and underwent reconstructive jaw surgery. Her mother, a psychotic, abused her verbally and urged her to commit suicide and once tried to strangle her. During a phase of depression and heart disease, she'd begun to communicate with birds she fed on her windowsill, and a mouse that lived in her radio sang to her. Still, she dodged anthropocentrism, a narrowing perspective, in her writing. Soured on humanity, she never had children or married.

Carrighar's Nome research base and ersatz colony was a late Victorian mansion she bought, the only house in town that had wallpaper and probably the first two-story house on the Bering Sea coast. A square tower with a pyramid roof sprouted at its front, and it was clad with clapboards on the first story and wood shingles on the second. Special arrangements had been made, because permafrost warped all the walls. A Jewish miner built it in 1903-04, a native of Germany, "a generous, whole-souled man" made flush by three major strikes during the gold rush.

This man, Jacob Berger, a man with "many friends in the Northland," owned two trophy dog teams, which placed first and second in the 1909 All Alaska Sweepstakes. Inaugurated in 1908, the Sweepstakes was the world's first organized sled dog race series. It ran 408 miles from Nome to Candle and back, traversing the Seward Peninsula twice, tracing the telegraph lines that linked Fort Davis, roadhouses, mining camps, and outlier settlements. The dogs, passing through the storm-swept waste of Death Valley, one of the waypoints, wore "canton flannel moccasins for their feet should they encounter icy trails; dark veils [of mosquito netting] for their eyes if the sun is too strong; and [rabbit skin] blankets in case of a cutting wind." Some lead dogs wore snow goggles.

In the 1910 race, the Dundee-born mushing legend Allan Alexander "Scotty" Allan came to grief when a snow ledge collapsed and he and his team tumbled two hundred feet down a sheer drop. He made it to Nome with "five dogs hitched, two in the sled, and three tied behind." The Sweepstakes four years later almost killed the future serum runner Leonard Seppala, who veered dangerously close to a cliff in poor visibility.

"What bull-fighting is to the Spaniard, horse-racing to the Kentuckian, a Marathon to the Greek, Derby Day to the Englishman, so is the annual All Alaska Sweepstakes Dog Race to the Alaskan," the Nome Kennel Club swaggered. As in today's football games, spectators rubbing shoulders on Front Street wore the colors of their favorite teams. "The first great race took place with all the pomp and ceremony that marks the carnival time in sunnier lands," a Kennel Club president remembered about these "famous Dog Days of Nome." She cared about the canine athletes' wellbeing, as Carrighar did about that of her lemmings. Female compassion had started to mellow the town's ragged edges.

The Sweepstake cash purse—$10,000 for the champion team's owner that year (versus a pocket watch for the musher)—drew a Russian fur trader to enter the 1909 competition. His ten runty Siberian huskies in their debut on American soil under a Danish sailor's command took third place, crossing the finish line looking as fresh as they had at the start. The betting odds had been stacked 100-to-1 against them. It was said that, had they won, they would have broken the Bank of Nome, and that their placing third might have been the result of a race rigged. More likely, the Dane's inexperience was to blame. Their surprise success marked the ascendence in popularity in Alaska of the "stoic little aliens," this wiry, foxlike Chukchi breed. The trader, less glamorously, had to sell some dogs to afford the return fare to Russia.

Today, still, it is hard to avoid the mania that grips this town for a few weeks every year. As evidence, I submit the siren's wailing during the Iditarod, which announces teams mushing in at all hours, ensuring that some spectators will greet them, even the last, the "Red Lantern" finisher, at the end of their grueling treks. Its lone howl sometimes woke me as I lay in bed, toasty under down, glad I did not have to be out there.

But I digress—again; Alaska stories, especially underdog stories, will do that to me. History is a rabbit hole that predates the Internet. And two degrees, rather than six, separate people in our outpost state. Let us return to Sally Carrighar in her new old digs.

Jacob Berger had based the design of his house on a pattern from an architectural book, modified for the harsh subarctic climate, with high-quality materials shipped from West Coast ports, even from New York and Chicago: "Much of the glass was plate; doors and sills were of extra strength; wainscotting was smooth-planed; shakes and shingles were of first-grade cedar." A round captain's window flanked each side of the master bedroom.

The apartment we rented on Lomen Ave. had an alcove that faced the street, with windows on three sides. I would sit for hours in an easy chair there, reading and thinking and watching the world go past, like a skipper on his bridge, or a lighthouse keeper in his lantern-room perch. Do not underrate the importance of windows where days are short, often drab, or linger all night in peach and lavender tones.

Unusual for the period in its size and number of windows, the Jacob Berger house looks like a rustic cross between the *Home Alone* home and a Transylvanian castle. When Carrighar moved in, an eight-foot bathtub sat in the middle of the bedroom, which was strange, since there was no second-floor plumbing. Hot water had to be carried one teakettle at a time. Wind entered not only through cracks in the walls but through the downstairs plumbing as well. At times, it was strong enough to lift her hair while she stood in the living room. Other sources relay that elsewhere on this coast because of the powerful winds "front doors had to be fastened permanently and an entrance made at the back."

The lemmings, less opulently, lived in habitats she had commissioned. One group was downstairs. The other, in a sort of free-range replica upstairs, was meant for restocking her first-floor population if necessary. She gained a reputation among some Nomeites of raising rats and letting them scurry all over her house.

Her subjects stayed busy, despite their new surroundings. She quickly noticed play involving a metered activity wheel—think hamster cage gym—and thought that her "little zoo functioned to everyone's satisfaction." Nests she repositioned were reassembled by the following morning in their old place. The lemmings had "more fire, more drive" than mice, and more impatience.

As in the apocryphal stories, after several months, her wards started to disappear from the glass-sided vivarium like Bering Strait sea ice in June. One under her care had fallen into the drip-cakepan beneath the oil heater and died days later, despite her giving it a soapy bath (an example for why oil extraction in the Arctic is never a good idea). Another, she found with its throat torn, a wound inflicted in fighting. Always, she heard them topside, "running about, spinning their wheel, chirring." And then, "from a certain day on," there was silence. With the help of an Inupiaq youth, Carrighar dismantled that room, sifting through the soil, barrels of grass, and driftwood she stored there to replenish her indoor tundra environment. But the fate of the final four, like that of twenty-four humans gone allegedly missing from Nome between 1960 and 2002, remains a mystery. The FBI, investigating, ruled that Alaska's harsh wildness was likely to blame. Still, as in the case of the vanished lemmings, foul play cannot be ruled out.

Shadow Catchers in the Land of the Midnight Sun

The man in the picture does not look like the bookish type. In a famous 1899 photo—a self-portrait in his trademark sepia-tone style—he sports a rakish felt slouch hat, turtleneck sweater, white canvas jacket, and Van Dyke beard, suggesting a better-groomed Buffalo Bill.

And yet, this former homesteader, this six-foot-two, thirty-year-old citizen of gold rush-era Seattle, launched the most expensive and expansive book project by an individual, the largest ethnographic enterprise ever undertaken in this country: *The North American Indian.*

Between 1895 and 1930, he amassed thousands of images from roughly eighty tribes. Of these, 1,500 large-format photogravure prints on fine papers made the final cut for his magnum opus of oversize folios accompanied by twenty text volumes. The bound books alone take up five feet of shelf space.

Awed by the fledgling medium, photography, Edward Sherriff Curtis's indigenous subjects nicknamed him "Shadow Catcher," but the record he left is much more substantial. He augmented his pictorial hoard with Hopi vocabulary, with biographical sketches of Nez Perce chiefs, with information about all aspects of Lakota life. On hundreds of Edison wax cylinders, he preserved stories, ceremonies, and music by peoples who, his fellow countrymen thought, would soon be extinct. But they survived Manifest Destiny, and the bereft turned to Curtis's collections to revive forgotten customs, to connect with a past that was quickly fading from view.

The man in the picture does not look like a family man either.

He was and he wasn't. Footloose, a workaholic prone to depression, he sacrificed wedded bliss on ambition's altar. His wife divorced him over his long absences in pursuit of his books. Living with his daughter Beth in Los Angeles, where they ran a studio, Curtis worked for Hollywood directors as a still photographer and cameraman (as on *The Ten Commandments*) when funds ran low. In 1927, homebound from his last trip to Alaska, he was briefly arrested for failing to pay alimony to his ex-wife, Clara. At the time of his divorce eight years before, Curtis had been nearly broke; while he paid his assistants, he himself was unsalaried, investing any profits in his studio and equipment.

He'd long ago alienated his brother Asahel, who had gone to the Klondike, by signing and publishing but not crediting Asahel for work he had done there. In a letter to *The Century Illustrated Monthly Magazine*, where the photos appeared, Edward falsely summarized exploits from his "trip over different trails to the Alaskan goldfields." He bragged that he had returned with "the most complete and the latest" sets of glass-plate negatives that showed the mad rush "more clearly and truthfully than can any mere pen picture." (He was referring, I hope, to the ink illustrations then common, not to writers' descriptions.)

In 1897, as a budding photographer of Seattle's elite apprenticed in Edward's studio, Asahel had joined the stampede to the Yukon goldfields with a camera he had built. He crossed on the Chilkoot Pass Trail the following spring. After working a poor claim and documenting the miners' efforts, he'd realized that "The lure of gold brought thousands to the Northland," though "working daily with it some of the romance was lost." In Edward's opinion, those 1,500 or so negatives sent home belonged not to Asahel but to the studio, which had sponsored the venture. Parting in anger, Asahel established his own Seattle studio and grew into a known landscape photographer, a booster for Mt. Rainier National Park, and a founding member of the Northwest conservationist club The Mountaineers. The brothers reportedly never again spoke with each other, not even at their mother's funeral.

Still, throughout his life, E.S. Curtis remained close to his second child and eldest daughter, Beth, his manager in Seattle who funded his Alaska venture and helped set up and run a new studio when he moved to Los Angeles. His daughter Florence, much less familiar with her absentee father, urged him to write and record parts of his life story during his twilight years.

A chance meeting on Mt. Rainier's slopes in the year Asahel sailed for the Klondike had Curtis embark on his own first trip to Alaska. When Curtis warned a party of climbers of dangers ahead, one of them struck up a friendship with the trim mountaineer. He was Clinton Hart Merriam, head of the US Biological Survey and co-founder of the National Geographic Society. Impressed with his work after a tour of Curtis's Seattle studio, Merriam asked Curtis to be the official photographer for the 1899 Harriman Alaska Expedition. Steaming north through the Inside Passage on the luxuriously outfitted *George W. Elder*, Curtis met another fan of Alaska: fellow expedition member and Sierra Club founder John Muir. More important, however, was the mentorship he received from professional ethnographers onboard, which, three decades later, would culminate in some of his most celebrated work, gathered in volume XX of *The North American Indian*.

Curtis left for his second cruise to Alaska on the steamer *Victoria* in the summer of 1927, accompanied by daughter Beth and the young ethnologist Stewart Eastwood. He traveled in less stately fashion this time, on a tight budget. After arriving in Nome, the trio continued to Nunivak, King Island, Little Diomede, Kotzebue, Selawik, Noatak, and Cape Prince of Wales. Curtis had never been happier, as the Native culture there still appeared to be vibrant and Alaska reminded him of youthful adventures in the Pacific Northwest. For the first time in his career, he kept a day-by-day journal.

Nome, on the other hand, was but a husk of its gold rush self. Its population had shrunk from 20,000 to 750, most of them Eskimos. Stores, shops, hotels, and gambling dens housed only the wind. Sidewalk boards were broken or missing. It was "a deserted mining town," Curtis wrote. They stayed at the Golden Gate Hotel, where "the floors sag to the four winds" and "If you want a bath, you arrange it for today and perhaps you will get it tomorrow." In a portrait he sat for, for one of the Lomen brothers, he looks professorial—round steel-rim glasses below a white wispy tuft sticking up from his balding dome; still trim, still sporting Buffalo Bill facial hair, plus a vest and tie; tendrils ghosting up from a cigarette leisurely held, his other hand cradling that elbow—an impression negated by a suit jacket boldly striped. The decades have engraved his brow. He looks quizzical, as if he were second-guessing the setup, lighting or angle. His pose seems somewhat self-conscious, studied. This photographer may have been more comfortable behind a camera than in front of one.

Curtis bought a fishing boat, *Jewel Guard*, which came with its previous owner. They called her a "mud hen," an alias for the American coot, a drab, tubby marsh bird with shortish wings. But she wore a white coat of paint, with dark elegant trimming, radiant as an albatross, on a sunny day. According to Beth, the skipper—Harry the Fish, a Swede—hated liquor, tobacco, and women. He had a reputation as a "sea coward" but may simply have been protecting his health, passengers, freight, and investment. The boat, about forty feet long, two-masted, with a cabin, Beth deemed "not so bad." Curtis, who had some experience with seagoing vessels, thought her "an ideal craft for muskrat hunting in the swamps but certainly never designed for storms in the Arctic Ocean."

While Curtis enjoyed hopscotching to Northwestern Alaska's islands and along its coast, a motion picture billed as *A True Story of Life and Love Among the Eskimos* wove a spell of polar lifeways for US audiences. This was *Primitive Love*, a silent docu-drama in the style of *Nanook of the North*, though much less accomplished than that grand opus of early Arctic ethnographic movies. The credits listed a certain Ray Mala, at the time of shooting fourteen years old, still largely unknown, as the assistant cameraman and playing himself.

Ray Agnaqsiaq Wise had first seen the wan December light of day in 1906 from inside a sod house in the mining camp Candle at the head of Kotzebue Sound, where glasses would ride if the Seward Peninsula indeed were a nose. His father was a Russian Jewish trader, his mother Inupiaq, and Ray would become the first Alaskan to grow into a Tinseltown figure, one of the few non-White actors who until then had been given a leading role. At the height of his career, "The Eskimo Clark Gable" worked with directors Alfred Hitchcock and Cecil B. DeMille (the latter of whom Curtis also assisted).

At fourteen, he had hired on as a ship's cook in Nome,

bound for Seattle. After losing his family to the flu at fifteen, he caught a lucky break in 1921, when Captain Frank Kleinschmidt, whom he might have met onboard, hired him to help with *Primitive Love*.

From 1921 to 1924, tracing the Proto-Inuit exodus in reverse, Mala served as the official cameraman for Knud Rasmussen. Then the man from backwater Alaska cranked out the newsreel of the finish of the serum relay run to Nome that kept American mainlanders riveted. The diphtheria antitoxin's arrival had to be reenacted in the morning for Mala, because when it had reached the town, it had been too dark for filming.

"Snowhouses" for the 1933 MGM production *Eskimo* (alternatively titled *Mala the Magnificent* or, chauvinistically, *Eskimo Wife-Traders*) were built near Nome. The book the movie is based on, by the Danish explorer-anthropologist Peter Freuchen, has a Greenland setting that the movie plot transposed to Alaska, so the cliché snow igloos are out of place. The first feature film in Inupiaq—or any Native American language for that matter—it still employed Asian-American actresses to play Mala's spouses. The glottal sounds of Inupiaq gave the technicians and their primitive mikes trouble, overloading the latter. After his breakthrough, Wise dropped his given name for the more euphonious and exotic "Mala," less of a challenge to most tongues than Agnaqsiaq.

The crew's land base at the Teller reindeer station was known as "Camp Hollywood." It saw Inupiaq extras striking for higher wages and Inupiaq strikebreakers replacing them. At one point, dog teams had to rescue the film crew caught in sea ice. The staff included dozens of cameramen and technicians, six pilots, and a chef from a four-star hotel in Los Angeles—many of the Native actors, for the first time in their lives, tasted bacon, cornflakes, and oranges. With the harsh summer sunlight, pink paint sprayed from aircraft dulled the snow's glare.

Mala performed his own stunts. According to Freuchen, who starred as the film's ship captain, the actor spent three afternoons trying to lure a wolf into attacking him. He was armed with a rock and a pistol under his fur parka while a rifleman provided backup. Mala managed to kill the wolf barehandedly, without himself getting injured, as shown in the film.

Ray Mala appeared in more than twenty-five films over three decades, cast in adventure flicks, embodying a Tahitian, a Hawaiian, an "Indian brave," and a "husky young Mexican bridegroom," all the while facing racist resentment. Whenever movie offers dried up, he returned to camera work. Mala's handsome face stilled prematurely in 1952, on a filmset, at the age of forty-five, when his heart failed. He had just completed *Red Snow*, the first movie to deal with the Cold War and the atomic bomb. Eskimo Sgt. Koovuk in this anticommunist feature helps to foil a secret-weapons test in Siberia. The Alaska Federation of Natives in 2013 petitioned to have a terrazzo-and-brass star added to Hollywood's Walk of Fame to posthumously honor this shining beacon among their own.

Film buffs will likely take exception to my exalted claims about Curtis's place as Alaska's ultimate lensman—from a craft point of view. He restored the dignity and past, if only momentarily, that had been taken from the Northwest's indigenous peoples.

Nomeites had warned the roving photographer against pushing his luck by launching so late in the season. Foolhardy, perhaps, but with only the last volume left to be finished, Curtis insisted on one more adventure.

Less than a week out at sea, the travelers struck ice while a storm walloped them. "The waves were ten times as great as our boat & we were shipping much water," Beth wrote. When, after nearly capsizing, *Jewel Guard* stranded on a sandbar, Curtis waded away from the ship, set up his tripod, and snapped her portrait.

After visiting Nunivak and grim Hooper Bay—Curtis guessed that 75 percent of the residents suffered from tuberculosis—Beth flew back from Nome to Fairbanks (the first woman to have done so) and from there traveled home to L.A. Curtis, Eastwood, and Harry the Fish labored on, to more remote communities. King Island, which Curtis described as a storm-beaten rock, in his opinion also was one of the most picturesque spots in the North. Unlike any other village on the continent, the hive of "box houses" clung to precipitous cliffs, shored up by driftwood stilts. It lay ghostly abandoned, as its inhabitants now summered near Nome. Curtis hoped to interview King Islanders there upon his return, to fill in cultural context. The photos he brought back from the island are haunting still lifes, time capsules of a society whose gaze focused outward, onto the vast, immutable sea.

Anchored off Cape Prince of Wales, Curtis and his crew received visitors, "fully 50 of them," walrus hunters in three large skin boats, who clambered on deck until Curtis feared that *Jewel Guard* would founder under the load. Curtis hired a local to act as interpreter at his next stop, Little Diomede Island. There, he got lucky with the weather, landed, and promptly went to work. The wife of a missionary told him it was the only perfect day that year; in fact, the finest she had seen in her four years on the island. Diomede's population had been ravaged by a flu epidemic, but the honeyed, late-summer evening light must have thrilled Curtis—he worked sixty hours, during which he slept four and a half.

Storms caught up again with Curtis at Kotzebue, where a pilot he'd hired got them mired and lost in the mudflats. The pilot later admitted that he knew everything there was to know about driving dog teams but not much about guiding big boats. A canoe excursion took Curtis and Eastwood to Noatak Village, where both worked hard for several days; Curtis found time to praise "the fine flavor of Noatak salmon trout" [steelhead or anadromous rainbow trout].

Working there, Curtis faced opposition from the

missionaries. Ironically, these were the "Friends," evangelical Quakers. Curtis, digging into the pre-Christian past, insisted on speaking to "Devil People": those who refused to convert and often were ostracized for it.

Curtis and his company only left Kotzebue on September 10. The days were getting short, the barometric pressure was falling, the land white with new snow, and the locals were putting up boats for the winter. The next day, a blizzard assailed *Jewel Guard*, with visibility "ten degrees less than pea soup." It snowed so heavily that flakes depressed the breakers. Harry the Fish frothed at the gills because they had not sailed sooner. The hull sprang a leak from seams that the tossing and pounding worked loose, and the ocean pressed in until the engine room floor lay a foot underwater. Threatened with freezing in place until spring, the skipper decided to run for Nome instead of beaching the boat for repairs. The crew manned the hand-pump, clanking away for half of the time. It was so cold that spray and seas slopping onto the deck bonded with snow into an ice carapace, which the men kept chopping off.

Curtis was fifty-nine, plagued by a bad hip and arthritis. He should have visited Serpentine. Canoeing up the Noatak instead, they had camped without tents in the rain, and now he was "numb from both ends to the middle." For a visual artist, he sure had a way with words. And, equally impressive, he kept scribbling them into the diary throughout their ordeal. He fell into his bunk each night wearing hip boots and a slicker, ready to pitch in on deck or at the pump at a moment's notice. Meanwhile, the storm smashed two schooners onto Nome beaches, drowning two men.

On the home stretch, *Jewel Guard* found her wings, more gull now than mud hen. She flew "before the gale merely hitting the [waves'] high spots."

Her crew in Nome had been given up for dead. Curtis, though, had been stoic: "You either make it or you don't." The main thing, he felt afterward, were the images that he had netted and saved in a tight box from ruin, the capstone of his career and some of his finest work. "Tonight I can sleep all night without thinking of storms," he rejoiced in his diary back at the hotel. A Nome banker acquaintance told Curtis that theirs had been the sole expedition into the region that did not ask for a loan or other assistance in order to exit that country.

Seen from a strictly commercial perspective, Curtis did not make it. In 1925, he surrendered the rights to *The North American Indian* to industrialist J.P. Morgan's son, who, filling his father's Oxfords, had stepped in years before to fund the costly project. Sinking into obscurity during the Great Depression, Curtis was hospitalized in Denver for mental and physical exhaustion. Except for corresponding with a Seattle librarian who rediscovered his work in his late years, he maintained few social ties. The man who once captured a US president's daughter's wedding, praised by Theodore Roosevelt afterward, would die penniless at the age of eighty-four, in the home of Beth and her husband, forgotten by almost everyone.

The ultimate praise for his life's work, albeit belated, came from those whom Edward S. Curtis had sought to honor. "Never before," in the words of Kiowa author N. Scott Momaday, "have we seen the Indians of North America so close to the origins of their humanity." Despite the nostalgia of his vision and erring about these cultures vanishing, Curtis's obsession has given us "indispensable images of every human being at every time in every place," wrote Paul Ongtooguk (Inupiaq), who graduated from high school in Nome but now lives in "tropical" Anchorage. Those words appear in his foreword to a book of recently resurfaced Curtis Eskimo photographs. The images, when Ongtooguk first saw them, "filled the missing pieces from my memory." The very best teleported him to his treeless home, "culturally and sometimes personally."

"Happy Jack and Wife"

An Insider Artist

When strong gusts flipped a small plane landing near Teller, on the Seward Peninsula, bound for Shishmaref on August 14, 1953, one fifty-year-old Eskimo hunter, trapper, and reindeer herder injured his knee and thereby lost all means of support. "No more work, no more hunting," he said about the event that caused a career change. "Is only way … drawing pictures." Like many in those days, this Inupiaq trapper had made a good living, earning far more than the local schoolteachers. While recovering, James Kivetoruk (Kivitauraq) Moses resumed a teenage habit now leavened by anecdotes, legends, and knowledge accrued over five decades during which the land had taught and sustained him. His larger paintings today fetch ten times the price of other Alaska Native artists'; the auctioneer's gavel normally strikes at $5,000 to $12,000. For the curators of one retrospective, his images "transcend the power of the photograph in translating the past into the present."

Orphaned at a young age, the kid born in 1900 near Cape Espenberg, at the south entrance to Kotzebue Sound, had lived with an uncle, an accomplished hunter and trapper. At fourteen, he'd apprenticed at a store in Deering, drawing in his free time. The store owner's wife, impressed by his talent, sent some of his output to Fairbanks, where eyes more attuned than hers could judge it.

Business boomed soon after his airplane accident. Moses started signing his images, generally undated, increasing their value for tourists, collectors, and museums seeking authentic depictions of fading lifeways. In "Honeymoon" (1964), he holds the halter of a reindeer harnessed to a sled with his bride on a second one. He issued best-sellers repeatedly—boats, polar bears, herders lassoing animals (the National Cowboy & Western Heritage Museum displayed him), camp and village vignettes—and worked in the plein-air mode and on commission too. A split panel by him illustrates the upside-down kayaker's "Eskimo roll," a self-rescue technique. A unique *umiak*-sailing piece assumes the perspective of a stalk-eyed crab on a beach, with the boat bucking atop frothing combers, partly visible, bearing down on that crustacean.

Years later, popular with tourists and collectors, he could not keep up with demand. Customers loved romantic scenes of "primitive man" pitted against nature, flashbacks of a society supposedly doomed. Ironically, critics label this cultural broker's oeuvre "outsider art." Coined in the 1970s, the term lumps together compositions by untrained, "naïve" painters and sculptors with little or no contact with the mainstream art world and often marked by disabilities shaping raw styles. While this definition makes the art sound rather crude, adjectives that describe it also could be "expressive," "unconventional," "nonconforming," and "genuine." In his forthcoming biography of Moses, the UAF art professor David Mollett, like many fans, values this autodidact's bridging of worlds in vibrant tableaus "from the rearview perspective of a man whose living conditions changed so much over his lifetime."

Having long ago traded sled dogs and furs in Chukotka and near his birthplace, Cape Espenberg, the bald, spectacled, willowy invalid Moses recalled with zest listening to Siberians who now languished behind the "Ice Curtain," bullied by commissars, clinging to scraps of their ethnic heritage. An Arctic Henri Rousseau, he painted hunts, walruses, voyages under sail, the ceremonial Wolf Dance, a revenue-cutter crewman and shaman competing at magic, and cryptic creatures: a nude mermaid on a floe's edge with her feet dangling in the water that he'd observed; a giant from a story, swimming among bergy bits; and a huge eagle abducting a man who thus grasped Earth's roundness in an Inupiaq version of the *Apollo 17* crew's "Blue Marble" moment. (His meticulous orb showed the international dateline.) Lesser known pieces—a toothy "Ike," a pin-up in a babydoll negligee—might have been whimsy or reaching for new marketplace niches. In his twenties, Moses may well have witnessed the arrival of Roald Amundsen in his *Norge* dirigible at the end of the Norwegian's transpolar flight. In one painting, awed Eskimo traders in a two-masted skin boat point at the named airborne craft that in his rendition resembles a black airplane bomb.

Moses' hunter-naturalist eye for detail matched a knack for narrative angles. He essentially was a visual storyteller, though he painted a good tale with words as well. (Fellow Inupiat accused him of sometimes stretching the truth a tad.) His colored-pencil, watercolor, and India ink landscapes and seascapes deftly rendered clothing, subsistence and social activities, ice, weather, even light and shadows typical of the seasons or hour of day. Species-specific fur, wood grain in boards, tan lines, chin tattoos, lip plugs, tonsure hairdos, and ashen cloud-bellies brushing against horizons segueing from powder blue to pollen reflect skills he kept honing. Seal blood spatters onto snow, shorthand for the brusque northern existence. Experts praise his "sophisticated mixed media technique" geared toward "dramatic departures from tradition"—conventions established through pictographic walrus-ivory carvings—and remark on his bigheaded figures, frequent frontal views, and stiff yet accurate postures, which all signal outsider art. He drew on paper, poster board, cardboard, and sometimes wood, canvas, or hide, initially in a small format. The lavish use of color distinguished him from his achromatic peers. Fittingly, perhaps, few photos of this man of humble beginnings survive for us to better envision him.

Moses remained a herder at heart. And modest. He never fully embraced the creative process, complaining about "Too much sitting" to one interviewer. Asked about his pictures' appeal, he admitted that they lacked refinement but stressed their hard-earned realism. They were true to the ways of the Inupiat, an oral culture's old literacy of the sea and land. "Young people try to be artists," he said. "They come up good artists, very good drawing because they were school. But no experience. Don't know nothing [about] living."

He always felt more comfortable speaking Inupiaq, hadn't finished second grade, and survived his five children. One mysteriously disappeared; one died while asleep, one from the flu, one in a plane crash; and one, when the Shishmaref store ran out of milk and bad weather delayed an emergency shipment from Teller by plane.

In 1975, weakened by strokes and surgeries, Moses, with his wife, Bessie Ahgupuk—the sister of another famous Inupiaq artist—resided in Nome, a non-Native commercial hub since Yankee-whaler days. Their cabin, abutting the Golden Goose saloon, sat a nugget's toss from foam-flecked Bering Strait beaches gray as graphite. Bessie, first acting as his bookkeeper, peddled a briefcase of Moses' nostalgia at local hotels. She kept a percentage of the profits for herself, she once joked. For an extra five dollars, she provided a handwritten summary of the subjects, of routines, beliefs, and a past beyond her clientele's ken.

The quiet octogenarian had stopped drawing after the death of one son but as his spirit ebbed in 1982 picked up a pen again. Bedridden in Nome's hospital, he sketched the artist as a young man brimming with strength and vitality. This final portrait was a family keepsake, not for sale.

Glacier Priest

Father Bernhard Rosecrans Hubbard, a Jesuit and geologist who led thirty-two expeditions to Alaska between 1927 and 1958, once listed the requisites of an explorer as "a strong back, a strong stomach, a dumb head, and a guardian angel." A strong back he certainly had, augmented by a boyish voice and a mop of black tousled hair. He always carried his mass kit together with food, camera, and other equipment, which added up to a burden of one hundred pounds. And his guardian angel worked overtime.

On his first Alaska venture, Hubbard braved the Juneau Icefield's crevasses. While surveying the effects of the 1931 Aniakchak volcanic eruption from the air, Hubbard and his floatplane almost crashed. He killed grizzlies on the land route to the still-active crater, where he posed with his dog Katmai at the rim before entering the brimstone mouth—both wearing gasmasks and heavy coats. One of the party's huskies fell into the Akutan caldera lake with a thousand feet of film in its pack. (It survived but was later preserved as a taxidermy mount.) Hubbard went that literal extra mile for a special picture; for one, his student crew of football players on the same trip tried to lasso a bull sea lion but stampeded the herd. Earlier that year, Hubbard had driven a dog team down the Yukon River from Nenana to Nulato. He raised woolly-haired Siberian Samoyeds from pups, which he then crossed with wolf hybrids for doughty draft animals. For him, tiny lapdogs—yappers more popular now than ever, it seems—were "animated carnations."

Alaska, perhaps not too strangely, had a tradition of daring, published priests. Archdeacon Hudson Stuck, the author of *Ten Thousand Miles with a Dog Sled,* mushed his circuit of remote parishes and was the first to summit Denali, North America's highest peak, led by a Native guide. They said that he had held mass in more places in which it never before had been said than any other priest alive.

A further requirement for being a modern explorer Hubbard could have mentioned is the ability to spin an exciting yarn for live audiences. In that respect as well, he had been blessed. "I'm a good showman," he admitted, adding that "God has given me the ability, and I'm using it for the work." General Patton, with whom Hubbard entered Vienna in 1945, concurred. He "talks very well when he forgets to advertise himself," "Old Blood and Guts" wrote in his diaries. In Europe, Hubbard lectured to the armed forces, a career he built upon after the war and which made him the highest-paid speaker of his time.

Wild country had long been calling to Hubbard; it brought him closer to his creator. Natural wonders were evidence of the divine shaping the world. When he was ten, his father bought a large tract of land south of San Francisco. Wielding gun and camera, Bernard roamed redwood forests in his free time, accompanied by his dog. He rode shotgun on a six-horse stagecoach, and scaled mountains and seaside promontories. Places like Aniakchak Crater or Katmai's Valley of Ten Thousand Smokes became sources of spirituality as well as testing grounds for scientific ambitions.

During studies for the priesthood at Innsbruck's Ignatius College, he proved himself in Tyrol's Alps, earning the epithet "Glacier Priest" from his guides. His interest in mountains and glaciers might rather have hindered his theological career. At Santa Clara, a California Jesuit college, he continued his order's intellectual tradition by teaching geology, German, and Greek in 1926. From 1930 on, his superiors freed Hubbard from all duties so that he could devote himself fulltime to lecturing, writing, and further explorations.

In 1937, three decades before the King Island Inupiat left their Bering Strait home to resettle in Nome, Hubbard fell in love with these "cliff dwellers" and their storm-besieged outcrop. At the time, it housed 190 people, a Catholic church, and a school in the only village. The church clung to a slope so steep that you could step directly from its snow burden onto the roof. The ways of these Ukivokmiut—honed between sheer drops and surf for millennia—were largely unknown to outsiders, and with their mainland move irrevocably changed.

Thanks to Father Hubbard, who added "documentarian" and "ethnographer" to his resume, a superb record of their traditions survives.

Fulfilling the wish of his predecessor, Father Bellarmine Lafortune, Hubbard helped to erect a bronze statue of "Christ the King" on a peak of the island that overlooks mainland Alaska and Siberia, as a beacon of peace between the two hemispheres. The crowned savior had arrived by *umiak*, unceremoniously, in a crate. To brighten the dedication, Hubbard ignited 150,000 feet of Hollywood films he had brought just for the occasion and that the Legion of Decency had banned. "As the celluloid sparkled and crackled," Hubbard crowed in an interview, the flames leapt up so high that "the natives on the mainland 30 miles away believed the Northern Lights had changed place." The islanders, in turn, carved two statues of Christ from walrus ivory, which Hubbard delivered to Pope Pius XII. Substituting for the sinful reels, Hubbard constructed and lit a hall to show his own films; his generators provided electricity for the village. Although they were silent films, Alexander Alurroc Muktoyuk remembered, they "really spoiled many of the King Islanders." His mother would in later years take him to see moving pictures at the Nome theater, for $1 per show for adults. Muktoyuk became "very addicted to the movies. Probably indirectly Father Hubbard's fault." The athletic priest also organized the island's first football match, on the only field available: sea ice in front of the village.

Hubbard shot more than twenty hours of black-and-white film (now at the Smithsonian) and nearly 4,000 photos: a kaleidoscope of Ukivokmiut customs and routines, many doomed to fade soon. Footage includes rare scenes from the men's *qagri*, a sort of club-house; of women splitting walrus hides; kayak and *umiak* races; funerals and the now defunct Polar Bear Dance; and children playing "Wild West stick-up."

In the same spirit, Hubbard hunted walrus with his congregation, using a "big game revolver," once missing four in a row before "a fifth slug brought down the biggest bull Walrus obtained this year in the Bering Sea." He mailed the forehead and tusks to Lt. Col. Douglas B. Wesson, vice president of Smith & Wesson.

To top things off, in the summer of 1938 Hubbard and an Inupiaq crew of eight, in an *umiak* propelled by outboard motor, cut a 2,000-mile arc that joined King Island, Kotzebue, and Barrow. Always mindful of his sponsors, Hubbard had an assistant paint the Agfa logo diamond onto the skin boat's hull before putting to sea. Spray constantly drenched the crew, which had been overdue for a week but arrived as search parties were being formed. A Thor Heyerdahl of the Bering Strait, Hubbard had embarked to prove that transcontinental journeys by skin boat were possible and, by inference, had been undertaken in the past. As a related purpose, he had studied the quilt of Eskimo dialects along that coast, which he linked to Siberian languages. "Civilization arose in Asia when Europe was a wilderness," he admitted, adding in the same breath that it toppled as it was currently doing in North America. He considered Russia "an oriental country." Ever the documentarian, he also decried the horrible injustice the movies had done the Eskimos by depicting their life as being lived in igloos, and brutish. "Their life is like that in the ordinary United States City, but with the sordidness removed," he defended his King Island flock. "In 50 years these people have had not one divorce, not one murder, not one suicide, not one case of venereal disease." These things, the Church cared about. Shamanism and animism—the belief that animals, too, possessed souls—or polygamy and spouse exchanges—vital arrangements in a hard land—or cultural alienation or "bone-racking" fevers hitching a ride with the missionaries? Not so much.

Still, combined with Hubbard's images from Aniakchak, Kodiak, Katmai, the Aleutians, and the Taku Glacier, his is one of the largest collections of motion pictures and photos made prior to World War II in the territory. Modern researchers appreciate the effort, though some of the cleric's contemporaries did not. "The too frequent moving pictures developed a craze for pictures in the [King] Islanders." In the patronizing view echoed by the General Superior of the Alaska mission, "they were no longer as simple as they used to be."

Naysayers notwithstanding, modernity and the media had arrived in the north.

Drawn to coastal settings, in 1943 Hubbard served on Attu Island as chaplain to the Seabees, the US Navy's construction battalions, or "CBs." Thus began his affiliation with the military, which culminated after World War II when he was asked to serve as Arctic Consultant to the US Coast Guard and Alaskan Air Command. But the man who befriended generals, who hobnobbed with Abbott and Costello, Disney, and Franklin D. Roosevelt, had a way with less glamorous folk too.

Before TV or the internet, newsreels and lecture circuits satisfied America's craving for visual stimulation, and Hubbard—a riveting narrator, author of three autobiographic books in the style of Teddy Roosevelt's—used multimedia presentations and oratory flair, and a few of his favorite huskies, to draw crowds. His science, according to volcanologists, anthropologists, and paleontologists, sometimes was flawed; he also feuded with mountaineer-photographer Bradford Washburn, a legend in Alaska, and promoted products in his films. Hubbard belittled the accomplishments of the younger explorer, perhaps jealous about funding. Washburn in turn called the priest "an out and out headline hunter."

Hubbard's skills with live audiences, however, were beyond doubt. The *National Geographic* contributor and mushing man of the cloth appeared on TV shows and entertained up to 7,000 people in lecture halls, including Carnegie. During two months in the war's last year, he gave nearly one hundred talks. "When you've lived in the north," he told a reporter, and have "come in to find your camp torn up by bears and had to eat your dogs when you ran out of food, you don't mind a little thing like a lecture tour."

In 1955 Hubbard suffered the first of five strokes (unsurprisingly, on a lecture tour) but, recovered from paralysis, returned to Alaska once more in 1958. He still clambered into and out of boats there, still driven, clutching his film camera with his limp right hand and operating it with his left. Santa Clara University, at whose infirmary he died, too weak to rise and go to the altar for morning service, in a sketch of his life credited Hubbard for melding "utter fearlessness with sensible caution, manly endurance with the warmest of hearts." Even physically disabled, at age seventy, he had had all it really takes to be an explorer in the traditional mold: determination, grit, bluster and competitiveness—and a few blind spots.

III. ART & INDUSTRY

The Deer Is Like Money

In the 1897 edition of *The Eskimo Bulletin*, between a sales ad for walrus heads and word of the discovery of ancient Eskimo armor made from iron slats, appeared the following news item:

> The success attending this third year of the mission herd of domestic reindeer at the Cape [Prince of Wales] speaks well for the faithfulness and skill of our Eskimo herders, all of whom are Christians. ... Each of them has driven more than 500 miles during the winter.

The author and publisher of those lines, Congregational missionary William Thomas Lopp, briefly served as superintendent of the District of Alaska reindeer station in Teller. The driving he mentioned referred to reindeer-drawn sleds whose drivers balanced on the runners in the style of dog mushers.

On Independence Day five years earlier, amid a flag-raising ceremony, cheering onlookers and a herd of fifty-three Siberian reindeer, district officials had opened Teller Station in Port Clarence Bay, a large, sheltered bight on the east coast of the Bering Strait. Those animals laid the foundation for a population of reindeer on the Seward Peninsula that would peak at 640,000 animals and create a booming industry that inexorably shaped the welfare of the region's Alaska Natives.

By century's end, commercial hunting had depleted whale, walrus and caribou populations on the peninsula, and starvation haunted the local Inupiat. Believing "God blesses aggressiveness," the Rev. Sheldon Jackson, a Presbyterian minister, missionary and Alaska's general agent of education, repeatedly sailed to Siberia in 1892 and imported 171 reindeer—the Eurasian form of caribou, domesticated or wild—to feed the Inupiat, compensating for game that had been overhunted. They called Jackson "the needle man," for the steel sewing needles he gave as gifts on his annual visits. Escorting that first shipment bound for Port Clarence on *Bear* under Healy were four Chukchi Siberian herders whom Jackson employed as instructors. In a badly faded photo from that time, crewmembers hoist a reindeer aboard, one man handling the pulley, the other the pointy end. Inupiat flocked from hundreds of miles away to see what the missionaries at Teller were up to. Their intentions were implicit in *The Eskimo Bulletin* and explicit in Jackson's reports to the federal government. The reverend—who stood just five feet tall but was colossally ambitious, egotistical and often tactless—considered reindeer "an important factor in the civilization of the Eskimos." In the eyes of another early-twentieth-century writer, "The Eskimo" was "naturally a communist."

The Inupiaq chronicler Inez Ayagiaq Black recalled how

the newcomers' dealings unraveled the cultural fabric of northwestern Alaska Natives. "When the young men started working, their lifestyle changed," she said. "They didn't eat only Eskimo food. Their clothing changed. They didn't use winter furs all the time, like the fur pants they used to wear."

Jackson taught Inupiat of both sexes English, math and domestic skills to prepare them for doing business with whites. Consider, for example, the following passage from a mission school language lesson sheet:

We-mok has ten deer.
They are big deer.
Some of them are fat.
Four of them are sled-deer.

Printed below this simple math problem were verses from abolitionist writer Julia Ward Howe's "Battle Hymn of the Republic" praising the fearful "grapes of wrath" and the beautiful lilies in which "Christ was born."

Underlying Jackson's agenda was his generation's overarching belief in Manifest Destiny. Reindeer would not only turn hunters into herders, he thought, but also "utilize hundreds of thousands of square miles of moss-covered tundra ... and make those now useless and barren wastes conducive to the wealth and prosperity of the United States."

Yet for millennia such "barren wastes" had sustained people who were neither ranchers nor miners nor farmers.

The North Country animals (fish and sea mammals) were their crops. "Any time that we wanted an 'apple,'" recalled Inupiaq leader Eben Hopson from Utqiagvik (formerly Barrow), "we went out and got it. We got what we wanted to live on, got what we needed."

In place of that footloose subsistence lifestyle, those Inupiaq apprentices selected by the mission instructors received five years of schooling, room and board included. Most were teenagers, some of whom the Great Death had orphaned. His first year, an apprentice earned the loan of two female reindeer (and any offspring they bore), the second year five, the third and each year after ten. At the end of five years, if judged sufficiently skilled, each was loaned enough reindeer to increase his herd to fifty head.

From the outset, tensions flared between the missionaries and their Chukchi instructors. Among other "transgressions," when the Chukchi were thirsty, they would lasso reindeer cows, kneel and drink directly from their teats, quaffing milk, to Jackson's dismay, "with as much enjoyment as if it had been pure nectar." More offensive still was their practice of leading the salt-loving reindeer by marking the ground with streams of urine poured from a sealskin bag. To Christian sensibilities, such behavior would do nothing to help civilize the Inupiat. How much more the pious would have recoiled had they known about the Chukotka custom of feeding a reindeer toadstools and collecting its piss in a bucket strapped to the animal and boiling it in a pot before sharing it all around, all to get as high as a priest in the pulpit who'd overindulged in sacramental wine. (Actually, the Chukchi imbibed this not simply to party but as a form of communion with ancestors.)

In 1894 the exasperated missionaries recruited sixteen Saami—seven herders and their families—from Lapland to replace the Chukchi instructors. A clause in their contract bound them to behave "orderly and decently and to show discipline." Each brought his own sled and herding dogs and would receive one hundred deer for three to five years of service.

On their transatlantic journey, carrying 500 tons of reindeer moss for the animals, these hardy landlubbers weathered temperatures well below zero and a nine-day tempest that ended up sinking their ship after it had delivered them safely in New York Harbor. One who had been fifteen when she crossed with her family wrote that, "The reindeer proved to be good travelers during the voyage, but the Laplanders were both homesick and seasick and having second thoughts about their venture into the unknown." White kids at schools in Alaska called girls like her "dirty little Lapp."

The Inupiat soon warmed to the "Card People," as they dubbed the Saami, whose traditional curled-toe boots and Four Winds hats reminded them of the garb of playing card jokers, jacks and kings. They learned how to lasso, harness, and milk reindeer, and to ride *pulka* sleds, how to make cheese, how to sew the curved-toe ski boots from the heads, and how to boil glue from the hooves. But the trainees still chafed at their subordinate status, the monotony of herding (compared to hunting or fishing), and the lack of immediate payback.

The Saami of course had stories, some of which would have resonated with the Inupiat in their worldview and gist, if not in the details.

According to one, Sun, who owned a reindeer herd, was being pulled in a sled across the sky. In early summer, a bear was his draft animal, making Sun bright and powerful. As the year progressed, he switched to a reindeer bull and then to a cow, growing weaker and weaker. In another tale, various hunter constellations in the heavens aim their bows at Sarvvis, the most important Saami cluster, "a big, fat reindeer with antlers" that incorporates Cassiopeia's W rack. An old woman on skis urges her dogs "Go chase, go chase!" promising the fat rectum as their reward. (Here, the Inupiat, with a humor equally earthy and a predilection for fat, would have smiled.) One by one, the pursuers give up as dawn blushes the horizon. The cosmic chase visibly plays out each clear winter night until, at the end of time, one arrow hits home. Then the deer will fall, and the world will end.

A third story addressed the origin of wild and domestic reindeer. Two sisters owned two roaming reindeer that returned every day to be milked. One sister was gentle and caring, the other rough, leaving bruises and scars. The mistreated deer fled into the wilds forever. All the wild ones descended from it, and domesticated deer from the meek one. Inupiat apprentices may have nodded before pointing out Tuttuġruk, "Caribou" (our Big Dipper) or reciprocating with a myth about a woman who gave birth to twins: the first grizzly and the first polar bear.

The missionaries had their work cut out trying to quell such rip-roaring nonfictions that explained how the world became the splendid tilt-a-whirl it still is.

Ironically, considering Jackson's stab at acculturation, the need to continually shift reindeer to prevent overgrazing required the Inupiat to lead more nomadic lives than they had as hunters and fishers. Shadowing the herds all summer, they walked or jogged up to thirty miles daily. "The deer run the herder," Saami instructor Andrew Bahr said. Inupiaq herder Chester Seveck, who tended reindeer for forty-six years, summed up the herders' existence. "We keep moving camp every ten days or two weeks to another grazing ground in wintertime," he recalled in his clipped English. "In summertime we keep reindeer on the coast near ocean side where flies and mosquitoes not so many."

In the winter of 1897–98 the owners of eight whalers trapped in an ice field near Point Barrow appealed to President William McKinley on behalf of their 265 stranded crewmen. As it was too late in the year for the US Revenue Cutter *Bear* to push through the pack ice, the rescue party disembarked at Cape Vancouver and traveled on shore, first stopping at Teller Station to purchase a herd—emergency rations on the hoof. In what would be known as the Overland Relief Expedition, they were to drive north "40 tons of meat."

Six men—including officers from *Bear*, station superintendent Lopp and Native herder Charlie Antisarlook—set out for Point Barrow in mid-December. Picking up more Inupiaq helpers along the way, they sledged provisions 1,500 miles by dog and deer while the men snowshoed and skied. As they crossed exposed Kotzebue Sound, they had to cut steps into pressure ridges and burn several sleds to keep warm. Approaching North Slope villages whose residents had never encountered reindeer, Lopp's men clarified that the animals were not caribou to be hunted. After suffering blizzards, frostbite, polar bear attacks, seventy-below temperatures and snow blindness, the men reached the stranded crews at Point Barrow by late March 1898, having lost only one-sixth of the herd.

That same year, with Nome in the grip of gold fever, outlying fortune seekers clamored for meat and regular freight and mail delivery. To supply their needs, Lopp and his herders established a "reindeer express" between Nome and the mining camps in the York Mountains.

Jackson's reindeer introduction plan had included a map of proposed mail routes spiderwebbing across the Alaska Territory. The first government route from the Yukon River Klondike gateway St. Michael to Kotzebue opened in 1900. It took two months to cover the roundtrip's 1,240 miles. The leg to Barrow was even longer, reportedly the longest, most dangerous mail run in the world, with marauding bears and wolves, and dicey river and sea ice, and wind obliterating trails and so loud that it disguised the cracking of said ice, and weather that froze at least one Saami mailman to death. Draft reindeer, despite taking longer to train, in many ways surpassed sled dogs, as the former grazed freely, while food for the latter had to be bought, fished for or shot and then carried. On the flipside, replacements for spent dogs could be picked up at every Native village. Hauling up to 300 pounds each, mail-service reindeer could cover thirty to fifty miles in a stretch. The animals rested at way stations, hoofing shrubby lichen from beneath the snow. In a land of few trees, fences of burlap, willow or blocks of lake ice easily held them. Some traveled 6,000 miles in a single winter. That said, most Inupiat preferred dogs, as reindeer kicked up snow into a driver's face and tended to slip and fall on glare ice. One storm toppled reindeer and overturned loaded sleds like toys. Rex Beach was caught in a bluster so bad that he had to lash his wrists to his sled's handle bars to keep from letting go of it.

With the arrival of the Lomens, the bulk of livestock husbandry shifted from the peninsula's missions to one centralized enterprise. Carl's initial reindeer sighting paints him as something of a citified "dude." While he was crossing the tundra near Nome in the summer of 1900, a herd stopped him dead in his tracks. Ignorant of the habits of reindeer, he feared they might attack. He also grumbled, like many a transplant, about "weather that would wear the patience of a clergyman."

Chances to score still abounded in the recent acquisition's most-populous city. In 1908 the Lomen brothers bought a photo studio, stocking it with cameras and glass-plate negatives acquired from other photographers. They soon mastered the craft while learning to keep their gear and fingers functioning at subzero temperatures. Cashing in on the soon-to-be-territory's aura and newfound popularity, the brothers sold their images as postcards and to various newspapers and scientific publications. In 1914 the family launched the Lomen Co., a meatpacking business at Elephant Point stocked with 1,200 reindeer purchased from an aging Saami. Within a couple of years, the enterprise was shipping meat to the Lower Forty-Eight. Commercial venison soon filled plates of china in Nome as well. Open day and night, Modini's Cafe on Front Street always had fresh reindeer meat (and ptarmigan) "for the traveling public" on hand.

In an ironic twist of the six-degrees-of-separation sort, Sheldon Jackson had fired the Norwegian Jafet Lindeberg who had refused to travel to Siberia to buy more reindeer. The Norwegian moved on to Norton Sound, where, striking it rich, he became one of the "Three Lucky Swedes," sluicing up to $1,800 a day from the ground—more than the price of a handmade motor car. Lindeberg then loaned money to the Lomens for starting their company by buying the reindeer of Saami herders. After selling his mining share,

Lindeberg, on a visit to Norway, convinced his old friend Leonard Seppala to join him in America. Seppala and his Siberian huskies Balto and Togo would garner fame for their role in the Nome Serum Run, which drew attention nationwide as "The Great Race of Mercy."

Carl Lomen, who boasted of the family's "many pleasant relationships with the native people," pledged that he and his brothers represented no threat to local herders, as they'd focus on national markets. By then, however, most miners had vacated the region, leaving no significant local buyers. Lacking the funds to build slaughterhouses or underground cold storages—natural freezers that took advantage of permafrost—Inupiaq herders couldn't compete on the national stage, not that they had any stateside connections.

Conflict over prime rangeland mounted as Lomen came to control the best grazing grounds, charging Native herders a user fee and collecting a herding fee for each Inupiaq reindeer that got mixed up with his animals. While the Lomens did hire Native herders and buy their excess steers, such were largely token gestures to maintain goodwill. Regardless, the recently converted pastoralists were far from throwing in the towel. With seed stock from the firmly established mission herds, additional Inupiaq reindeer stations sprang up in Iliamna, Barrow, Kivalina, Nulato and as far inland as Bettles. On a US Bureau of Education map from 1917, they, and the attendant boarding schools, look like red pimples on the nose of the aforementioned angry gnome.

In his 1954 memoir *Fifty Years in Alaska*, Lomen gave patronizing dues to Native resilience and good humor. "Civilized men," he wrote, "would become despondent living under like conditions, but the Eskimo meets them lightheartedly. He exhibits no concern for the morrow." Pages later, the entrepreneurial meat-packer contradicted himself with a quote from Inupiaq herder William Allokeok of Shishmaref: "If you wish a good living from your deer, you should think and plan how to care for them. If you don't, your herd will decrease."

Neither did the Lomens shy away from abduction. Nunivak Island had been declared "public domain," open to grazing, ignoring Nuniwarmiut prior claims. The brothers promptly filled the vacuum with reindeer from Golovin. To the chagrin of the shaman Nayagnir, crewmembers of SS *Ketchikan* dropped them overboard, one by one, when stormy seas prevented their landing. This burl of a man, with a facial disfigurement from a gunshot, opposed the brazen land grab openly and threatened to kill the animals, which had been so terrified that they tried to climb back onto the freighter.

A ship captain of the company snatched "the outlaw Eskimo," whom Carl Lomen deemed "insane and dangerous" and whom locals accused of terrorizing that island for years. He was thrown into Nome's federal jail, where he languished without legal representation. Knud Rasmussen, after interviewing Yup'ik informants in the course of his Fifth Thule

Expedition, noted that Nayagnir "was forbidden to speak his own language in prison, and as he could not speak any other, he did not speak at all for a whole year."

Fellow islanders tended to avoid Nayagnir—shamans often were feared in their own communities. Two enemy shamans, one from Selawik, the other from the Kobuk River, once dueled long-distance with lightning bolts. The Sealwik sorcerer, when he converted to Christianity, coughed up a piece of jade, the source of his power from nearby Jade Mountain. Even after his death, people dreaded him and would not build on his former house site. One of Nayagnir's contemporaries related how footprints that shaman left behind changed into animal tracks, possibly those of a wolf. The troublemaker was also thought to have flown across the Etolin Strait on his return from Nome. Rasmussen described him as "a man accustomed to finding himself alone against a crowd, and with his own little tricks of self-defense."

Unfortunately, no amount of skill and dedication, or protection by spirits, could guarantee an Inupiaq herder's success. By 1896, Jackson had changed the apprenticeship terms so that no animals could be earned during the period of instruction, and Native herders could no longer expect the loan of a starter herd on graduation. The new rules also specified that when an Inupiaq herder died, half of his herd reverted to the mission.

Lopp and others sincerely concerned about Inupiaq livelihoods raised the alarm, prompting a 1905 Interior

Department investigation of the mission stations. It found that the missions, their supervising Scandinavians, and the government itself, not Native herders, owned most of the 10,000-plus head then in Alaska. Jackson, singled out for his conflicting interests as the district's agent of education and field agent of the Presbyterian missions, resigned, and a new policy was implemented to place more reindeer into Native hands. Instead of having to qualify through apprenticeships, Inupiat could simply purchase reindeer from fellow herders, though they were still not permitted to sell female breeding deer to non-Natives. Only through a legal technicality had Lomen been able to buy his original herd, as no sales restrictions had been imposed on non-Native herds.

Alas, the government reforms benefited few Inupiat, and most of those only temporarily.

Among the few truly successful Native herders was "Sinrock Mary." Born Changunak in 1870 to an Inupiaq mother and a Russian trader father, she was raised in bustling St. Michael. Growing up trilingual, she worked as a linguist and interpreter for Jackson and Captain Healy before achieving fame herself as the "Queen of Reindeer." (It seems as if, in those days, everyone had a nickname. It distinguished between persons of a similar name but was never spoken in that individual's presence.)

In 1889 Mary married Charlie Antisarlook—the Teller Station herder who a decade later would join the Overland Relief Expedition. The couple moved to Cape Nome, where

Charles had established a modest herd, the first owned by an Alaska Native. When her husband succumbed to measles in 1900, Mary worked diligently to maintain the herd, selling meat to local businesses and the Army station. Her second husband wasn't interested in reindeer, so Mary adopted eleven children, among them little ones the epidemics had orphaned. She transformed them and other Inupiat into "deer men" able to manage their own herds.

At one point "Queen Mary" reigned over the largest herd in the North Country. Through her children she also managed to uphold Inupiaq traditions such as gathering berries and greens, fishing, and preparing skins for sewing. Conniving to cheat her out of her inheritance, rumrunners and drifters slurred the stately, curly-haired woman, threatened and sued her, shot at her deer to scatter them, killed some and left them rotting on the tundra, and proffered her liquor to cloud her judgment. One Swedish schemer pretended to be her third husband, while relatives of her dead husband, inflamed with a new kind of fever—the lust for unearned wealth—tried to disown her, stating that Inupiaq inheritance rules favored males.

Changunak had long witnessed the effects of greed, disease and lawlessness. Miners staking claims within grazing ranges often destroyed the natural reindeer and caribou forage by burning off vegetation. Scores of other reindeer were lost to rustling. With the proliferation of Nome honky-tonks and home brewing, alcoholism became rampant.

The encroachment on Inupiaq hunting and fishing grounds brought new diseases—smallpox, influenza, measles, etc.—to which Alaska Natives had little resistance. By century's end more than half the Native population in northwestern Alaska had died. According to Sister Frances Kittredge of the Cape Prince of Wales mission, whose sister Ellen had married Teller Station superintendent Lopp, hardly any Inupiat over fifty years old remained, and few younger than five. "There is hardly a family where someone is not gone," she wrote to her mother.

The 1916 influenza epidemic practically wiped out Sinuk, aka "Sinrock," the village from which Mary took her nickname and where she tended her herd. Lomen, who paid his helpers in cash, lured ever more herders away from the widow, who could only pay in reindeer and whose herd withered away in the absence of competent care.

In 1915, to better integrate herding into Inupiaq culture, Interior's Bureau of Education began organizing weeklong annual fairs in centrally located settlements. As described by Lomen, these were splendid affairs, versions of Rocky Mountain fur rendezvous that echoed the ancient trans–Bering Strait barter gatherings at Sisualik, a spit near Kotzebue. Clanging brass bells and the old man grunts of sled deer announced the arrival of delegates representing herds from all points of the compass. The herders wore fine costumes, while harnesses blazed with dangling yarn pompoms, and hand-carved walrus ivory buckles and clasps fastened the straps.

At times, the pageant resembled a fashion show. Spotted Siberian reindeer made flashy garments. *Pukiq*, snow-white fur from an animal's throat or belly, was especially valued. It looked dashing on chocolate-colored summer hides or in contrasting panels or inserts of geometric motifs, like checkered or zig-zag parka hems. White deer leg skins made for fancy mukluk boots. Surviving photos of duotone skin rugs sewn in that time, whose designs mimic Navajo weaving, hint that some items were meant for collectors or other commercial markets.

The fairs adopted a flag—a red reindeer on a white field bordered in blue—which snapped in the arctic breeze beside the Stars and Stripes. Attendees field-dressed animals, cooked, shared stories and sang. "They had races using one sled deer, then two sled deer and then four sled deer and eight sled deer," longtime herder Seveck recalled. There were shooting and heavy-pull contests (with 1,600-pound loads of sand), men's and women's snowshoe races, and bow drill fire-starting and snow-melting competitions. In one popular rodeo contest a man roped and then harnessed a feisty bull reindeer, drove a distance and then sped back to the start. When herders wanted to perfect their throwing skills without disturbing their grazing animals, one of their own would play the target, scampering about with antlers atop his head. Another amusing winter exercise for ropers,

Ellen Lopp wrote in a letter, "was to go to a long hill, get some children to coast down on sleds or barrel staves, and lasso them as they went sliding down."

After the flu epidemic of 1918 killed most veteran deermen, the fair, having been held only three times, never resumed.

Fall and spring roundups continued as social events. Families camped at the corrals and chipped in on such tasks as separating out the respective herds, choosing steers for future draft duty and castrating newborn calves. Castration allowed selective breeding and improved the meat of steers that skipped the fall rut. It also made males more docile for pulling sleds. Gentling a fawn to collar and harness could turn into a rodeo, with the animal bucking and running until it settled down. A single long rein tied to a sled deer's antler tines allowed the driver to execute turns. A family culled its herd for food and clothing and tallied how much it had grown. As cows sometimes bear twins and calve annually after becoming yearlings, well-serviced herds could swell by more than a third every spring. Like the Saami, the Inupiat ear-notched reindeer for identification, as their fur is too thick for branding.

Exponential growth. Investment and interest. Supply and demand. By the late 1920s, many Inupiat had joined the capitalist venture. For the first time they owned live animals individually. "The deer is just like money," herder Cudluck Oquilluk aptly put it.

And therein lay the seed for the industry's demise. Despite Lomen's salesmanship, his attempts to endear "America's New Health Meat" to a nation raised on beef, mutton and pork yielded only modest results. Seeing their returns threatened by reindeer meat, the big beef producers fought the Lomen Co.'s every effort to ramp up sales. Reindeer hides earmarked for glove-making fetched good prices at Seattle auctions, and thousands of reindeer were slaughtered for their leather alone. As outside markets collapsed, people fed excess reindeer meat to dogs or used carcasses to bait fox traps.

The Depression and mysteriously crashing herds—a "great die-out" between the 1930s and '50s—doomed large-scale herding in Alaska. Still, the Department of the Interior's Alaska Reindeer Service in 1936 counted fifty-seven herds grazing between Kodiak Island and Barter Island on the Arctic Ocean coast.

A flurry of protests from Native herders precipitated the 1937 Reindeer Industry Act, which transferred all non-Native herds and equipment to the Bureau of Indian Affairs and, therefore, to the Inupiat (until 1997, when a court decision reopened the enterprise to non-Natives). Lomen in particular had been a target of Interior Department investigations for about a decade. At the liquidation of his depleted herd in 1940, the government paid just three to four dollars a head, whereas in the industry heyday a reindeer had sold for upward of sixty-five. "By the late 1930s the Eskimos of Alaska had taken both legal and cultural control of what was originally designed to be a project of assimilation," environmental historian Roxanne Willis observed.

Precipitating a crash of the Seward Peninsula herds in the winter of 1938–39 were wolf kills and losses of reindeer the Inupiat believed had tired of being herded and wandered off to join migrating caribou. Seveck had vivid memories of those weeks, the twilight of an era. "Three big herds of reindeer follow the caribou and lost completely," he recalled. "The caribou very wild and travel day and night. We must let them go because we could not catch them. They too fast for us to follow." Years later, runaway reindeer from the Kobuk–Selawik herd were shot 400 miles to the east, north of Fairbanks, along the Steese Highway. Hunters there mistook them for caribou, despite the ear clip marks their owners had made.

The last great trail drive left Kotzebue Sound in 1929, an epic five-year trek plagued by wolves, storms, deserting Saami herders and mosquitoes that stampeded reindeer into the wilds. The Canadian government had contracted with Lomen to deliver a herd of 3,000 reindeer to the Mackenzie River delta, as officials there also wanted reindeer stations to boost Native economies. But herding failed to root in Inuit culture, as it had with the Inupiat.

Alaska's Inupiat and their Yup'ik neighbors, who'd adapted to changes in nature over millennia, were not particularly upset by the reindeer's decline. The endeavor had brought more toil than reward, and many men gladly spent more time with their families again, embracing the ingrained, engaging subsistence way of life.

Interviewed at age eighty-three, Seveck reminisced about what the ex-herders sought to reclaim, a time before businessmen came into that country. "Many Eskimo people were old ages, brave and long life," he said. "Never sick, only dying by accident and starvation. They works together. They hunt together to help one another. They divided equally things among themself."

Reindeer herding on the Seward Peninsula is not obsolete but a living, if downscaled, tradition. During the 1960s, Alaska Native owners were selected to become private reindeer herders with designated ranges. In 1968, the Bureau of Indian Affairs took over range management by issuing grazing permits and monitoring range conditions. Soon after, modern management techniques, in part developed with the University of Alaska Fairbanks Reindeer Research Program, were applied to herding. With passage of the 1971 Alaska Native Claims Settlement Act, Alaska Natives were drawn deeper into free enterprise. Several regional and village corporations sought to revitalize reindeer herding as viable economic ventures.

Approximately twenty reindeer herders currently graze 20,000 reindeer in western Alaska. These owners belong to the Reindeer Herders Association, part of the Kawerak, Inc. Natural Resources Division. This nonprofit arm of the Native corporation assists with bettering herd management and developing a sustainable industry to support rural Alaskans.

At summer roundups near Teller, a helicopter—hovering like a monstrous dragonfly eight feet above the ground—has been used to help funnel reindeer into corrals. The pilot was Donald Olson, a medical doctor, Alaska State Senator, and the great-grandson of one of the original Saami herders.

Nowadays, the most lucrative reindeer product is no longer meat but velvet from the young antlers. The dun to chocolate-brown fuzzy skin supplies antlers regrown yearly with minerals. Pulverized in sports supplements or Asian folk remedies, it promises manly vigor at ten bucks an ounce. In clinical tests, this elixir improved the sex lives of aging male mice. Between 1987 and 2003, western Alaska "Viagra" generated ten million dollars. A testosterone booster advertised to bring up your moxie within a month, it has also been used to accelerate healing, and to treat weak bones, weight loss, cold hands and feet, and slow growth in children.

For caribou, champion antlers serve as a *visual* means of seduction. A bull's recurved, wrist-thick brackets can flare into NBA-star palms with dozens of stiletto digits, the "points." In the cervid fall competition, cranial grandeur defeats rivals while signaling health, seniority, dominance, the smarts to dodge wolves, and the wherewithal to sire hale calves—all turn-ons for the less endowed cows. Still, as push comes to shove, the odd bleary-eyed bout sees both combatants starving to death, tines interlocked.

The only reindeer within miles of downtown Nome today, is Velvet Eyes. A pet doe, she waits patiently in the back of a pickup for her owner to finish his shopping at the Alaska Commercial Company—a Nome latter-day trading post. He raised her from a fawn, and she is twelve and fond of blueberry pancakes. She is but a shadow of the string of white reindeer the Elks Club paraded down Nome's main artery on December 10, 1908, with the club members dressed in white top hats and fur coats. Or, more so yet: of Santa's bunch, in 1923, which endured "a very windy snowy dark day" harnessed to a red sleigh while he handed out presents to every wide-eyed child at Holt's hardware store on behalf of the Lomens, on Christmas Eve.

Airborne, tripping, sometimes intimidating, Santa has uncanny traits that intrigue anthropologists. Shamans on reindeer sleds visited Finnish Saami households on the winter solstice, dressed in red and white, symbolic of the psychedelic fly agaric mushrooms they ingested. Snow burying the *gamme* sod houses of many families forced the visitor to enter through the roof's smoke hole.

A 1925 silent short film shows Santa in his North Pole workshop visiting Eskimo neighbors and taming and harnessing his sled deer. It's "a fantasy actually filmed in Northern Alaska" that toured the US around Christmastime. In the denouement, the shockingly skinny protagonist wiggled down a Nome chimney. Lomen reindeer played the parts of Donner, Blitzen, and Co.

NOME

LOMEN BROS

Qiviut Fever

There's a substance on the outskirts of Nome that makes certain people take risks, hoard, and hungrily crave ever more. Those who search for it walk hills and ridgelines with hawk eyes fixated on the ground. An ounce of the stuff, laboriously processed and refined, can net them $100, though many hold on to it.

The fortune seekers are not crusty, unshaven Outsiders pulled here by Jack London or reality TV, however. They are much less conspicuous local women who defy northern stereotypes: teachers, homemakers, wildlife biologists, artists, craftspeople.

The stuff that ignites their creativity and passion for collecting is qiviut, the sable of wools, the lush undercoat of muskoxen. Unlike raw sheep wool, it contains no oils like lanolin, which benefits people allergic to other natural fibers. Having fallen to the rifles of caribou hunters and whalers, muskoxen were reintroduced to the Seward Peninsula in the 1970s; it took decades to establish these herds, so people caught on to qiviut more recently than on Nunivak Island, from where that seed stock came—it in turn had been transplanted onto the island from Greenland.

Several herds hang out in Nome, and I mean *in* Nome.

Wildlife officials say that they hide among us from bears, as it were, since hunting the roaming mops close to town is illegal. So, the beasts rest and digest, or play King of the Hill on a vacant lot across from the Alaska Commercial Company store. You see them drift through neighborhoods or clip the green runway margins as you take off in an Alaska Airlines jet. Wary of traffic hazards, Fish and Game wardens have posted a blowup grizzly alongside the small-plane airstrip to deter the archaic cud-chewers; the puffed-up sentry sports a chest patch drenched with bear-urine repellent sold online as "Predator Pee," a number one, not two, bugaboo, acting like an electric cattle exclosure that supposedly triggers bovine fear.

All this may suggest fun and games, but cornered muskoxen pose serious threats. Huskies chained in backyards have been mauled, and in 2022, an Alaska State Trooper in Nome was gored and bled to death when he tried to shoo muskoxen away from his kennel. Residents fearing for their children have called for the culling or removal of herds.

Light as a cloud, soft as a baby's breath, and eight times warmer than sheep wool, the lustrous, chocolate-brown to smoke-gray or vanilla fiber for which we risk our lives lies beneath guard hairs of a muskox's shag. The difference is similar to that between a bird's contour feathers and its down. Muskoxen wear two coats, so to speak, with the outer, coarser one shielding them against wind, snow, and rain. It's the principle of a hiker's garment layering: an outer, waterproof shell above thermal underwear.

While horses and mammoths died out on this continent, muskoxen weathered the last Ice Age and, thanks to their deluxe insulation, they face winter storms with iced-up beards, comfy at forty degrees Fahrenheit, some surviving at seventy below. Unlike caribou, the boulder-shaped stoics never run far, because they easily overheat. With the Arctic heating up four times faster than the rest of the globe, the muskoxen's coat may become maladaptive. And they already live in the northernmost margin of possible range in Alaska, lacking a farther north to flee to.

A small clan of Nome women gathers and cleans the gossamer gold before color-sorting, spinning, dyeing and knitting it, fashioning splendor from scratch.

Come spring, muskoxen itchy and hot under their fleece even in coastal temperatures shed hanks of the silky fluff over a period of just two weeks, speeding the process by rubbing against or rambling through willows and alders. Even the wind can shred and scatter it from their beefcake bodies.

The first challenge for crafters like my then-girlfriend, Melissa Guy—a public health nurse with an interest in ethno-botany and a novice to qiviut's secrets—is finding enough high-quality wool on the tundra early on in the season. To her, "looking for qiviut is like a walking meditation." Ideally, she gleans her wool before it collects too much plant debris and rain turns it into dreadlock burrs. Nonstop summer sun also bleaches the qiviut, whose protein bonds become brittle. Those who dare get theirs closer to the source, at the risk of being charged by a browsing muskox. "I always want to push how close to the animals I can get," one picker admits. There is a thrill in that beyond the mere tickle of cheap acquisition, that something-for-nothing-but-labor sensation. Many a time, my heart flatlined—*No thump. No thump. No thump*—when a brown hump breached a thicket in which I was trailing muskox gifts, only to be revealed as the back of an ox, not that of a griz'. And I've stalked a herd close enough to hear the calves' bleating while avoiding eye contact with their guardians. They simply stood there, ruminating, but failed to grasp what all the fuzz was about.

My strangest find ever was a bird's nest woven from down and qiviut, a cobwebby off-white cubby, a dream home built in a red-alder fork.

The skin trade through Nome's online exchange network is brisk, as hunters who keep the meat often sell hides. Knitters comb up to four pounds of underwool from one hide, glad for each fiber bonanza. The less fortunate comb exposed, rugged country—bear country, no less. Luckily, with the onset of May, there is plenty of daylight for that. A climate we've unhinged and two-foot-long lungworms encouraged by it (digging in to cause verminous pneumonia) will leave many more carcasses for the reaping. *If* found fast enough.

Most Nome knitters send their raw qiviut to a fiber mill, to have it spun into yarn. Hardcore devotees like high school teacher Lynn DeFilippo will have none of that. Ironically, she considers herself a lazy spinner: "I want only the finest qiviut to spin now. I don't want to sort or clean or pick through my stash."

Twelve years ago, a woman in Interior Alaska taught DeFilippo—who in turn has taught other women. She was "no wretched spinster hag," according to her disciple, but someone who ran sled dogs and guided big-game hunting trips and jet-boat safaris. DeFilippo remembers thick skeins drying in the rafters of her mentor's log cabin and crates, from which spilled a rainbow of handspun yarns. (She later learned the woman used hair from her dogs.)

You can spin manually by using a spindle or by using a spinning wheel. Spindles, which predate the wheel's invention, come in as many forms as chipped flint arrowheads. Often crafted from precious woods, spinning wheels yield more yarn faster, but the attraction of spindles, Melissa says, is that they're easier to pick up for a try-out by beginners, and cheaper.

With a deft flick, DeFilippo animates her spindle, which hangs from a strand of teased-out fiber and rotates with the hypnotic ease of a spinning top or prayer wheel. The basic, prehistoric tool torques energy and fiber into thread, thin and even. Practiced hands feed it more wool, and yarn quickly spools onto DeFilippo's spindle.

Hunting for qiviut, seasoned crafters scan the landscape for other ingredients they'll use later on. After fermenting for months inside of Mason jars with ammonia, chopped lichens with tongue-twisting Latin names are coaxed into releasing sublime tie-dye tints. To untreated wool, the branches of Lapland rosebay—a tiny, purple-blooming rhododendron—lend a soft rose tan and to alum-treated wool a rich autumn gold. The needlelike leaves of Labrador tea conjure shades from beige to caramel and, with yarn soaked in an afterbath of copper, a creamy tundra-green. Enhancing color longevity, copper, alum, iron and chrome act as mordants, fixatives for evasive one-of-a-kind pigments. Cast-iron pots or copper cauldrons simmering for ten hours or longer on a wood fire in somebody's backyard might suggest a cookout.

But the resemblance ends when a spinner with a stick fishes skeins of exquisite brilliance from their dye bath. Like winemaking or concocting pottery glazes, dyeing with nature's materials—mostly with plants or minerals—is part alchemy, part adventure. Even slight variations in the materials or procedure can cause stunning gradients. Meticulous note-taking ensures dyes stay consistent in hue when cooked up in separate batches. Experimentation, however, does beckon. Chance or circumstance—like the soil in which lichen grows—adds to the crafters' palette.

Mindful of qiviut's warmth and value, knitters prefer fishnet designs in lacy scarves and stoles and blend it with silk, merino, or other fine fibers in hats or bulkier garments. Interest in qiviut spreads like a gene through female bloodlines, rippling far beyond Nome; 250 Alaska Native knitters from remote coastal villages sold their creations through the Oomingmak Musk Ox Producers' Co-operative, which also bought raw qiviut from Bering Strait residents. Not much came from Nome, because "a lot of people in Nome do their own stuff with it." They always have been a crafty bunch.

At least three North American farms—counting one in Palmer—raise muskoxen to satisfy the demand for their wool. For the UAF Large Animal Research Station, it's an important source of funding. There, captive muskoxen let themselves be combed in a squeeze chute like those used for cattle branding. Aware of social hierarchies and recognizing human individuals, though, they'll try to bully new caretakers. When they feel threatened in the wilds, they form a rank, a breathing bulwark in front of their calves; one bull even tried hooking the landing gear of a low-flying plane with his horns. Their keepers emphasize that, unlike yaks, captive-born muskoxen born never become fully domesticated. With docile ones, whole blankets of fleece can be peeled off their flanks, shoulders, and rump, totaling about four pounds. It takes two grooms an hour with a patient animal holding still.

The UA's Northwest Campus in Nome teaches qiviut processing, which it plans to do in other communities. Kirsten Bey, a former lawyer, helps organize these classes. She best sums up qiviut's snowballing appeal: "It's rare. It's exotic. It uniquely embodies the mystique of the North."

Heartbeat of the North

The crowd at the Nome Recreation Center goes wild as the octogenarian in a wide-legged crouched stance accelerates. His mukluk-clad feet pound the stage timed to the drummers' salvos. In the crescendo, which almost drowns out the lyrics, the King Islander aims an invisible rifle at make-believe passing geese overhead and recoils with shots fired, synced to accented drumbeats. A little later, a white-haired lady of similar age dressed in a blue-calico *atikluk* joins him with restrained sinuous motions, feet modestly planted together. The applause swells as audience members rise. Dozens throng onstage for the finale open to everyone, a "happy dance" invitational. Its thuds reach into the pit of my belly.

Drum dances formerly took place outdoors also, sometimes behind makeshift windbreaks of stretched canvas or mammal skins. In notoriously breezy Nome, with spectators watching from rooftops, an upturned *umiak* walrus-hunting boat often shielded performers as a windbreak.

In the Alutiiq language of Prince William Sound and the Alaska Peninsula, *cauyaq* signifies both music and the drum, the oldest of all instruments. (Ugandan chimps pant hooting and knuckle thumping tree roots in individual rhythms message each other that way.) In the adjacent Unangan, Yup'ik, and Inupiaq cultures too, drums, dance, and song form a trinity. While Native groups throughout Alaska boast equally vibrant traditions, fans rank Eskimo drumming and dancing supreme, for its muscular elegance, its raw vigor and grace, "ecstatic harmony," in one anthropologist's words.

Thunderous claps on animal membranes have roused northerners since "many grandfathers ago." Hoop drums unlocked deep-sea or lunar realms for Eskimo shamans during séances. Symbolic of cycles, they centered communities. Greenland's permafrost has yielded 4,500-year-old drum fragments. Handles and frames unearthed on St. Lawrence Island belong to instruments last heard in Old Bering Sea culture settlements two millennia ago. Stickmen pecked into Afognak and Kodiak boulders depict Alutiiq ancestors wielding drums. Modern-day ethnic drumming, in the words of the aural historian Jack Loeffler, "reenacts mythic moments," priming the consciousness of participants to embrace "meaning that extends into antiquity."

North Slope elders recall drumming's origins. Seeing that humans were lonely, Eagle Mother told one hunter to prepare the first *kivgiq* or Messenger Feast. Then she taught him how to build a wooden box-drum that sounded like her metronome heart. The faint beat heard from a distance on one such occasion near Old Shishmaref spelled out an invitation: those who heard it passed on word about the festivities to those who had not.

For centuries, drums underscored action in curing rites, divination, and trance journeys to other worlds, where shamans appeasing spirits rectified breaches of taboos. The *kivgiq*'s three-day sessions ensured that animals hunted for food would reincarnate. Dancing and singing also honored forebears, interpreted myths and experiences—a shared history—and invited spirits to winter feasts. In the Bering Strait, December was "Time of the Drum." The tuning, done by dampening the skin drumhead to keep it from tearing, has its own song. One, borrowing from a missionary who taught some Inupiat his style of music, employs the syllables *do-re-mi* as part of the lyrics but stripped of all context. After decades of suppression, innovation is flourishing. A modern "Float Coat Song" song mixes a traditional boat dance with promoting life jacket safety for youths. In the same spirit of innovation, odd instruments were requisitioned. In 1944, Eskimo servicemen danced in Fairbanks traditionally, uniformed, but in mukluks and gloves. A bass drum borrowed from Ladd Army Airfield lads urged them on, with the Dive Bombers' logo blazing on the drumhead.

By the 1930s, Yup'ik and Inupiaq villages had abandoned masked dancing, certain songs and rituals, and mask and drum manufacture. Epidemics killed many shamans and elders; food shortages, wage labor, and boarding schools further frayed the tribal fabric; missionaries discouraged, banned, or inverted practices seen as "devil's frolic." A rare image from the 1920s, taken at the Catholic mission in St.

Michael, Norton Sound, says it all. Girls aligned in traditional *kuspuk* tunics and dance poses sway and semaphore next to a man not beating a drum but squeezing a button accordion, a typical sailor's instrument. As part of a renaissance in the late 1960s, people reclaimed traditional dancing, learning it from ethnographic recordings, luckier neighbors, performing visitors, or through workshops or instructional videos. Tony Keyes from Wales, up the coast, where there had been no singing, no drumming, no dancing for fifty-seven years, rejoiced at the resurrected musical culture of his village: "You should never say something is dead; nothing is ever dead … it was sleeping." Dancing, as portrayed by Sally Carrighar in her memoir *Moonlight at Midday*, could be an act of defiance. When one Inupiaq Santa in Unalakleet broke character and lapsed into traditional moves, children and parents cheered while the missionary, in a huff, fled the building.

Dances and songs, often commemorating events like the first plane to ever land in a village, can't be appropriated. Some circulate among kin exclusively. Etiquette requires special permission and that other singers credit a composition's owner(s). Others were exchanged between villages or trading partners. Drummers could be waterborne, announcing the arrival of traders, as they did while approaching the gunports of Otto von Kotzebue's brig *Rurik*, singing "to the accompaniment of a tambourine."

A knack for making the oversize tambourines often runs in families. The craftsman steams or boils two- or three-inch-wide spruce strips for pliability. He bends them and closes a hoop of up to two feet in diameter by drilling holes for tying the ends together. Scraped whale-liver membranes, walrus-stomach linings, caribou hides, or, in the Gulf, bear lungs, seal bladders, or halibut guts, stretched tautly and tied with sinew to a groove around the rim, have provided drumheads, which can be painted with spirit-helper designs. Lastly, a sturdy notched wood, bone, or walrus-ivory handle is lashed to the frame, which formerly consisted of split driftwood cores. Drumsticks were shaped to fit the individual form of a drum and the player's hand. The handle of one "fine drum" collected in 1906 in Wales was an ivory bird with beads for eyes and the movable legs of a man.

Drummers chant in unison, with soaring, nasal voices. Filler syllables replaced long-lost lyrics. Each village cultivates a unique style and repertoire. Percussionists, holding drums like they would hand mirrors, dipping them lightly, hit the rim, drumhead, or both, with a supple willow wand, producing clicking taps or deep, rich, often sharp, resonances. The tone changes with the drumhead's tension, affected by moisture. Yup'ik drummers strike its face, Inupiat the underside. "The men" in the *qargi*, Joseph Senungetuk remembered, "would visibly perspire and strain to keep the dance at a frenzied pace, once the opening stanzas were cautiously elaborated upon." Nowadays, women may drum but do so rarely.

The one-time Alaska resident and composer John Luther Adams described Eskimo "angular melodic contours" and "explosive drums." He deemed this asymmetrical throbbing "more sophisticated and more energizing than the steady 4/4 backbeat of rock 'n' roll."

"After a strong dance group from the Arctic coast," he writes, "even the best rock bands sound rhythmically square." Listening to Eskimo drum songs at their full volume sends all your blood rushing to the head and feet, with a new hammering filling the middle. Good vibrations, indeed.

Drummers cue in the dancers, picking up or slowing the pace, a dynamic that Cordelia Qiġñaaq Kellie describes as "entwined." The drumming subtly builds up to its final beat, getting "a little bit more intense and elevated and emphasized," which tells the dancers exactly when to stop. To outsiders, this looks a lot like telepathy. Kellie thinks that dancers formerly faced the drummers, moving toward them, an arrangement that new settings changed. Unlike in the *qargi*—a burrow-like community chamber-workshop—dancing no longer occupies sacred, ritualistic space. "We have performances now. We have performances to external audiences and a stage," Kellie says. "Where do we dance now? We dance on stages, we dance in convention centers, we dance in gyms, in front of so many people."

Dance styles reflect the limited space of communal quarters, the Inupiaq *qargi* or Yup'ik *qasgiq*, men's houses operating as workshops and ceremonial chambers. Yup'ik male dancers mostly kneel, twisting arms and upper torsos like frantic, fluid traffic cops; women stand rooted, spell-weaving, knees flexing, "willows bending in the current of the stream," communicating by hands. At social dances in Wales, men sometimes danced with their back to the crowd, heads hanging low, and women disguised by their long hair, while spectators guessed their identity based on their style. At winter dances in the *qargi*, snowballs from buckets were used to cool the faces of infants and "to refresh parched drum skins."

Sewing, harpooning, butchering, sled hauling, paddling, and courting all have been translated into kinetic shorthand. Snowy owl feathers raying Yup'ik men's dance fans stress sweeping movements; caribou throat-fur tufts in the women's highlight restraint. On sepia photos, bare-chested male dancers wear skin gloves, out of respect for paraphernalia they handled, or from a fear of evil-spirit contagion; the gates to the shaman's otherworld could swing both ways. In Wales, Susan Bernardi recorded, gloves were "made of white drill cloth or, in some instances, deerskin wrist-length gloves decorated with fancy stitches." At one Whale Dance carnivore harvest festival, a shaman drummed while a masked whaling crew of eight danced. Dancers today don cotton or work gloves, but elaborate gauntlet gloves may still tinkle with bone, bird beak, or ivory amulets, for secondary percussive effects, or with brass shell casings. They also set visual accents on the dancers' sharp gestures.

Dancers often mime—the best *become*—sea mammals or birds, an imitation founded in rites that feted animal spirits before returning bones in awe to the sea. A swaggering King Island mask dance encapsulates bull walrus nature. Creature calls enliven, or inspire, performances: seal barks, wolf howls, bird shrieks, whale song, walrus grunts. An ancient King Island loon song contains the line "I wish I were able to sing just like that bird." Complex phrases suggest the loon's bobbing and preening; a wide ascending interval in a blanket-toss song mimics the thrill of being aloft. Grotesque masks, motions, facial expressions, or the replays of comic hunting mishaps defuse conflict within close-knit societies, especially in the dark, housebound months. Canadian Central Arctic shamans faced off in mocking-song drum duels, gaining prestige in Inuit bouts of Yo Moma or The Dozens.

"The drum will heal your soul," the Nome musician Bryan Muktoyuk promises. Neuroscience supports what Native peoples have long known about the good vibes. Drums engulfing an audience release endorphins like those from a runner's high; they reduce stress, lower blood pressure, and enhance immunity. They boost Alpha brainwaves linked to bliss that induce meditative states. Brains ultimately tune in to these cadences. This not only coordinates group behavior but individuals' thoughts as well. When folks groove with each other, they more likely see harmony in their surroundings. Any immersion in rhythmic group activity—be it work, worship, or play—strengthens cohesion. A known music psychologist has identified human contact, communication, and emotional support as elixirs for mental wellbeing. These social factors also ground the therapy of a drumming shaman, "one who knows" hypnotic power, in the Tungus term's meaning.

Additionally, Eskimo quick-stepping fosters nimbleness and keen observation crucial in subsistence pursuits and non-verbal learning environments. Last but not least, singing maintains Native languages, aligning youngsters and elders, past and future generations. "Drums awaken our roots," they say in Bethel. Regardless of the region, all practitioners dance as if their forebears were watching.

Utqiaġvik, as one example, fields 200-plus dancers and drummers in five formal groups. St. Lawrence Island, Point Hope, Little Diomede, Nome, and Wainwright are further hotbeds. Small villages stretch their resources as they host several visiting troupes at a time. Many tour stateside and a few abroad. You can catch them gaily compete at the World Eskimo–Indian Olympics in Fairbanks, on Alaska campuses, at Bethel's Cama-i ("Welcome") festival, or at Alaska Federation of Natives conventions. The tribal funk band Pamyua—a Yup'ik-Greenlandic-African American quartet fusing gospel, Inuit drum-songs, South African a cappella, and Pacific Islander chants—gives the world Arctic jive.

Some pupils start stomp shuffling as toddlers. Isabell Elavgak has taken her kids to rehearsals a few times a week since they were babies—one was only five days old. "Now they know how to sing," she says. "They find all kinds of toys to use as drums." A pulse weakened over twilight years has rebounded; vital, steady, booming, assured.

Dressed to Survive

Humans, underendowed for high latitudes, to endure and even thrive there learned to slip into skins of creatures better suited to cold. Step by northward step, sub-Saharan brains contrived comfier, smarter microenvironments. Our species in fact prospered, going global, during the Pleistocene, the last chapter in Earth's saga of ice ages. Functional, well designed, expertly made, skin couture expressed the wearer's skills, wealth, local or ethnic identity—it still does—and pleased the animals' spirits. It was crucial in telling friend from foe, too, outdoors, at a long distance or with faces often hidden by hoods. "You make one style and it's kind of like a family design," explained Bobby Lynn Qalutaksraq Brower.

It is said that in the high Arctic there were few singles, because it took a couple to survive: a man to provide skins and meat and a woman to tan skins and sew them and keep them in a good condition. They lived and worked "encased in an artificial environment," as one ethnographer put it. Furs were currency also. Finished clothing changed hands for money or goods. An Inland-Eskimo old-timer I interviewed remembered traveling downriver to the Kotzebue fair as a young man to trade pelts of wolves he had trapped—desired for ruffs—for his first rifle. The wife of an old shaman (Punginguhk, who had challenged the whaling captain) made mukluks, a parka, mittens, and sealskin pants for a captain of USRC *Bear* (the one the knife had chased; no hard feelings there, apparently). The Inupiat bleached sealskin for aesthetic reasons by weathering it on drying racks and applied the word for it to Europeans, when those first showed up on the scene.

Charles Francis Hall and the proponent of a "friendly Arctic," Vilhjalmur Stefansson (born: William Stevenson) braved a mind- and limb-numbing climate in garb tested over millennia. Stefansson claimed that a family could live as comfortably in Ultima Thule as they could in Hawaii, in part based on their manner of dressing. "The Needle work of these Cloths does great honour to the ingenuity of the Ladies of the Country," Captain Cook thought, "to be excelled by no People under the Sun." For Cook's Lieutenant James King, Seward Peninsula Eskimo clothing was "made with a good deal of Taste." Pilots and flying game wardens donned moose-hide gauntlets, caribou parkas, or all-fur flight suits and the mountaineering priest Hudson Stuck wore lynx-paw mitts and a beaver hat, since Athabaskans of the Interior wore beaver "to the great advantage of health in the severe winters." A loose fit allows air to circulate, carrying moisture away. Roald Amundsen, who favored fur clothing for Antarctica, remarked on this: "Both the inner garments and outer anorak [the Greenlandic parka equivalent] hang loosely around my trousers; I think it is excellent and the only way to wear such hides if one wants to avoid sweating." Many of today's outdoors people consider caribou footwear and beaver mitts superior to synthetics.

This concludes the book's Native outdoor gear endorsement section.

The Seward Peninula's Kaweramiut had a legendary culture-hero who invented clothes after a cold spell caused by an orbital irregularity in which plants withered and animals died and people succumbed due to a lack of caves in that country. This superman of yore, bear-riding Ekeuhnick, "looked at the dead animals. He skinned some of them and took the hides to cover his body. He took some skins to wrap around his feet." Others quickly followed his example, and soon "they were not so cold and they could look at the changed world around them." Realizing that snugly tailored clothes would be even warmer, "using the Power of Imagination," Ekeuhnick invented the needle, together with the ulu—any Inupiaq woman's most-prized possession before the age of sewing machines. He found a piece of bone; sharpened it at one end; drilled a hole into the blunt end; cut "strips of skin-like strings" and took thin tendons from the animals whose skins he had used; and finally threaded his needle. He "bound the edge of the skins together" into a shirt, a pair of pants, and soft boots protecting his feet. For a long time thereafter, the narrator concluded, "the clothing of the people was made according to Ekeuhnick's pattern."

The legend stunningly matches conditions in northern latitudes during intervals like the Younger Dryas (between roughly 12,900 and 11,700 years ago) and the Little Ice Age (circa 1300 to 1850 CE), the latter one of the chilliest periods since that late-Pleistocene dip. The Trail Creek caves, whose finds I described in my author's note, might well have harbored Ekeuhnick's kin. William A. "Old Willy" Oquilluk, a drummer and former reindeer herder at Mary's Igloo who committed the legend and others to paper in the early 1970s, just in time (helped by a counterpart Anglo scholar), stressed the importance of physical cultural evidence of past crises and opportunities for humanity:

> If people want to, they can see these places [the caves] for themselves, too. The young people and the children coming along should see how their ancestors used to live by the land.

Ekeuhnick's ensembles—of lightweight, very warm, water-resistant, and strong caribou skins—facilitated survival at –55° or below. Dense underfur trapping air under long guard hairs conserves heat, as does layering. And the honeycombed guard hairs contain tiny air bubbles, much like synthetic Hollofil fiber. In clinical trials, skin-clad subjects stayed warmer than those in expedition or army winter getups.

A Lomen Brothers photo from 1914 shows Makpii, an Inupiaq girl, at age three, in front of a house in Nome. She was the youngest survivor of the doomed HMCS *Karluk*, a Canadian Arctic Expedition vessel that lodged in sea ice in 1913 and was eventually crushed. Makpii on that sunny day wears a fur parka, mittens, and mukluks. She smiles, perhaps glad about having been rescued with her family and the few remaining crew members. Her father, Kurraluk, had joined the team as a skilled hunter, bringing along his wife Qiruk and her sister Qaualuk. The young girls helped keep the trapped explorers cheerful during dark times. Makpii and her family returned to Point Barrow after the ordeal. As Ruth Makpii Ipalook, she later lived in Barrow until her death in 2008 at the age of ninety-seven. Her mother had mended the sailors' clothes and sewed new ones from seals her husband hunted, thereby improving their odds. Another Inupiaq needlewoman, the twenty-three-year-old "female Robinson Crusoe" Ada Delutuk Blackjack, cast away for two years on uninhabited, cliff-bound Wrangel Island in the Chukchi Sea, off the north coast of Siberia, hunted foxes and sewed sealskin parkas.

The feel of animal skins next to yours each waking and sleeping hour, and owing your life to them—in skin boats, as well—must change your relations with those fellow beings.

Expert seamstresses in the Bering Strait region, normally older women, engaged in a different form of skin sewing, striping the chins of girls with *tavlugun* tattoos. They used bird bone or ivory slivers (later, steel needles) threaded with sinew they'd blackened with soot mixed with urine, which limits scabbing. The striation proclaimed a girl's coming of age, her ability to endure pain, and, as did nicely tailored clothes, her readiness to become a wife, mother, and homemaker. She would hold her head high, with the same confidence that her pair of dazzling mukluks bestowed. On St. Lawrence, ink lacework scrolled across cheeks and the back of women's hands sinewy from ceaseless labor. Equally intricate thigh tattoos were believed to ease childbirth. Newborns got acquainted with beauty through them—the first thing they saw as they slid from the womb. Inupiaq men who had fought bravely in battle received *tupit*, often four parallel straight lines on each cheek. A young man's first whale could be honored with miniature flukes at the corners of the harpooner's mouth. Like clothes, tattoo styles also demarcated kinship and ethnic belonging. In Eskimo societies, stitched bodies constituted the body politic.

While it empowered women, this was another custom the missionaries condemned. The wrong sort of stigmata, with *Leviticus* 19:28 as their strongest indictment: "Ye shall not make any cuttings in your flesh for the dead, nor print any marks upon you." Together with drum dancing and shamanism, it spelled backwardness, pagan ways, vanity. With a younger generation returning to their roots, Eskimo facial tattooing has seen a resurgence, providing continuity with homelands and ancestors. The scars healing are those of historical trauma. The flesh is pierced for the living *and* dead.

The centerpiece of Yup'ik and Inupiaq dress was the

hooded parka. It could be worn with the fur inside and another over it, fur facing out. The word—Unangan, but of Siberian origin—arrived with the last wave of indigenous New World colonists in small watercraft. While modern materials replaced animal hides in certain contexts, the basic parka design persists. A wolf or wolverine hood ruff's uneven hair length creates a calm-air pocket in windy conditions, a safeguard against facial frostbite. Wolverine hair also sheds frost condensate from exhalations. One type of soft frill, the famed "sunburst" or "sunshine" pattern, encircles a woman's face like petals a daisy's disc. Tests have shown it to be the most effective hood by far in slowing heat loss. "The Rolex of ruffs," one seamstress calls the lavish trimming that graced wedding parkas and sometimes combines wolf *and* wolverine. During trail tea breaks or before entering homes, travelers whapped their clothes with a caribou-antler or wooden "snowbeater," as melting snow weakens fur's insulating properties.

Mottled, Alaskan-bred Siberian reindeer sparked an early nineteenth century fad of piebald apparel with striking contrasts. Women's parkas with spacious hoods cradling babies boasted checkerboard panels offset with tassels or trims. Elaborate Seward Peninsula parkas, with the typical bicolor hems of calfskin from domestic cows that came into fashion in the twentieth century, could take four years to make, including the procurement and preparation of the materials. Summer skins sometimes were preferable—shorter-haired, not as warm, they're less prone to shedding and easier to tan. Thin, pliable reindeer calfskin yielded the best parkas; a large fall bull's back, sturdy boot soles. Rare materials, or those that could be obtained only through trade with neighboring groups, were especially valued —beads, certain shells, inland furs, or the skin of dried salmon, for example.

Aptly named "gores"—inserts shaped like walrus tusks, cut from white short-haired caribou or reindeer skin and running from the neck down the chest—were a distinctive Northwest coast marker. "Long time ago," Brower recalls, these tusk-like gussets were "used to scare the walrus or maybe to make the walrus think you are a walrus. To get close to them when you're out hunting." Siberian Natives told explorers that to their east lived people with tails. Such rumors sprang from the sometime Inupiaq custom of attaching wolf, fox, weasel, or wolverine tails to parka waists, which transferred hunting prowess. Strips of wolverine fur on the front of women's parkas, also called "tails," signaled wealth.

People strutted their stuff and best parkas while dancing during the Messenger Feast and on other important occasions, and gave ornate ones to guests as gifts. Parkas customarily functioned as burial shrouds, keeping the deceased toasty in the afterlife. Linen parka covers preserved the luster while fishing or gathering berries, and white ones allowed hunters on the sea ice to blend in.

Dry grass, rabbit, or ground squirrel socks lined knee-high mukluks: caribou leg-skin boots loose enough for good blood circulation. Their wide tops let moisture escape. Skin off the backs of animals' legs lacked thin spots caused by their kneeling. Hooper Bay's Neva Rivers wore mukluks (from Yup'ik *maklak*, "bearded seal") "all the time ... except in the summertime, when we usually went barefoot or used short little boots." Caribou skin pants and mittens completed the outfit. A skilled seamstress could make one in a month.

For milder, wetter coastal seasons between Barrow and Bethel, sealskin, lacking underfur, was ideal. Waterproof boots with crimped soles shaped like small tubs factored most when snow and ice became slush. Sublimely patterned, porous ringed-seal skins are durable as well as breathable. Their natural oils, retained through a special tanning process, repel water. A waterproofing stitch with sealskin sinew, which swells when wet, joined crimped, dish-like, tough bearded-sealskin boot soles to "stovepipe" uppers shaved or with the fur left on. Strips sewn onto the seams also prevented leakage. Sealskin was handy too for pants, mittens, and lighter parkas. All outerwear had to fit properly. Formerly, for tape measures, on St. Lawrence Island, "They use their hands from thumb to middle finger," according to Estelle Oozevaseuk.

Where reindeer or caribou were absent and minks, otters, or muskrats scarce, birds sufficed. "Water just rolls down their feathers," the Yup'ik elder Frank Andrew enthused. Reversible parkas served differently in either rain or cold: plumage on the outside, under an optional gut shell, or against the skin.

The avian target species, thicker-skinned diving birds, were netted or downed with bolas, then skinned, de-fleshed, and repeatedly rinsed. Birds ready to migrate after the fall molt provided the plushest skins. A parka of pigeon guillemots, eiders, puffins, emperor geese, or oldsquaw ducks could last two years. St. Lawrence women tailored parkas from twenty murres with whale or reindeer sinew, and form-fitting socks from two loon bodies. Unangan parkas incorporated 140 cormorant throat skins.

Lydia Apatiki from Gambell, who revived the obsolete craft there, likes charcoal-gray crested auklets, with white-breasted parakeet auklets for flashy chest panels. Yupik Day "show and tell" at their kindergarten inspired her. She couldn't remember any islander having sewn a bird-skin parka in a long time. So, she asked an aunt how to make one for her grandson.

Kayaking and tide-pool hunting required a different kind of protective gear. Gut parkas, diaphanous raincoats of bearded seal, sea lion, bear, walrus, or whale innards, surpassed European raingear before rubberized mackintoshes, and the Russians commissioned some cut like overcoats for their merchant-ship crews. They sometimes were worn while flensing a whale, messy work. To make one, first, the intestines—250 feet in a sea lion—were cleaned, inflated, and air-dried, and then split open and cut into strips. St. Lawrence Islanders hung them up in cold, sunny weather, which turned them uniquely supple and white. Even plain gut parkas took one month to finish but lasted only about five. Tightened with hood and wrist drawstrings, short ones cinched around the kayak cockpit's coaming with a hem tie, for a sprayskirt–paddle-jacket combo. Puffin beaks, resembling parrot beaks but colorful, feathers, dyed baby-seal fur, and dyed yarn worked into seams adorned ceremonial versions. Fox gland oils impregnated sea lion–gut galoshes. After World War II, rubber ensembles replaced these Native XTRATUFs and Helly Hansen tops.

Army demand for skin clothing suitable for the Arctic, which predated World War I, gave rise to a Native women's cooperative during World War II. The Nome Skin Sewers fulfilled orders for 26,000 pairs of mukluks and thousands of reindeer parkas and sleeping bags, as well as snowshoes, sealskin trousers, and fur socks. In 1944, they sold $200,000 worth of goods to members of the military. When that operation folded, Polet's Curio Shop took over production, training Inupiaq seamstresses on skin-sewing machines—sweat shop assembly-line work had arrived. About 500 women in the region found employment that way. With each year, the quality of Eskimo fur craft made for markets declined. Sears Roebuck began to affect the local taste. With tourism budding, Kotzebue elders posed in their fancy parkas for pictures in exchange for hard cash.

All the world's money, however, could not replace the pride in locally sourced snazzy handiwork, in having envisioned and fashioned it.

Working the Ocean's White Gold

Sculpting walrus tusks is an act of transformation, turning animal into art. At the same time, it is revitalization: what is inert once more becomes animated. Lastly, it's the thrill of discovery. *What hides in there?* the carver asks, exploring a smooth arc with callused hands. A shape already inheres in the material, waiting to be liberated.

Throughout the Bering Strait region and Arctic's coast, the earth has given up walrus ivory artifacts thousands of years old. Saws, adzes, files, gravers, bow drills, and the odd crooked knife fashioned bolas, harpoon heads, rests, and foreshafts, armor, amulets, lip plugs, figurines ... Inupiat keen on currency engaged in "ivory mining" on beaches at ancient village sites, selling their finds to curio traders.

The practice of manufacturing things of transcendent beauty from the sea's white gold continues to thrive. In Savoonga on St. Lawrence Island (the "Walrus Capital of the World"), nearly every resident has a relative who is an ivory carver. They sell their creations to tourists or mainlanders living there, to private collectors and galleries, and to gift shops and wholesalers like Maruskiya's of Nome, whose window on Front Street brims with finely wrought treasure, a subarctic Tiffany's. Inupiat from King Island, another sea-mammal hunting outpost, likewise market their wares through this store.

Before contact with Europeans, Eskimo people had little access to metal or wood and therefore cultivated the craft of carving bone, soapstone, and walrus ivory; more durable than wood, the curved canines were easier to process than stone. They yielded ancestral images and everyday items: sled runners, snow goggles, needle cases, fishing lures, dice-like gaming pieces, thimbles, fancy combs, arrow straighteners, and scratchers tipped with claws that drew curious seals to breathing holes. Soot or red clay rubbed into patterned grooves looked pretty while adding magic and meanings. In the seasonal round of never-ceasing activities, December, when the sun barely peeps above the horizon, was *sainatovick* for the Inupiat: "Carving Time." With the influx of sailors, traders, miners, and missionaries in the late nineteenth century, new demands broadened Native repertoires: scenes from life, scrimshawed on entire tusks, ornamented tobacco pipes, letter openers, watch fobs, and sundry souvenirs and collectors' items. Styles changed, from semi-abstract representations of humans and animals and geometric compositions to large-scale graphics and naturalistic designs: flags, roses, sleds, boats, hunts, and cliché (and incorrect for this part of the North) igloo encampments—often copied from illustrations or photos the customer provided. Some artifacts truly deserved the name "curio." I offer as proof:

one engraved nineteenth-century ivory meat tenderizer with a puppy head.

Ivory carving morphed from subsistence into a cash enterprise also in Saint Michael, Teller, and on Nunivak Island. "Hundreds of Eskimo men turned out thousands of ivory cribbage boards, gavels, umbrella handles [with a few grips formed like a woman's hand], and figurines for the local stores," according to the anthropologist Dorothy Jean Ray. In Nome, observed Edward S. Harrison, "the men circulate through the streets … with their wares under their arms, offering them for sale to passers-by." He commented on the (to him) bizarre practice of copying advertising illustrations from newspapers onto walrus tusks, including one for a face powder.

One of the Bering Strait's most prominent ivory artists was Angokwazhuk, born in Ayasayuk village near Cape Nome around 1870. In 1892, when Angokwazhuk was nineteen and living on Little Diomede Island, *Mary D. Hume's* first mate Hartson Hartlett Bodfish, having heard about his talent, invited him to winter on the whaling ship. The youth soon began to speak rudimentary English and to play the accordion. The sailors came to like his sunny disposition, calling him "Happy Jack." Like the Nome painter James Kivetoruk Moses, he was another great outdoorsman driven to the creative life by an accident. The year before he met Bodfish, he'd been detained on one hunting excursion with a partner on an ice floe for a full month. His companion died, but Angokwazhuk made it to shore and dragged himself home. He had suffered severe frostbite to his feet. His mother, detecting signs of gangrene, ordered a man to cut them off near the ankle. In the 1890s, the survivor sailed on whaling vessels to San Francisco and into the Beaufort Sea, off Alaska's northern coast.

He learned the scrimshawing craft from sailors on board but quickly impressed his own vision onto the scrimshander's raw material, walrus tusks. His early engravings boast a parade of comical figures—highly patterned, two-dimensional humans and animals reminiscent of Russian folk art or illuminations in medieval Gothic manuscripts—which playing cards may have inspired. Angokwazhuk gradually shifted toward a more realistic style: a Big Diomede village scene, with a figure holding up a king crab; a dozen-dog sled team; reindeer herds, ptarmigans, polar bears hunting walruses; a pipe-smoking prospector panning for gold; and his signature image: the hare. He carved representations of "Mutt & Jeff" (characters of the first daily comic strip); a steam whaling ship model with a bone foremast and twisted reindeer-sinew rigging; a pocket-watch effigy whose hands never moved; and slews of grinning, baby-Buddha-like Billiken figurines—the mascot of the Alaska-Yukon-Pacific Exposition, a world's fair held in 1909 in Seattle. He began copying postcards and magazine photos and mastered the art of portraiture. He depicted Theodore Roosevelt, himself, and one of his wives. With a fine needle, he captured halftones and textile textures. He clearly kept the tastes of his customers in mind and also produced commissioned work, some of it for miners. An ivory Rosh Ha-shana (New Year) greeting from Nome, dated to 1902, ranks among the finest of his output. It shows a couple in formal attire believed to have run a store there, the man top-hatted, with a patrician's beard; the woman, possibly wearing a wig, in a Belle Époque dress. Their faces flank Hebrew characters and a gold inlay Star of David.

His peers praised him. "When Happy Jack worked, he worked it perfectly, exactly. You can't even see the marks on his things," his brother-in-law Michael "Big Mike" Francis Kazingnuk said. Big Mike could not do the same, even when he tried to imitate Angokwazhuk's handiwork. Before he died in the 1918 pandemic—too soon, middle-aged, at the peak of his career—Angokwazhuk schooled fellow carvers, loaned them tools, gave them ideas, and even sold their pieces for them. In the process, he changed Eskimo art. Happy Jack, in Ray's words, "was the first to recognize that ivory carving of the future was to be done for a different purpose and for a different culture than before."

Impostors jumped at the chance of money to be made. A Seattle jewelry-souvenir company operating since the 1910s mechanically etched fake Eskimo items, signing them with names like "Nunuk" and "Nuguruk," whereas most of the Nome art at the time remained unsigned. The typical northern motifs mass-engraved on the Seattle knockoffs usually adorned *elephant* ivory.

In the years around Happy Jack's birth, the Alaska Commercial Company at St. Michael bought walrus tusks and gave or sold them to men for engraving, since no walruses lived in the area. Elsewhere, large-scale commercial exploitation of the animal's tusks, blubber (for lamp oil), meat, and skin (for drive belts in industrial machinery) caused Arctic populations to plummet from hundreds of thousands to 50,000 by the 1950s.

Luckily for the carvers, a second source of raw material lies underfoot: Modern Michelangelos dig fossilized walrus teeth from the normally frozen ground around prehistoric hunting camps during summer's brief window. They chance upon them beachcombing or hunting, as rivers and wave action uncover ancient wealth. Minerals from the embedding soil tinge these gems creamy-white, bluish, or a deep, chestnut brown. An unworked fossil walrus tusk fetches about $500, depending on size. It is perfect for chiseling: soft enough to be carved with hand tools yet hard enough to be polished like stone, without need of lacquer or any other finish (fresh tusks must be seasoned before they are carved or they will crack). These nevertheless are formidable weapons.

A female protecting her calves sank a landing craft carrying Russian scientists, and at least one walrus lunging knifed a Zodiac. James Kivetoruk Moses painted a bull goring a polar bear. A crewmember elsewhere shot at a charging walrus through an umiak's bottom. No problem; hunters plugged holes in the hull with blubber until they could haul out and properly patch the damage. Beyond defense and display functions, three-foot grapple-hook tusks clear lanes through brash ice, break open breathing holes, and assist flexing flippers and necks in wrenching bodies as heavy as sedans onto beaches or floes. The genus name, *Odobenus*, overstates this last behavior, making the walrus a "tooth-walker."

Alaska Natives who traditionally hunted the species shielded under the 1972 Marine Mammal Protection Act can continue to do so and sell byproducts—whiskers, skulls, ivory—that have been modified, upgraded into art. Though it's illegal to take fossils from state or federal lands, Alaska Natives and non-Natives may use fossilized walrus (and mammoth) ivory. In Nome, the center of Eskimo carving, out-of-state tourists watching the Iditarod or disembarking from cruise ships like to buy locally carved ivories. Unfortunately, many don't understand the difference between legal walrus and illegal elephant ivory. Like anti-fur and anti-whaling campaigns, bans on elephant ivory trading and polar bear trophies have harmed the standing and financial security of Native Alaskans. Alaska galleries complain that sales for some artists have dropped 40 percent since the ivory ban. The buyers' uncertainty spells hardship for carvers and their families, as in this cash-poor region, art pays for clothing and fuel. To make matters worse, works by fictitious "Eskimo" carvers, frequently mass-produced and from poached elephant tusks, infiltrate markets.

The white gold—or "abnormal economic pressure," in the

language of one official report—can bring out baser metals in human nature. In 2015, near Cape Lisburne, 300 miles north of Nome, surf laved twenty-five walrus carcasses. Locals said several had been riddled with bullets or beheaded for their tusks. Twelve calves lay amid the ruin. The meat, which could have fed a whole village, had been left to rot. Under federal law, to prevent headhunting, much of it has to be used, as it has been and is traditionally, the flippers, heart, liver, and tough skin included. Steve Oomittuk, a Point Hope subsistence walrus hunter and whaler who had had a bad spring hunt that same year, like others in his community had been angry to see good meat go to waste. The US Fish and Wildlife Service built a case against the suspected culprits. Four men were charged, and sentenced two years later. In addition to being fined and put on probation, and made to perform 500 hours of community service, the guilty had to apologize publicly to the village council and whaling captains, and to give presentations in coastal settlements about hunting ethics, and to hunt for three years to fill the freezers of Point Hope elders.

Currents *do* wash ashore walruses dead from natural causes (or nowadays, toxins). Seventy-nine stranded within ten years between Elim and Unalakleet alone, two villages bracketing Norton Bay. Beachcombing near Cape Nome, Melissa and I came upon one such bloated mound once. It had announced itself with a gag-inducing stench, and the sight of the melting fat berg had been disturbing.

Today's carvers have changed with the times as their forefathers did. Instead of bow drills and files, many now prefer dental or electric tools. In the old days, the carver's teeth clenched a carved wooden bow drill socket—the mouthpiece—while a spindle with an iron or flint bit bore down on the ivory, twirled by a hand that wielded a bow strung with a leather thong, like Paganini playing *prestissimo*. (I've started campfires by a similar method, sawing away and breaking a sweat, and, believe me, it isn't easy.) The bow itself, made from split walrus bone, engraved with lively scenes, could be a work of art.

Carvings remain a ready cash source for villagers stranded in Nome. An expecting Inupiaq father, staying at one of the town's few, pricey hotels, posted a set of six ivory dice on Facebook for sale while awaiting his boy's delivery.

For tracery, Sharpies have replaced graphite, India ink, charcoal from burned grass mixed with oil, or charcoal or gunpowder or cigarette ash mixed with blood. Souvenirs can no longer be had for tobacco, flour, or nails. Statuettes with inlaid baleen eyes or trim, engraved with lines filled with black pigment and set on fossilized ivory bases, cost thousands of dollars apiece, as do embellished skulls with the tusks in place. Regardless of trends to modernize tools or techniques, the creative process and artistic sensibilities remain unchanged. Still, the carver, observer of physical and spirit realms, makes them tangible for the rest of us with his vision and skill.

ESKIMO BERRY PICKERS, NOME, ALASKA.

Got Stink?

Names can be misleading, or even belittle the bearer. Referring to different plants, the unflattering term "stinkweed" knocks an herb more salubrious than cannabis, with qualities just as intriguing. The northern herbalist's go-to for countless complaints, it would make Dr. Oz swoon.

Related to tarragon and variously called "caribou leaves," "wild sage," *sargiġruaq, cheye'uk*, or "Aleutian mugwort," three Artemisia or "wormwood" species are the Eskimo and Athabaskan equivalents of chicken soup or udder-warm milk. Stinkweed is one of the two most important and commonly mentioned Yup'ik and Inupiaq medicinal plants, and nearly every ethnobotanical reference written in Alaska mentions it. Said to heal a hundred diseases, juice of stinkweed was administered during the Covid-19 pandemic. Its taste, though, suggests anything but the white blandness of milk. In the dry tongue of science, Artemisia is "a self-limiting medicine" whose bitterness "discourages excessive consumption." Many of the sixteen species that thrive in Alaska have roots in Beringia. In the Old World, the silver leaves of certain kinds bound it to the moon and Artemis, goddess of the hunt, who was also responsible for women's reproductive health. Believed to induce miscarriages, the moon plant has been credited with warding off evil spirits, unwanted energies, as if herb magic had anticipated *Rosemary's Baby*.

This cure-all from the sunflower family smells much better than its name leads you expect. Northwesterners wipe their hands on the fragrant sprigs to cover butchered-walrus or gutted-fish smells, and stuff crushed ones inside socks or rubber boots to prevent athlete's foot and mask malodors. Aromatic oils released from wet foliage placed on heated rocks mentholate sweat bath interiors and cut the steam's bite. They spice up herbal smoking mixtures, Native tobacco substitutes when the trade kind was dear. Leaves burned in smudge pots or rubbed onto skin repel mosquitoes and gnats. Smoldering stinkweed's acrid punch keeps flies off drying racks festooned with fish and meat.

The list of medical applications reads like a nineteenth-century snake-oil ad. Infusions are sipped daily as a tonic. Soaked-leaf poultices soothe and purify after a loved one's death or during equally taxing times. It stops bleeding, disinfects wounds, and alleviates skin rashes and arthritis, fevers and gum disease, muscle and headaches, bruises and sprains. It clears up congestions and asthma, fights colds and coughs. Packed onto a person's chest, it became Vicks VapoRub, but sourced locally. Nome old-timers mixed it with bear grease for relieving muscle and joint pains. It is said to ease pregnancy and addiction recovery, yields eye and body washes, sore-throat gargles, and sometimes nutrients: raw, peeled shoots, dipped into seal oil, are edible, if rather acrid. It rids guts of intestinal worms. Ingested in large doses or over long periods, however, it is poisonous, causing paralysis, kidney failure, erratic breathing, numbness of arms or legs, or delirium.

Typically seen as women's business, leaf-picking lacks the excitement of prospecting or of killing a moose, except when blundering into a muskox or grizzly on the alder-studded tundra. Contrary to stereotypes of the male breadwinner, in some hunter-gatherer societies, plants that women collect contribute most of the calories and prove more reliable than migratory big game. Berries, beach greens, sourdock, fire-weed, wild rhubarb, and *masu* or "Eskimo Potato"—the root of alpine sweet vetch—had an important if subservient place in the Inupiaq diet. Surprisingly, mushrooms were not on the menu, taboo to touch, maligned as "that which causes your hands to come off." The Yupik saw in them evil spirit ears and the Inuit shit dropped by shooting stars. A Greenlandic cannibal monster lathered up with their slime as soap. Yet the same fungiphobes did not flinch at the half-digested lichen inside a caribou stomach or at "stink flipper," walrus or bearded seal buried in a barrel on the tundra and left to ripen for three months to a fine Stiltonesque ("very blue" in the words of one gourmet) flavor that lingered for hours. You wiped with artemisia after handling that.

Like sewing, berries, and qiviut, Eskimo herbalism largely falls into the female domain. Thomas Punguk from Golovin, sixty-five miles east of Nome, recalls his mother gathering: "Ugly looking greens, flowers; she put away flowers, roots and stuff. Tell me what they're for, I forget most of it. But my wife knows a few; she has a few herbs put away for her own use, and they work for her. I never try it yet."

Herb doctors in our past used to get burned at the stake; nowadays, they amass homeopathic fortunes. In the Inupiaq world, they still serve their people directly. Norton Sound Health Corporation employs tribal healers. One, who became a National Guard combat medic and traveling health aid and received the Alaska Federation of Natives "Healing Hands" award, credits early experiences with plant medicine, in particular stinkweed, for her choice of a career. To help renew interest in traditional medicine, herbalists offer workshops in salve-making at schools and cultural centers.

MaryJane Anuqsraaq Litchard, an Inupiaq healer and artist in Nome, believes midsummer sunlight imbues plants with a special energy. Dried, they are storable for a year without losing potency. The children of the Point Hope gardener Shirley Ipalook, who prepares a stinkweed cleansing tea, "can just feel it working in their body ... like a tingling." Herbal treatments, often practiced by individuals for decades, were passed on along family lines. As in the Old World, herbalists mostly are women, their societies' traditional foragers. Alaskan elders remember stinkweed helping measles and tuberculosis patients. Elmer Goodwin's Inupiaq grandmother had a remedy for everything. She taught him to combat headaches by putting stinkweed leaves under his tongue, like "you see cowboys in the movies doing snuff." And "It's pretty close to Tylenol."

Southcentral's Dena'ina Athabaskans (with whom I celebrated a part of my first Alaska winter and one Russian Christmas at Lake Clark), and others flogging themselves with wormwood switches while taking a sweat, can taste the herb while doing so. This hints at the active ingredients' easy absorption into the bloodstream, which has been widely documented. Steam-bathing Yup'ik flagellants enjoyed the stinging sensation.

Though few species have been analyzed thoroughly for their pharmacological merits, some, like Tilesius' wormwood (*Artemisia tilesii*, named for the man of mammoth acclaim by yet another Baltic German serving a tsar), contain a restorative substance resembling codeine, which accounts for the plant's analgesic effects. Artemisia's chemical cocktail boasts nine essential oils extracted by steam distillation, one of which—absinthin—as a mild narcotic affects the brain region that processes pain and anxiety. Artemisinin has been shown to target certain cancer cells and malaria. Absinthe, a famous fin-de-siècle wormwood bitter, improved digestion by increasing liver and gall bladder secretions. Inducing a dreamy state in the drinker, the "Green Fairy" spurred artistic creativity and wanton lying about and, like opium, it was quickly banned. Stinkweed's current reputation exceeds Native circles. It is made into incense and into sprays to foil insects invading organic gardens. Tilesius' wormwood, the Yup'ik *caiggluk*, loves disturbed soils; cultivars planted on toxic mine spoils assist reclamation and, elsewhere, erosion control.

Herbalists, including Mary Jane Litchard and Colleen Yaari Walker from St. Lawrence Island, who works with the Alaska Native Heritage Center, sell teas and salves at local events or online. Walker only cuts stems and leaves, preferably in the fall when they start turning brown—she thinks herbs are most potent then. And "We don't touch the roots," out of respect for the plants, "otherwise you'll kill them all." Many traditionalists stress that medicine should be harvested in a pure state of mind to compound its powers. Tia Holley, with roots on King Island, thanks the plants—"This will help a lot of people with pain or with skin issues"—before leaving a strand of her hair as compensation. The truly devoted insist on crushing herbs manually and with love, not in a blender. This is where medicine-making, like berry-picking or drumming, can become rhythmic meditation. What may sound like New Age mysticism rather reflects a medical concept that banked on prevention and which often assigned spiritual, not physical, causes to illness. Hence shamans acted as much as bonesetters as they did psychotherapists.

Where drugstores are rare and links to the past remain strong, herbal fixes supplement modern pharmaceuticals. "Today, if you are out camping and do not have modern medicine, or your medicine is not working, use the stinkweed,"

Golovin's Florence Willoya says. But many people no longer trust in that old-time prescription: "They would rather go to a doctor …" Asthma inhalers' nebulized albuterol, for instance, largely replaced the burning of stinkweed on embers to calm wheezing coughs. According to Willoya, younger generations disregard the miracle weed, resorting to it only when other medications fail. Unfazed, Julia Brown of Kongiganak administers wormwood to her children and grandchildren. Because she wants them to learn, she insists. "Even if they do not like the taste, they consume it." As with many a bitter pill, habituation appears to be key. "Quit being so stubborn, I think it tastes better than the cough syrup," a fan of stinkweed wrote in a letter to the editor at *The Nome Nugget*, "and if you give it to them as babies then they don't mind taking it."

Where else in this country are childrearing and home remedies two epistolary peas in a pod broached publicly with a third, by the same reader, calling for a pipeline along the Iditarod trail?

The Fabulous Kidney Stone

It shines like the drapes of northern lights: vibrant, viridian, mysterious, apple to Kelly green, gummy-bear yellow, rarely lavender or pinkish-gray. The Chinese fittingly call it "Stone of Heaven." Confucius praised it as an object exquisite and mysterious as the earth also, because it appears in the hills and streams. Han Dynasty royalty was buried in plated suits of it, and corpses whose orifices had been stoppered with plugs carved from it—the yoni eggs of their day—never decayed. The Spanish *piedra de ijada* "stone of the flank," which spawned jade's English name, referenced amulets that the Conquistadors reported the Aztecs were using to treat diseases of the kidney, liver, and spleen.

More common than Asian jadeite, and therefore less valued in the Far East, but less hard, easier to work, nephrite (from Greek *nephrós*: "kidney") in large deposits seeds the ground in Alaska's northwestern quadrant. The Kobuk River watershed's is the only known nephrite lode in the United States. Both varieties cooled and congealed along the margins of tectonic plates as products of metamorphic compression where seafloor slips under the buoyant continental crust into the planet's mantle. Nephrite—a tough aluminum silicate—in the process experienced much less pressure and stress than jadeite; it settled closer to the surface, where erosion often exposes it. Nephrite's specific hues flow from its iron content. Translucence, textures, fractures, inclusions, and patterns also determine the price. Only jadeite comes in imperial green, which gem dealers most prize, but none occurs in Alaska.

One of the westernmost Brooks Range peaks, a dome straight from Scheherazade's tales lies jam-packed with this fruit of Earth's loins. A bush pilot relates that "when a person flew over it and the sunlight was just right, the whole thing turned jade green." Nephrite at angles of repose on its slopes outweighs dump trucks. The US Navy's Lieutenant George Morse Stoney, who in 1884 gathered Jade Mountain samples for the Smithsonian, first charted it for the English-speaking world. Frost, snowmelt, and rainstorms pry blocks from its heights and trundle those into Jade Creek, a Kobuk River feeder. You find the best quality as a rule in stream-rolled boulders, which have been smoothed as if in a rock tumbler. Often, a brown weathering rind that has to be cut away before the polishing with diamond-infused grit disguises the moss-green marvel within. The interlocked crystals of some cross-sections sawed with diamond-coated blades suggest a satellite photo of taiga threaded by silt-bearing rivers. One like that adorns the hall at the UAF Museum of the North, donated by a woman freighter and mail barge operator, the "Tugboat Queen of the Arctic," based in Kotzebue. It weighs as much as three concert grand pianos but, dense and wondrous as a meteorite, has the dimensions of a coffee table.

Like muskox wool, gold, or walrus ivory, jade is a pan-Arctic connoisseur token of wealth, though less widely appreciated and procured. Since the 1899 Seward Peninsula gold rush, prospectors have been aware of its presence. The region's Inupiat have gleaned from the peak's tool-stone sites since time before time. Intercepting caribou of the Western Arctic Herd on their fall migration at Onion Portage, 118 miles east of Kotzebue, people combined Kobuk River hunting with rock hounding at Jade Mountain. Jade rubble on a peak near the delta at Noorvik represented the remains of a sumptuous see-through house a shaman had helped spirit there for her proteges.

Two orphaned cousins from Hotham Inlet, that story goes, went to Jade Mountain to obtain blocks for building a house. They zipped above tundra—*whoosh*—on the lower jaw the grandmother of one had loaned them, which had transformed into an airborne sled. (Note the physical resemblance between the bone and the actual vehicle; the magic mandible is a culturally appropriate flying carpet, a teleporter of its place and time.) *How did she eat in their absence?*, one wonders. Perhaps, fasting was part of her sacrifice.

At the mountain, the cousins secured the jade by besting its owner in a dancing and drumming duel. Returned home, the boys, clearly apprentice shamans, restored grandma's jawbone, and she put a roof over their heads in one night, while they lay asleep. As a result of her witchery, they become affluent, influential men. Two other youngsters desiring the mountain's jade spent the rest of their lives as marmots, likely because they had no such protection.

One present-day homesteader on Dahl Creek with better mojo, following suit, encased the fireplace in his log cabin's living room with walls of the mineral.

Did that hearth stone recall the crucible of its formative years?

In the distant past, at the very beginning of human knowledge, when a different path still seemed possible, such sentience—which may look like a writer's conceit—was the uncontested truth. Literary critics later denounced it as a "pathetic fallacy." But in the Eskimo–Inuit universe before contact with missionaries, all things were animate, possessed of an individual spirit or soul: *inua*. This worldview, "animism," encompassed waves, sea ice, the moon, auroras, the winds, sleds, harpoons, ceremonial objects ... and *nuna*, the land, including the stones she had birthed. Humans and animals shifted their shape, and it was wise to never offend their indwelling power. A large stone outside the village of Wainwright had been a legendary shaman. The local Inupiat offered it scraps of meat and blubber to ensure hunting success. Hudson Bay Inuit believed that highly skilled shamans could consult with and seek assistance from any stone whatsoever. "If the shaman's wish be fulfilled," Knud Rasmussen wrote, "the stone will emit a grumbling sound."

The West Greenlandic term for a shamanic "rubbing stone" (*agiaq*) was applied to the violin when Danes first introduced that instrument. Such stones, rubbed together or against a flat boulder or in circles on the ground or skipped off a lake's surface, induced trance states in initiates during which guardian spirits might appear. Remember that before you stone-skip the next time, unless getting gulped by a polar bear doesn't bother you.

Throughout Greenland and Arctic Alaska and Canada, it was taboo and brought bad luck to destroy *inuksuit*, the often human-shaped rock cairns that functioned as navigation aids and markers of graves, fords, good kayak landing spots, fishing, egging, healing, and historical sites, as well as of meat caches and dangerous places. With the literal translation of the singular *inuksuk* as "to act in the capacity of a human," *inuksuit* have variously been described as "silent messengers," "helpers to humans," and "stone people who live in the wind."

Compare that attitude to *Habakkuk* 2:19: "How terrible it will be for the one who says to a silent stone, 'Get up!' It cannot tell you what to do." A blustering blazing shrub, on the other hand, will.

Defying certain trends, hip modern Westerners acknowledge the minds of stones, and not just metaphorically. For the Sardinian sculptor Pinuccio Sciola, born on an island of megalithic menhirs, stone is alive and can speak, and engraving it can release sounds that have been trapped in it for millennia. The material's physical properties allow it to vibrate in the contact, which makes it sing like glass, metal, or water, "giving voice to the earth's bowels or the depths of the sea." Confucius, too, had rhapsodized that jade struck will chime with a note "clear and prolonged, yet terminating abruptly"—pure music. Our home planet, the blue marble, as a whole has been hailed, and by a *science journalist*, as "a stone that eats starlight and radiates song." Stone communicating expresses poetic rather than scientific truths, a contrasting way of grasping the continuum of existence, one no less important.

In a mundane, commercial context (if such a segregation makes sense to you), jade from the Kobuk in bead form circulated as currency. It is still sold in Nome gift stores, where it provides income for Inupiaq artisans. Elders remember Siberian Yupik Eskimos venturing to Kotzebue to barter for the sea-colored stuff. Hrdlička bought several Jade Mountain axes from Nome dealers for the National Museum's collections. In Diomede, he obtained a good antique hafted one from the teacher's wife, though she parted with it reluctantly, since it had belonged to her grandmother. Jade axes cropped up in mounds excavated near Barrow. "Eskimos often undertook long journeys for their procurement," Hard Liquor wrote. Conversely, jade traveled widely from its upriver source in exchange for coastal products, especially seal oil and sealskins. Jade instrumentalized humans, one could say, to get around.

If gold was a useless loud king, jade was the versatile taciturn handyman. Tools and weapons with jade components were dear enough to be handed down from generation to generation, or to be dug from sand-drifted ancient settlements: adzes and chisels, hafted with ivory, antler, or bone; drill bits (in place of the more common shorter-lived squirrel incisors); whetstones; ornamental lip plugs or "labrets"; harpoon points; arrow barbs; spearheads, also worn as charms; skin scrapers (one extant specimen has a mammoth-ivory handle); knives, including ulus; and hammerheads for crushing caribou bones to extract marrow. In pre-metal days, Point Hope whalers farther up the coast wielded *qalugiat* hand lances to deliver the coup de grâce, made of a nephrite blade mounted on a long bone attached to an eight-foot wooden handle. "Axestone" cobbles also came from the Kiana hills and from stream gravels in the Shungnak headwaters. The word Shungnak itself echoes the Inupiaq term for jade, *isingnaq*. A creek by that name salted with top-notch nodules of the substance joins the strait north of Cape Krusenstern.

Regarding names: none is tied to Kobuk jade as intimately as Marvin "Muktuk" Marston's. During the 1950s, the mineral and the man, in his own words, became synonymous. In 1943, the founder of Alaska's Territorial Guard and dogsledding commander of its tundra army of Scouts had visited a homesteading couple on the Shungnak, lured by jade's luster and a story he'd heard at the Kotzebue trading post.

The trader, a "delightful character" with "long curly white hair down to his shoulders" and married to an Inupiaq woman, knew about a 250-year-old lamp gouged from a jade lump, lit by seal oil soaking a braided-grass wick. Its maker had set out to craft "the finest lamp ever made." That man had carried two jade lunkers in a willow root basket on his shoulders, one piece in front and one behind, "so they swung freely." He had walked seventy-five miles back to his village, possibly Kiana. After his death, the lamp had been placed on his burial mound and become a shrine at which travelers left fish or ptarmigan offerings. The trader had promised an Inuk familiar with its whereabouts 100 pounds of flour to bring him that lamp, which he he'd received months later. A Smithsonian curator, whom the trader had invited, had deemed the item "too young" to be of interest to the museum.

With directions from the Shungnak homesteader, Marston set out for Dahl Creek and its nuggets of many tons, wanting a fragment for carving a jade lamp himself.

After finding a choice chunk Marston estimated to weigh 100 pounds, he strapped it to his packboard and lugged it to Kobuk Village. A log bridge across the creek broke underfoot, and with each step he sank ankle-deep into muck, down to the frozen layer. Groaning under his load, the fifty-four-year-old major and future delegate of the Alaska Constitutional Convention wondered if he'd grown too old. At the scales of the Kobuk trading post, he gasped at his treasure's real weight: 164 pounds.

Seeing Jade Mountain's lode as a boon to the Native economy, Marston asked Territorial Guard Captain Joe Sun from Shungnak to stake a claim for the Inupiat. A war correspondent witnessed the semi-precious whacker in Marston's Nome office, and when his story broke stateside, it unleashed a mini-boom.

Jean Joiner from Nome was one of the Anglos to whom the lapidary hoard called. He had a mine near Jade Mountain on Dahl Creek and in the 1960s told a story about an "upright walking bear" he had shot in the back and killed there. The creature, inspected up close, strongly resembled a hairy man. Scared, believing he would get into trouble, Joiner had cut up the slain Bigfoot and thrown the pieces into the creek. Years later, he shared the secret with a Bureau of Land Management area manager at the Nome office.

A numinous aura wraps around Iñgisugruich. Only shamans could visit there safely and only after purification rites. Tales like that of the orphans must have been spread, at least in part, to keep trespassers from a coveted commodity. The risk inherent in these quests surely increased jade's worth.

Non-Natives who'd appropriated sections of the mountain sent bargeloads of jade to Seattle and from there as far as China and later Germany, supplying carvers and collectors—one shipment was sunk off the Aleutians. Soon, almost all the area's surface had been picked clean; the glassy green now had to be quarried to get the papery version. That and the long transportation to processing centers made it expensive. No one in Kotzebue had a scale fit for one particular jade monster to be flown out and estimated at 9,500 pounds. The flight crew guessed that its weight fell within the small plane's carrying capacity. The Anchorage end of the airline lacked equipment to unload such freight, so "it flew around our system for 3 days until they figured out a way."

A monolith the size of a rhino, which had taken five years to transport downriver, lingered on the outskirts of Kotzebue like a milestone to nowhere. Argentina's dictator Juan Perón had ordered it for a statue of his wife, the flamboyant "Evita" whom Madonna portrayed in a movie. After his overthrow in 1955, it sat in town for some time in the company of a few more, covered with a white shroud, yet another roadside attraction of parking barriers "likely worth $50,000 each," according to one Fairbanks stone mason. (Disclaimer: I could not verify the Perón episode, and it may belong to the same realm as Little People and Sasquatch stories. But I've summarized it here as further proof of jade's uncanny heft in our imagination.)

When jade was designated the official state gem in 1968, yields from the forty-mile branch of the Kobuk became sculpted civic displays. The "Alaska Stone"—a marbled tablet slabbed from the coccyx of the continent's spine—was installed inside the Washington Monument in 1982. As the obelisk's latest and uppermost dedication plaque, it towers above the National Mall, courtesy of the Northwest Alaska Native Association, the corporation that now owns the Kobuk claim.

Jade brightened the passage of statehood papers. Over a decade after his Shungnak search, Marston had finished a lamp from his haul, obsessed with the trader's account of the famed lamp, which had disappeared. In 1956, Marston's creation, with a tip of fused gold nuggets, graced a table in the gym that would henceforth be known as Signer's Hall, where I enrolled for courses on my first day at the University of Alaska in Fairbanks. The lamp's diaphanous panels soldered with silver tinged the snow-scape of the constitution about to be signed. Recounting his foraging trek for the convention's other delegates, Marston compared the path to statehood to those travails. "I don't want to brag, but I broke all records—Harvard and Yale records—in the leg and back lift," he told the delegates. He thought jade appropriate for the occasion. It had been here when mastodons roamed the land, he explained, "and in the light of the ages past we could project the dream of the future." The lamp fashioned from it looked rather crude, roughhewn and weighty but durable, whispering "Riches! Riches spiritual *and* material!," much like the young state itself.

The litmus for Alaskans would be to which degree they could cling to their humanity in pursuit of the latter kind of plentitude. What would their purification rites entail? Which "festivals of atonement" should they have to invent (robbing eminently quotable old Nietzsche here)? Would they be able to listen to stone? Would they remember the light shed by jade?

IV. JOURNEYS

Into Cold Air

On Front Street, outside City Hall, a bronze bust of Nome's most famous visitor, explorer Roald Engelbregt Gravning Amundsen, greets tourists and fellow adventurers—mushers at the Iditarod Trail Sled Dog Race's finish line. The beak-nosed old salt looks a bit green around the gills, and gulls sometimes treat him unkindly. He deserves better.

Amundsen last set foot in this town at 5 a.m. on May 16, 1926, in the company of four men, conveyed to shore by the launch *Pippin*. Nome kept seeing dozens of diphtheria deaths, despite the serum Leonard Seppala, another Norwegian, had delivered in a run for the ages by dog team the previous year. The stern fifty-four-year-old Amundsen, a star worth following, stood at his career's apogee.

He had departed Ny-Ålesund, Norway, on Spitsbergen's westernmost tip, five days earlier aboard the semi-rigid airship *Norge* with fifteen others bound for the North Pole. *Norge*, named after Amundsen's homeland, had departed Rome on March 29 and journeyed to Svalbard's Norwegian-ruled islands via London and Leningrad. The silver-cigar hulk, dull pewter when clouds shuttered the sun, was the brainchild of Colonel Umberto Nobile, an aeronautical engineer and World

War I Italian air service officer whose bearing befitted his last name. *Norge*, 347 feet long, was considered medium-size. Hitler's future, ill-fated *Hindenburg* measured more than twice that. Still, with her rubberized membrane braced by a metal frame fore and aft and plumped by 670,000 cubic feet of pressurized hydrogen—the equivalent of more than seven Olympic-size pools—she was no mere blimp, no manatee. She could travel at sixty-two miles per hour, half the top speed of that era's fastest racecars. Three engines in gondolas held by steel cables hung underneath. Their propellers faced rearward, and they even had a reverse gear. An underslung bag between her external control cabin (the "bridge") and the hull contained the keel, a steel gangway allowing the crew movement along her full length. That space, resembling "a flying storehouse," had been loaded with tents, reindeer-skin sleeping bags, skis, snowshoes, for those who could not ski, with shotguns, rifles, ammunition, a sledge, and a canvas boat, all hanging from struts like art in a gallery or flies in a spider web. It was the equivalent of the survival kit kept in the back of today's bush planes.

Hydrogen buoyed *Norge*, more volatile than helium, but cheaper, with better lifting capacity, and more widely available. At heart, regardless of bulk, she was just a mobile, flammable egg.

Amundsen had bought *N-1* (*Nobile 1*) from the Italian government and re-named her to honor his homeland. With Nobile as pilot, Amundsen as the expedition leader, and

Lincoln Ellsworth, the American sponsor-sportsman son of a millionaire (and recipient of a Nome mammoth tusk) along for the ride, *Norge* cast off at 8:55 a.m. on May 11 to make history.

So far, it had been smooth sailing, a chilly cruise at 3,000 feet.

Ink-black water gaped in the fanged pack ice below. Polar bears startled by the monstrous, booming apparition dove into the sea. Belugas hid under floes. Near the magnetic pole, *Norge*'s compass twitched nervously.

The scene transported Amundsen back to 1906, when he'd made his reputation. Over three years, he and his crew of six had sailed the seventy-foot whaling sloop *Gjøa* through the long-sought Northwest Passage between Greenland and Alaska. That labyrinthine maw had claimed the lives of countless men. Jailed by ice and "wild with eagerness to get to a telegraph office and send the news to the world," he had sledded from Herschel Island to Eagle, Alaska, on the banks of the Yukon River, 1,000 miles round-trip, his quest all but completed.

Amundsen joined Captain William Mogg, whose whaler *Bonanza* the ice had stove in east of Herschel Island, and who carried the mail of his men and would request supplies for their overwintering. An Eskimo couple with two dog sleds guided the party. Somewhat scornful of explorers, Mogg was allegedly well content to huddle in his furs on the sled while Amundsen broke trail on snowshoes ahead of the dogs. "I landed at Eagle City in tatters," the Norwegian recalled in an interview with a tad too much swagger, "with a 60 below temperature … and but one board [of firewood] left in my sled."

Having found his stride, he had then led the first group to the South Pole in 1911, in a Nordic ski race of epic proportions, and, capably, on the trek home. His competition, Robert Falcon Scott, failed to do so, dying a martyr.

At 6 p.m., *Norge*'s port engine stalled. The switch to the third, starboard motor—silenced thus far to save fuel and as a reserve—went smoothly. It started with a roar and the Italian mechanic attending the dead one, cussing for hours, found the glitch: ice had clogged the fuel line.

At midnight, Ellsworth turned forty-six. Ninety minutes later, on May 12—sixteen hours after leaving Ny-Ålesund—*Norge*'s shadow fell on the pole, or would have, had there been sun. Sextant readings confirmed their position. Nobile put the airship into a tight circle, lowering her to 300 feet. The crew dropped three flags from a window: Norway's indigo, white-bordered cross on a red field; Italy's Tricolore; and Old Glory, a nod to Ellsworth funding the venture. Weighted with spears, these national claims augered into the ice. The crew celebrated, relishing their single hot meal: meatballs from a thermos cask, swimming in grease. Their hydrogen gas and engine fuel cargo made cooking and smoking too risky.

Norge, sniffing safety, pointed its blunt muzzle south, toward Alaska.

One must remember that the grim stretch under her keel had never before been traversed. A lot could hide in that vacuum. The papers gushed about what they might discover. "Crocker Land," an elusive landmass sighted once only in the Polar Sea, beckoned the intrepid. You may think of Nome as "the North," but it's as far south of the pole as Mexico City from Kansas, one hundred miles shy of the Arctic Circle, at the same latitude as Fairbanks. (Yet it decidedly looks and feels like the Arctic.)

Alas, conditions deteriorated inside and out. "Three big heads had to live under the same hat," Nobile quipped in his memoir. Ellsworth had been mediating the bickering, which predated the launch, over who should be in charge. Relations between Amundsen and Nobile, already tense in the cramped, freezing, noisy cockpit, soured when the Norwegian noticed that the Italian flag fluttering pole-ward was bigger than the other two. He later scoffed that the airship under Nobile became "a circus wagon in the sky," but, credit where credit is due, told funny stories in midair to lighten the mood.

Since that milestone crossing, ice had sheathed *Norge*'s exterior guy wires. As vibrations flaked off shards, the propellers hurled them against the behemoth's fabric, where, sounding like gunshots, they tore ragged cuts. The sleep-deprived crew rubber-patched several. They used up all their cement fixing her wounds but luckily lost no gas through leakage. Fog now engulfed them. Radio contact had been lost. Under the mental strain and pelted by snow—as if in a disaster flick in which things progressively fall apart—they imagined seeing the mainland.

Terra firma first materialized west of Barrow at 6:45 a.m. on the 13th, like a mirage. *Norge* droned over the whaling community of Wainwright a little later. Amundsen and his engineer, Oskar Omdal, recognized a cabin in which they had stayed during the 1922-23 Maud Expedition. They'd shipped a Junkers plane on *Maud* to Point Hope and from there to Wainwright for an earlier stab at the pole. Amundsen, with Omdal copiloting, had wanted to fly from there to Svalbard in the spring, but when spring arrived, the plane with the fuel needed couldn't take off, and they'd scuttled the plan.

Peering down through *Norge*'s snow-streaked windows, they saw figures on the roof of the small Wainwright house waving at them.

As if they had not endured enough between the weather and crabby company, a gale blew up, pushing them westward, out into the Bering Strait. *Norge*'s hide shuddered under the onslaught. The buffeting caused significant drift. She was a "dirigible," direct-able, steerable, unlike passive hot-air balloons, but only on good days. They regained control somewhere near Serdtse-Kamen, Cape "Heart-Stone," a walrus haul-out and cliff brow on northeastern Siberia's Chukchi Peninsula.

Back on course, near Teller, they followed a ravine amid the landscape's milky monotony. Without warning, a blast of wind pushed the airship toward a flanking hill. The windows had fogged up, so Nobile, taking over the wheel, ordered the navigator to stick his head out. A warning of impending doom—black rock ramparts looming in front—came almost too late. Nobile, pulling into a steep climb, managed to dodge the hill but feared he'd lost an engine gondola. The engineer in that pod swore he could have touched the rocky crest.

Since visibility had been poor and their compass on the fritz, they'd guided their vessel as mariners did, gauging the sun's position above the horizon. Thankfully, in May, it never dropped below that boundless, uncaring line. Approaching their destination, with the hull blocking the lode star, the Norwegian navigator, Hjalmar Riiser-Larsen, clambered up an outside ladder to the top of the gasbag. From there, his sluggish fingers gripping a sextant, he "shot the sun" and fixed their latitude.

Unfortunately, the same sun caused the hydrogen to expand, lifting *Norge* like a child's runaway Mylar balloon. The increasing pressure threatened to burst Amundsen's bubble. Nobile opened valves to bleed the envelope. The airship, however, rose faster than gas could be released. "Fast to the bow" sent crew members scrambling up the inclined keel, shifting the balance. At the same time, all engines were revved full ahead. *Norge*'s nose dropped, ending the deadly climb seconds before the gasbag would have ruptured.

After a night to remember, a night without darkness

other than that of the soul, at long last, at 1:30 a.m., the radio operator picked up a message from Nome.

Where are you? Awaiting news.

Army and Navy radio operators had been crowding the ether with calls. The papers speculated that Amundsen, with his well-known sense for the dramatic, withheld his exact position for a grand entry. *Airship Norge bound Nome, Alaska, please any hear*, the St. Paul station in the Pribilof Islands received at one point. Interference prevented a response.

At 3:30 a.m. on May 14, *Norge* reached Teller, an Inupiaq-Eskimo coastal settlement sixty-three miles northwest of Nome, their original destination. Residents spotting the airship from their windows first mistook it for an odd cloud and then for a flying whale. It was as if one of the prophesies of the legendary Maniilaq finally had come true. This drumming Inupiaq seer, born on the upper Kobuk before 1830, had foretold the coming of people with fair skin and fair hair; that taboos would no longer be obeyed; and iron sleds riding the sky; and outboard motors—boats propelled upstream by fire—and that "Someday people would travel against the wind merely by sitting down."

With the weather worsening, Amundsen chose to end the flight here, 3,393 miles from Ny-Ålesund. They'd been awake more or less for three days, fueled by coffee and sandwiches, though with subzero temperatures the coffee was cold and the sandwiches brittle shingles.

They circled for two and a half hours, hoping for a lull.

All hundred-some villagers crowded onto the sea ice, including fourteen-year-old Elizabeth "Betty" Pinson, who'd lost both legs to frostbite at age six when the 1918 influenza pandemic killed the grandparents she'd been visiting in their sod igloo. Kind-hearted folks had ordered and paid for prosthetics. Blue-eyed Betty, the main source on *Norge*'s time in Teller, was the daughter of an Inupiaq mother and a shipwrecked German sailor who became a trader there. On shore leave in San Francisco in 1896, her "papa" had been shanghaied and put on a whaler bound for Point Barrow, where he fell in love with the Arctic. (He had also prospected in Nome with Jafet Lindeberg.)

Upon the airship's approach, the two village-storekeepers had left their doors ajar, their wares unattended. The kids around Betty clung to each other or to their mothers or clapped hands over their ears to drown out the racket. A few hid in closets, thinking the world was about to end. Most of the assembled Inupiaq only knew even cars from pictures.

A voice from up high—Amundsen's, boosted by megaphone—announced the imminent descent, whereupon one storeowner grabbed the bowline and headed *Norge* into the wind. The airship hoisted several people off their feet, bucking, reluctant to end its voyage. But boat anchors soon tethered her to Grantley Harbor's ice.

The two men who emerged from *Norge*'s belly couldn't have been less alike. Nobile—photographed on a different occasion in full uniform, with medals, jackboots polished, slender, dark-eyed, clean-shaven—cradled his terrier Titina, an adopted orphan that hated flying and trembled despite her wool jersey. Hardnosed Amundsen, after eating draft animals on his 1912 South Pole quest, had concluded that "it is anything but a real hardship to eat dog flesh." He may have disembarked *Norge* first, in a ratty old parka and earflap hat, unsmiling as ever, the irises above his gray handlebar mustache blue as the ice of which he had seen so much. In fact, to coordinate the mooring, the mechanic Ettore Arduino already had parachuted in, mistaken by Betty for a falling door. His two superiors were no longer on speaking terms and bunked separately with their crews in the two local stores' dorms. Nevertheless, Amundsen probably felt like the "Three Lucky Swedes" who had started Nome's gold rush (one of whom actually was Norwegian, you may recall).

Nobile ordered *Norge*'s gasbag to be deflated by pulling the release cords right away, to avoid damage. But a gust rolled the airship, which to Betty sounded "as if a million tin cans were rattling around inside." No one was injured.

The crew handed out cookies, candy and Italian oranges. "It was like Christmas all over again," Betty remembered. Amundsen, this time spared a 700-mile slog, reported their safe landing to Nome through a small radio in the village.

For weeks, Teller buzzed with news of the handsome European strangers who became friends and romantic interests. And it seemed as if every woman in town wore a blouse or dress of airship silk from the hull. This was the middle layer, brownish, oiled, sandwiched between tightly woven linen and the tough metallic skin; the women had bleached the silk with kerosene to a nice, creamy beige.

Dogs dragged *Pippin*, the launch Amundsen hired upon landing, on a sled fourteen miles across the frozen bay to water. The ride to Nome was "a most difficult one," with fog and gyring sea ice, a cold, gloomy voyage. Ellsworth commented upon arrival that he was "hungry as a horse."

They were, as the *San Francisco Examiner* headlined it, "Decidedly Not Heroes in Nome." They did not find that, as Indiana's *The Journal Gazette* had promised, "Neither 'sourdough' nor Eskimo could suppress his curiosity and excitement." The welcome differed quite from that two decades ago. On that November day, fresh off the Northwest Passage, Amundsen paraded through town in a wagon, posed for group photos, and hosted admirers on *Gjøa* before being feted by burghers and boisterous miners and toasted by the Norwegian consul at the Golden Gate Hotel (where, from its roof, a spark would unleash the 1934 fire). Initially, this time, *Rome to Nome* banners had been duly strung on flag-lined Front Street. One hundred men had been readied to pull *Norge* to earth in a roped-off, cleared landing field. Rival Lower Forty-Eight newsreel men in two charter planes had raced from Fairbanks to Nome and without delay on to Teller, an adventure itself during the infancy of aviation. The Bering Strait town that no longer boomed felt let down, betrayed. Bunting was scrapped, the reception committee disbanded, disappointment openly voiced.

Teller and gale force winds, had stolen the glory. In Rome, meanwhile, bells pealed and throngs in the streets belted out patriotic songs. To Amundsen's chagrin, "This salaried airship commander on a Norwegian ship, which belongs to an American and myself," had reaped that honor "which is not rightly his." What a crusty, bitter, vain sod he was.

The Italians dismantled *Norge*, crating and storing her engines and salvaged parts in a two-story wood-frame building in Teller, to await shipment to Seattle by freighter. The storage house, listed in the National Register of Historic Places, still stands. Pieces of the balloon envelope kept surfacing unexpectedly, and a chair and fuel tank are in the Alaska Aviation Museum in Anchorage. Other mementos may have been converted to quirky ends, as is customary in the high north.

Nobile was promoted to general and hailed for his "conquest" as a hero of Mussolini's fascist state—*Norge* bore the regime's classic Roman fasces (a symbol of imperial power: a bound bundle of wooden rods often including an axe) emblazoned on the front of her bridge. What is it about malignant narcissists and phallic symbols (nowadays, again, rockets)? How did people not see burning, collapsing, city-bombing zeppelins as omens of doomed ambitions?

In 1928, two years after they landed in Teller, seeking fame for himself and his country exclusively, Nobile crashed *Norge*'s sister ship *Italia* northeast of Spitsbergen, stranding Titina and nine surviving crewmen on the ice. Putting aside old grudges, trying perhaps to top the news stories, Amundsen and a crew set out on a rescue mission. From Tromsø, Norway, they left in a Latham flying boat—Amundsen, the Norwegian pilot Leif Dietrichson, and four Frenchmen—never to return. Except for a wing float and fuel tank off Norway's coast, no trace of the men or seaplane was ever found. It took forty-eight days for all the *Italia* crash survivors to be rescued.

Discussing dirigibles in 1926, Ellsworth and Amundsen had agreed that in addition to carrying heavier loads and being able to stay airborne longer, airships had other advantages. Airplanes had to land if an engine failed; an airship crew might repair one aloft. And touchdown by plane through fog, on ice, spelled "certain death."

Perhaps Amundsen sensed that he'd used up all his lives. "If only you knew how splendid it is up there," he told a journalist in 1928. "That's where I want to die."

Nobile, criticized for the *Italia* flight, disgraced in his native country, continued to work with airships in the Soviet Union.

Amundsen had unmoored *Norge* at Svalbard just two days after Richard E. Byrd and Floyd Bennett returned from *their* polar flight in a trimotor Fokker. Byrd's claim of having been first, like those of Frederick Cook in 1908 and Robert Peary in 1909, has been disputed. *Norge*'s accomplishment, the first polar transit from Europe to America, soars beyond doubt.

Dateline Adventurers

Traversing the Bering Land Bridge, bands of Siberians craving mammoth or milder climes became the first Americans, dateline adventurers before datelines existed. Daredevils 14,000 years later filtered back, though by then the route had been flooded. One, Lynne Cox from southern California, wore only goggles, a Speedo swimsuit, and a bright yellow bathing cap to avoid resembling a seal.

The marathon swimmer who'd claimed the English Channel record at fifteen dreaded sleeper sharks—whale, walrus, and seal parts have been found inside their stomachs. She also feared rips sloshing between Little and Big Diomede that doubled the distance and could have swept her into the Chukchi Sea. Accounting for drift, fighting the "big dishwasher," guided by Inupiat with a rusty compass, who were keen to meet estranged kin, Cox swam the 2.7-mile inter-island stretch in two hours and five minutes, stroking seventy times per minute through disorienting fog; cameramen in fins could not keep up with her. She checked on her shoulders, afraid they'd turn blue, while the sea sucked heat "like a huge vampire." A subcutaneous wetsuit of 35 percent body fat saved her. In Nome, before freestyling from today to tomorrow across the International Dateline, the woman who hates cold showers had carb-loaded and acclimatized to thirty-eight-degree brine. Helped ashore on rocky Big Diomede, she thawed out with hot-water bottles in a sleeping bag. "I do this because I can," she said, and "to help open the border… and promote peace." Relations between the US and USSR had been tense until Soviet leaders lifted the "Ice Curtain" for Cox, for the first time in five decades. Before she waded in, two Soviet ships had parked their steel behinds in the strait, to which the US had responded by scrambling fighter jets. Reagan and Gorbachev toasted a nuclear arms treaty and Cox's contribution to perestroika later that year.

Cox might have known about Lillian Alling's 1927 attempt to reach Russia. A Slavic immigrant, homesick, she was thirty, Cox's age, when she braved the unknown. Lacking steamer fare, Alling left New York a year after Amundsen's zeppelin extravaganza on what grew into a three-year journey. But "I go to Siberia," uttered in a throaty accent, didn't cut it with constables who jailed her near Vancouver for vagrancy. The broad-faced, "wraith-like," taciturn exile spent thirty-mile days on the muskeggy, buggy Yukon Telegraph Trail, arriving in Dawson in mismatched men's shoes, with a knapsack, and an eighteen-inch iron bar for protection against men. Kids there mocked her broken English. Rumors that the "Mystery Woman" was a grand duchess or counterrevolutionary spy were just that. "Writes novels," and "perhaps a criminal," guessed others who met her. (Which would be worse as a reputation?) When the pack-dog a kind linesman had provided died, she may or may not have skinned it and stuffed it with grass. Having wintered as a domestic at Dawson's St. Paul's hostel, a children's home, she repaired a skiff and, chasing the outgoing ice, stopping at cabins for sleep and for food, sculled to the Yukon delta. The tide hijacked that boat while she sat and ate on the beach there. She was last seen pulling a two-wheeled cart outside Nome, beyond the old Teller reindeer station, Amundsen's landing site. Cape Dezhnev and Slavic homelands beckoned: the Chukchi Peninsula's easternmost point lay a mere 109 miles away.

She possibly crossed. Responding to a 1972 article about Alling, one reader related a Russian friend's story. The friend in the fall of 1930 had watched officials, ringed by a crowd, question three Diomeders disembarked at Provideniya's waterfront—a white woman with the trio said she'd come from America, walking "a terrible long way."

At least one other person tackled the strait's fifty-six endless miles, like Alling, out of nostalgia. In 2018, to join his Chinese wife and son in Guangdong, John Martin, a homeless, six-foot two-inch Anchorage man raised on a Soldotna homestead, sailed a dinghy slightly bigger than himself down the Tanana and the Yukon, tacking north, past St. Lawrence Island, sighting the Diomedes, and beaching at Lavrentiya, Chukotka. He carried little more than a compass, blanket, water and grape juice jugs, salmon bellies a cannery donated, and *The Crown of Truth* for spiritual orientation.

After being detained in Anadyr, where he wrestled six months with apparatchiks, Martin flew back to Alaska. He'd already quit twice, before even spotting his country's coast, hoofing it, years ago, stopped by too little ice on rivers he therefore forded swimming.

Few have completed the direct crossing on foot. The first on record, the German trader Max "Mike" Gottschalk, was "a legendary and unscrupulous trapper from Nome." He was another contender for the original Sea Wolf—"cognac," in the words of one acquaintance, to Cap'n Alex MacLean's "milk and water." He once painted his boat so it would look like his competitor's. He peddled alcohol to the Chukchi, and the Bolsheviks, wanting him dead or alive for murder, placed a bounty on his head. Elizabeth Pinson, who watched Amundsen's landing at Teller, called him a "brigand of the Far North" who "did things the way he wanted, legal or otherwise." Her father, a trading partner of Gottschalk, told her not to trust him any further "than you can throw a bull by the tail."

In the fall of 1912, he became shipwrecked with a Norwegian naturalist and another skipper and part-time trader when pack ice off the north Siberian coast crushed both schooners "to matchwood." They were able to save most of the natural history specimens (caching those among rocks on the shore) and $2,500 worth of furs, plus a whaleboat, with which they made Cape Dezhnev ("East Cape"). There they embarked for the Diomede Islands in an *umiak* before the onset of freezeup. Landing on Big Diomede, the three men again wrecked when sharp rocks smashed their boat. They got to shore with only their rifles and the bundle of furs. For three months, they subsisted wholly on walrus meat. Driftwood sheltered them and kept their life flame stoked.

At the end of February, "pack ice began pouring through the Straits," promising a solid path to the neighboring outcrop and back to the American mainland. With their possessions strapped to their backs, they reached Little Diomede but failed to convince the Inupiat to take them across in an *umiak*.

The Diomeders were well aware of the perils in sledging on sea ice. Even before first contact with Russians on Little Diomede Island in 1732, Bering Strait Eskimos had converted kayak frames into sleds pulled by leaderless three- to five-dog teams harnessed in a fan pattern. Their owners usually walked or snowshoed in front. The built-up "railed" sled described in nineteenth-century accounts dates at least to the mid-1500s, based on runners and pegs excavated at Kotzebue. Dog traction has been credited for the rapid expansion of Thule culture whalers along the north coast—from the Bering Strait to Greenland within two or three centuries. After more frequent encounters with Cossack traders, Yup'ik and Inupiaq mushers began riding sleds, standing on runners and gripping handle bars, and used larger, faster dog teams and single-file or tandem-hitch setups better suited to wooded terrain.

Gottschalk and his partner, having taken the furs from their cache in March, set out again, at twenty below, with a sled and sixteen dogs bought from the Diomeders. Told to stay close, Gottschalk drove the loaded sled, mushing far ahead, while the second man trailed him on foot. Before long, Gottschalk whipped the dogs onward, speeding them toward Cape Prince of Wales.

Unknown to Gottschalk, his partner, after falling three times through the ice, struggled back to the Inupiaq settlement. The naturalist thereupon headed east to pursue the fur thief. Relying on a wobbly pocket compass, he wandered for thirty-six hours in darkness or fog across the milling ice, sometimes detouring a mile around a fissure a few yards in width. Depleted of strength, having yelled when a light punctured the gloom, he was finally carried to the house of the doctor in Wales. As soon as he could, he swore out a warrant for Gottschalk's arrest. The third man later showed up in Nome "with a few toes and fingers shy," noted the US Marshal at Teller. Gottschalk, set to be tried in the summer, jumped bail and returned to East Cape. There he killed a Russian officer who tried to board the fugitive's boat. The naturalist at long last sailed on *Bear* to Siberia, where he retrieved his collection.

In a 1938 letter to the Smithsonian, Gottschalk described how he had traveled at an angle "to allow for the northward current" shifting the ice. A skim of young ice on "leads"—open channels, whale and walrus highways—had meant trouble for his companion. Gottschalk the wretch, despite his load, had likely been spared by his sled's greater weight distribution and speed. The prevailing currents pushed floes that delivered him seventy miles northeast of his intended destination.

Gottschalk confessed that it had been a risky trip, one he would not wish to repeat. "But then I am older now and that may be the reason," he added, attempting to burnish his bad-boy reputation. He enclosed a sketch of his route but never mentioned the Norwegian or furs. In his version, he had wrapped his freezing partner and driven him to Little Diomede, where he soon died. As Pinson's papa had said: Gottschalk was a shady narrator, a con artist. He was a fitter, tougher Donald Trump of the ice. Still, channeling the Beringians, the two men had proven that the strait could be traversed largely on foot, if at a price.

Equally lucky souls in modern times arrived by standing on a paddleboard for eleven hours or, threatened by shifty seas, were choppered out. Two kayakers caught between freeze-up and hell shivered a long night in mummy cocoons, stuck in slush that soon set like concrete. "There's success, there's rescue, and there's death," said one of them, a five-time Everest summiteer and veteran of both poles who embraced the middling outcome. Another six, straddling jet skis for a TV stunt, scootered into a Russian restricted zone and, betrayed by their headlights, straight into four-day custody. *Four days*—did John Martin laugh? Perseverance and courage, not bluster, earn respect: the Soviets greeted Lynne Cox not with a tank but with biscuits, tea from a samovar, and a warm hug.

Wheels to Fortune

In late February, as the days grow longer and somewhat milder, down-clad athletes flock to western Alaska for the Iditarod Trail Invitational. "The world's longest and toughest winter race," like the famous mushing event, honors the life-saving Serum Run. Fat biking, running, and skiing, pulling sleds and often pushing their vehicles (and their luck), thrill-seekers cross the Alaska Range into the frigid Interior—and into vales of deadfall, snowdrifts, and overflows—before sighting the coast on the Bering Strait. Members of this confederacy of pain are likely unaware that they're following the tracks of velocipedists who swift-footed toward gold over a hundred years ago, back when the state was a territory.

In 1897, greenhorn mobs boarded steamers bound for the Klondike goldfields, while bicycles, invented eighty years earlier to counter horse shortages after the Napoleonic Wars, had become a nationwide fad. Sears, Roebuck & Company offered surprisingly modern-looking "Yukon" models for ladies and gents. The cavalry officer and polar explorer Adolphus W. Greely considered bicycles equal to the telegraph, perfect for quickening long-distance communication through mechanized messengers. Robert Service, the Bard of the

Yukon who missed the rush there by seven years, commuted by bike from his cabin to his Dawson bank teller job and to court his stenographer lady friend. Dr. Arthur Conan Doyle, the creator of Sherlock Holmes and a one-time Arctic traveler, in 1896 had endorsed the conveyance: "I believe that its use is commonly beneficial and not at all detrimental to health, except in the matter of beginners who overdo it." Other physicians feared that, combined with sunburn, the exertion and the effort to maintain balance could cause "bicycle face," a possibly permanent condition characterized by a clenched jaw and bulging eyes. Today's racers know that bicycle face is nothing compared to the lost noses and cheeks of severe frostbite.

As soon as news of the bonanza broke, a New York syndicate pledged to build a bike path to it, "a roadway, lightly constructed of steel, clamped to the sides of the mountains where it is not possible to arrange for a roadbed on a flat surface." The plans included a roadhouse every fifty miles as a refuge for riders ("especially the wheelwomen") to hide out during particularly inclement weather. The schemers proclaimed they would have nothing to do with "common methods of transport, such as railroads, boats, pack horses, dog-sleds, and Indians." A Palo Alto bike dealer promptly sold his inventory to drag a ninety-pound sled loaded with photographic equipment across White Pass. He put the bicycle on the sled in rough spots but made up for lost time downhill and on frozen lakes.

Commercial single-gear models were advertised as the miner's best choice, as were snowshoe attachments clamped to the frame and bicycles with a ski instead of a front wheel. The tellingly named Seattle hardware firm Spelger & Hurlbut sold merchandise obtained from Chicago's Western Wheel Works factory, and one reporter wrote that by 1900, "scarcely a steamer leaves for the North that does not carry bicycles." The Rambler Road Wheel, which dealers touted for Alaska conditions, came with a detachable, easily repaired tire with heavy tread. The Klondike Bicycle, probably never built, sported solid rubber tires, weighed about fifty pounds, and, in the words of one 1897 guidebook, was designed "more for strength than appearance." Shrunk-on rawhide wound onto its steel tube frame would allow prospectors to handle it comfortably in low temperatures. It was a shape-shifting cart—the rider, dismounted, would haul a quarter-ton of goods on four wheels before retracting one outrigger pair and pedaling back to pick up the next load.

Bikes proved to be more efficient on hard snow than on boggy, boulder-strewn summer terrain. Dawson stores peddled them to tenderfeet, and a local newspaper speculated that canine freight teams were doomed. Best of all, even a ready-made snow bike cost only a fraction of a sled or the optional dogs.

"Dog-punchers" eyed bicyclists guardedly, as they did East Coast dandies or cabin-fevered odd ducks. One can hardly blame them. Bizarre do-it-yourself arrangements flourished. Two fellows, anticipating the Yukon debouching from Lindeman Lake, had left New York with conjoined bikes. Between those hung a rowboat with their possessions. With roadhouses spaced about twenty miles apart, the 400-mile Dawson-to-Whitehorse trail on the Yukon saw hundreds of wheelmen in the spring of 1901. Trading shank's mare for iron ponies, they'd mastered the eye-straining trick of staying in the two-inch parallel grooves firmed up by sled runners.

Cold-weather cyclists were gearheads then, too, although by necessity. Some wore a flannel shirt or a onesie "union suit" inside a fleece-lined overall, topped by a mackinaw coat or drill parka, plus two pairs of thick wool socks inside felt boots not so snug as to cut off circulation, a beaver-fur ear-flap hat, fur nose guard, and fur mittens. Many riders strapped a fur robe or bearskin over the handlebars. The mukluks of one rider wore out and his toes bruised severely on the ice. Fastened behind the seat, the canvas pannier of yet another rider contained a spare shirt and socks, more woolen underwear, a journal in waterproof covering, pencils, and several blocks of sulfur matches. At the roadhouses, a peeling nose signaled a salty trail dog; without it, people might think you had come in by "hot-air stage," a sleigh covered with canvas, with a stove inside.

When gold rushers had staked every claim "from sea-beach to sky-line," often with markers rough-cut from willows, and each pull yielded less or even nothing of value, the action moved on. Gold strikes near Nome (in 1898), Fairbanks (in 1902), and Wiseman (in 1903) shifted the human tide. Again, wheelmen rode cold and hard, if not consistently fast, taking advantage of frozen-stream highways to riches, which could be as smooth as pavement.

On February 22, 1900, likely ignorant of Arthur Conan Doyle's advice, the trading post owner Ed Jesson left Dawson on a bike he bought with gold dust after a man who'd ridden up from Skagway sold it to the Alaska Commercial Company store. Young Ed owned an exceptional dog team but spent eight days taming this newfangled beast, which looked like a "white elephant" attached to his hands. He took dozens of headers into the snow, and after each one, his mutts climbed on top, nearly smothering him. "We will have to put him on the woodpile until he comes out of it," old-timers commented when he'd announced his plan.

Jesson arrived in Nome five weeks and 1,348 miles later, bruised, tired, and almost snow-blind. Abrasive gusts had stalled him. Fueled by mush, griddle cakes, coffee, and muskrat mulligan, he had skirted open water, dodged ice jams—or head-butted them—and zipped full-tilt over glare ice, overtaking a big Norwegian on skates who had been dunked. At times, kiting before the wind, he backpedaled to slow down. A small bottle of mercury at one stopover cabin froze solid, which meant temperatures dipped close to minus forty degrees. Somebody had planted a ghoulish trail marker: a red, shorthaired dog balanced on its nose, stiff tail straight up and paws at a trot, "like a circus clown doing his trick."

Initially, Jesson, not yet having learned to steer with one hand and rub his numb nose with the other, vise-gripped his handlebars two-fisted. On a good day, he covered one hundred miles. Sharp north winds kept him from crossing Norton Sound at the current location of a safety cabin on the Iditarod Trail, grounding him three days at a busy roadhouse. Then as now, congealed grease, frozen bearings, rock-hard "Flintstone" tires, and knee, elbow, or collarbone fractures were common. One solo traveler on the Yukon River, after lying immobilized in the snow for five days, had to have both legs amputated by an Army post surgeon. Miners in Nome held a benefit at the Grotto Saloon for a pair of better-fitting prosthetics for him. Taking falls in tailwinds of sixty miles per hour, cyclists saw their rides skid away on glassy river ice unless they held on. "I have ridden bucking horses and been bucked off many a time," one of them confessed, "but I never saw a bucking horse that could get from under me as quickly as that wheel."

At −40° temperatures, boiling water tossed up blossoms into a crystal-dust mohawk. In such cold, air pumps shatter, pedals and cranks snap in half, wrenches adhere to finger-tips, and even the obese wheels of today's cyclists expire spontaneously. (A single speed demon in 1908 had so many flats that he stuffed rope into his tires to make it home.) On his 1,000-mile journey, Jesson carved wooden replacement pedals, each of which lasted only a day. Having bought nuts and bolts, he hacked a more durable one out of sheet metal, helped by a missionary. Still, he praised his boneshaker. "It didn't eat anything, and I didn't have to cook dog feed for it."

Starting in March of the same year as Jesson, Max Hirshberg raced spring's thaw from Dawson to Nome, where people stole tents and moved houses while the owners were out prospecting. His departure had been delayed by blood poisoning—while fighting a hotel fire, he'd stepped on a rusty nail. Drivers of dog teams he approached en route veered off-trail and restrained their barking packs from nipping his heels. Other riders, meeting mushers at blind corners head-on, created snow angels or augured into drifts. Near his trip's end, Hirshberg fell through ice on the Shaktoolik River and almost drowned. Struggling for two hours in ice-cubed water, he lost his watch and a gold poke worth $1,500 but managed to save his bike. When he got marooned on an ice floe, he jumped to shore, grabbed a driftwood log, and, like an overdressed gondolier, poled his ride back to land. Just east of Nome, Hirshberg crashed and busted his chain. Unable to pedal or brake, he threaded a stick through his mackinaw coat for a sail. For once, the wind blew from the right quarter, yet it forced him at times to steer into snowdrifts to stop his wild flight. He turned twenty during his adventure.

The last original spring stampeder, the sea captain John Sutherland, rolled into Nome, overdue and presumed dead, sixty-two days after hightailing out of Dawson. When he first glimpsed Norton Sound, the ice had already gone out. He walked his bike, detouring 360 miles through swamps with mosquitoes thick as smoke. The bicycle frightened a group of Athabaskans, who shot at Sutherland because their shaman said all the fish would die if the weirdo lived. Fortunately, soldiers from a nearby fort came to his rescue. The next day, the Natives brought peace offerings and punched the Scot to see if he was real. One tried to buy his magic hoops. Having lost twenty pounds, Sutherland tipped the scales at 230 pounds regardless. "I rode my bicycle night and day," he said. "Sometimes it rode me."

While two-wheeled traffic may have irked grizzled Yukoners, the cheechakos' locomotive antics amused indigenous spectators and drew crowds. "White man he sit down, walk like hell," one wisecracked when, showing off, Ed Jesson encircled a camp. Others, hollering "Mush!"—the traditional dog handler's command—urged the passing figure to speed up.

Hardy women and men still get to Nome by parking their butts, shunning heated snowmachine or cushy airliner seats. With their snotsicles and waxy cheeks, their breath plumes and hulking silhouettes, they may resemble team Donner or Robert F. Scott's doomed Antarctic crew. But they remind locals who know their history of earlier sprinters in spring. What is transport for some, for others is mettlesome sport: a personal dare and homage to a hell-on-wheels past.

Image Notes

These are visual trophies—each, I hope, tells its own story—and I thank the institutions that preserve and make them available to the public.

p. 4/5 (Frontispiece): A rare Edward S. Curtis photo of an *umiak* under sail approaching Kotzebue. This is a photo from one of more than 200 forgotten original negatives discovered a few years ago, a selection of which appeared in the Curtis Legacy Foundation's book *Unpublished Alaska*. Inupiat of the region keep identifying family members, and in rare cases their own, much younger, faces in these photos. The foundation, through its Descendants Project, supports Native voices and stories. For this, it photographs relatives of people in the Curtis images with a nineteenth-century camera and lenses for glass plate negatives that create effects similar to the originals. Courtesy of John and Coleen Graybill, Curtis Legacy Foundation.

p. 8: An Eskimo grave on the tundra, made of driftwood, includes necessities for the afterlife. 1935. Library of Congress.

p. 10: Glimpses of a different world—an Inupiaq woman reads *Woman's Home Companion* in this Lomen Brothers photo taken between 1903 and 1915. Glenbow Museum.

p. 16/17: A 1776 map titled *The Russian Discoveries* (cropped), by the London cartographer Thomas Jefferys, shows the most important achievements of the Great Northern Expedition or Second Kamchatka Expedition from 1733 to 1743. It includes the sea routes of Vitus Bering and his second-in-command, Aleksei Chirikov, but mainland Alaska still appears as a blank, amorphous blob. Western Alaska is labeled "Land indicated by the inhabitants of Kamtschatka, which according to some navigators, may be seen from Bering's Isle," westernmost of the Commander Islands. Even the extent of the "Land of the Tschuktschi" (Chukotka) was "not yet known." Early modern cartographers believed that the Strait of Anián—a semi-mythical body of water documented from around 1560—marked the boundary between North America and Asia and permitted access to a Northwest Passage from the Arctic Ocean to the Pacific. The strait's name probably derived from Ania, a Chinese province mentioned in a 1559 edition of *The Travels of Marco Polo*. Published in *The American Atlas: or, A Geographical Description of The Whole Continent of America*. The geography department of the St. Petersburg Academy of Science had printed the original version in French, in 1754. Wikimedia Commons.

p. 18/19: The captain of an Arctic whaler in the Bering Strait collected this "map" that a Chukchi hunter allegedly drew on sealskin between the 1860s and 1870s. It may be a pictographic record of the events of one year in the region—similar to a Plains Indian "winter count"—or simply of scenes from daily life. It contains calendrical references (celestial bodies) as well as stylized beaches, bays, and heights that match actual landmarks. A Siberian Eskimo perhaps painted this skin, as the marine mammals hunted on it are more typical of that group. The representation of reality on the next page spread holds information about gold and coal; this rendition shows reindeer, polar bears, bowhead whales (even a pregnant one), and the competition: New England whalers. Each map emphasizes what matters most to members of the respective culture. The illustration is from Walter James Hoffman, "The Graphic Art of the Eskimos Based Upon the Collections in the National Museum," in *Annual Report of the Board of Regents of the Smithsonian Institution … for the year ending June 30, 1895.* Washington DC, Government Printing Office 1897.

p. 20/21: US Geological Survey, map of Alaska (cropped), 1898. It outlines the gold and coal fields and Fort St. Michael Military Reservation together with principal steamer routes and major trails. Topographical features gradually took shape, with the "void" being filled from the coast and rivers outward, and an imaginary line now separated Russia from the US, Asia from North America. Library of Congress.

p. 22: Michael Healy's former ship, the US Revenue Cutter *Bear*, in the "roadstead" (a sheltered, near-shore anchorage) at Nome. Lomen Brothers, ca. 1914. Library of Congress.

p. 44: A tent city, including a drugstore tent, grew on the black, gold-bearing sand beaches fronting the town. The Lomen Brothers took this picture in 1900, at the height of Nome's gold rush. Library of Congress.

p. 64: It is unclear if the title "The Giants at Work" refers to the high-pressure hose and monitor nozzle employed in "hydraulicking"—working placer deposits—in Glacier Creek's Miocene Ditch in 1910, or to their operators. One promoter of mining enthused about water hurled from the monitor "with such force that it tears a hole in the hill-side and makes great boulders dance like little pebbles beneath the stream from a garden hose." Photo by Lomen Brothers, Library of Congress.

p. 80: Nalukataq, the Inupiaq Blanket Toss with a walrus skin, was part of the feasting that followed a successful whale hunt. Originally, it may also have served to give a person elevation in a flat country to spot game on the tundra or whales out at sea. This is a rare photo by Dr. Samuel J. Call from circa 1898, before the Nome gold rush. Call, a surgeon on USRC *Bear*, accompanied Sheldon Jackson to Siberia to fetch the first reindeer for Alaska. He participated in the 1897-98 overland rescue mission to supply whalers trapped in the ice near Point Barrow, for which he received a Congressional Medal. During the early years of the Nome rush, he privately practiced there. Library of Congress.

p. 98: This Bell P-63 Kingcobra fighter aircraft crashed on Christmas Eve 1944 at the Nome airfield, killing the pilot, Major Nikolay Markovich Senchenko. Most of these Russian pilots had only had a few hours of training at Ladd Field on the US aircraft they were about to fly across the Bering Strait. Library of Congress.

p. 120: "Working to beat the devil" in Nushagak, 1900. The Yup'ik shaman "exorcising evil spirits from a sick boy" might in fact have tried to cure him of the White Man's curse, one of several introduced illnesses. Traditional healers lost influence, helpless when faced with new infectious diseases and hounded by missionaries. Library of Congress.

p. 130: An encounter in 1900 on Nome's unpaved streets encapsulates contrasting cultures. Children were often the mediators, quick to learn and to adapt to new influences. More than half a century later, they supplied Nome's Lemming Lady with rodents. Library of Congress.

p. 140: Ũgiyakŭ, a Yup'ik woman from Nunivak Island, wears a hooded gut parka decorated with hair, and a nose ring and lip plug "labrets" made of beads. This E.S. Curtis photo from 1929 typifies the portraits for which this artist became known. A note on the negative sleeve identifies the woman as "Sophie Weston's older sister, Elsie Williams' aunt," and the ornamental material as coming from dog tails dyed red with berries. Library of Congress.

p. 154: Another Inupiaq artist whose injury in a harsh environment forced him to switch careers: the ivory carver "Happy Jack" Angokwazhuk and his wife, Assongoyi, by Frank Hamilton Nowell, 1904. "We have a photograph of everything in the great North but the pole itself, the Seattle-based photographer and former mining agent boasted about his business." Assongoyi is wearing keys on a chain around her neck, and Angokwazhuk's parka shows the region's typical walrus-tusk gussets. Library of Congress.

p. 160: "Mother Hubbard" on King Island nurses an orphaned polar bear with Carnation condensed milk, while Mageik, the explorer's favorite dog, watches. Blue-eyed Mageik looked like a reincarnation of Jack London's protagonist Buck from *The Call of the Wild*. Part Siberian Samoyed (a woolly-haired, spitz-like reindeer-herding breed), she herself was a celebrity: her painted portrait graced a menu cover of Alaska's first cruise line. Mageik accompanied Hubbard on stateside lecture tours, and he had her preserved as a taxidermy mount, as he had Wolfe, a three-quarters timber wolf with "huge paws for strong going on rough ice or snow." Hubbard also honored his northern dogs with a collection of *Saturday Evening Post* articles anthologized as *Mush, You Malemutes!* (1932). Department of Archives & Special Collections, Santa Clara University.

p. 170: "A Rebellious Captive," a white reindeer roped on the tundra near Nome by an Inupiaq herder. Notice the 1920s-style straw boater. Lomen Brothers, between 1900 and 1930. Alaska State Library.

p. 194: Eskimo fur trader in Nome, circa 1900 to 1916, by the Lomen Brothers. Library of Congress.

p. 202: An Inupiaq dance near Nome in 1900. The bucket probably held water for moistening the drumskins to avoid tearing the skins. Library of Congress.

p. 212: A kayaker wears a waterproof paddling jacket made from guts in this Lomen studio portrait from 1900. He holds a toy *umiak* he made for a son or, more likely, for the curio trade. Library of Congress.

p. 224: A King Islander drills a walrus tusk for a cribbage board in this Edward S. Curtis photo from 1929. Library of Congress.

p. 234: Berry-pickers in Nome, between 1900 and 1930, by the Lomen Brothers. Unlike photos of hunting, it is rare to find historical images of Eskimo women gathering plants. This reflects a male-observer bias similar to that of earlier ethnographic studies, not the activity's actual importance in the yearly subsistence cycle. Library of Congress.

p. 242: During World War II, the old and the young served together in Marvin "Muktuk" Marston's brainchild, the Alaska Territorial Guard, though the unit never saw combat. Here, riflemen march behind a much younger standard bearer. After the war, in an attempt to jumpstart a small-scale jewelry industry similar to ivory carving, several Inupiat traveled to Mexico to learn jade-working and silversmithing at Taxco. The experiment failed; jade recovery and processing created very few jobs in Northwest Alaska. Vern Brickley Collection, Anchorage Museum, B1998.014.1.2648.

p. 254: *Norge* on Spitsbergen, at the mooring mast. Her old name, *N1*, can be seen. National Library of Norway.

p. 268: The Serum-Run racer Leonard Seppala poses with sled dogs from his kennel in this Lomen Brothers photo from 1924 or 1925. From left to right: Togo, Karinsky, Jafet (what a jokester, Seppala), Pete, unknown, and Fritz. Seppala was the first American to breed and popularize Siberian huskies superior in strength to the Kotzebue area's native malemutes—rangy half-breeds. Nomeites at first had maligned the much smaller dogs as "Fuzzy-wuzzy Lap Dogs" and "Siberian rats." But they could trot eleven hours straight with a speed of nine miles per hour—the average pace of longer-legged, unburdened, human marathon runners. Jafet Lindeberg had obtained the first litter of Siberian pups, intended as a gift to Amundsen for his drive to the North Pole. When Amundsen canceled the expedition, Seppala inherited the dogs, caught the bug, and went on to win the All Alaska Sweepstakes—three years in a row, before World War I terminated those races—and silver in the 1932 Winter Olympic Games at Lake Placid. Willem Dafoe, who played Seppala in the Disney movie *Togo*, and John Wayne, after filming *The Spoilers*, both claimed to have lived in Nome—an indication of the town's cachet. Carrie M. McLain Memorial Museum, Nome.

p. 276: Miner with minimal equipment panning for gold near Nome in 1916. Library of Congress.

p. 286: The German emigree "Captain" Frank Emil Kleinschmidt on a "Day of Blood" in 1909 that he described in *The Pacific Monthly* also as "Bringing Home the Esquimau Bacon." A tour operator for rich trophy hunters, Kleinschmidt roped a polar bear cub swimming with its mother and hauled it aboard his vessel during the 1911 Carnegie Museum Expedition (shown in 1911's *Eskimo Life*). The former World War I cinematographer who filmed from the trenches, from an airplane, and from a submarine staged a throwback polar bear archery hunt for *Primitive Love* (1927). His most successful production was the 1925 short *Santa Claus*, shot in Nome.

His parka in this photo sports the fancy "sunburst" ruff. Ron van Dopperen, Wikimedia Commons.

p. 296: "Eskimo Highkick" (6 feet, 5 inches), during the July 4, 1915, festivities. The highkick is one of the disciplines at the World Eskimo-Indian Olympics (WEIO) held since 1961. Photo by Butler, Mauro & Co., a Nome drugstore. Library of Congress.

p. 302: In this Lomen photo from 1900, an aerial tramway conveys passengers from steamers to shore while freight is being barged in below. Nome lacked a deepwater harbor and wharf and had to improvise disembarkments. That was true for the entire coast. When *Bear* lay moored outside the Port Clarence Reindeer Station in the fall of 1894, ready to deliver the first thirty-two Siberian animals, Saami herders "landed the deer by throwing them overboard and letting them swim on shore." Library of Congress.

ESKIMO HIGHKICK. NOME ALASKA
6 FT. 5 IN. JULY 4th 1915

Suggested Readings

Aim high, but try to check out at least a few of these:

Allan Alexander, Allan. *Gold, Men and Dogs.* G.P. Putnam's Sons, 1931.

Anderson, Wanni W. *The Dall Sheep Dinner Guest: Inupiaq Narratives of Northwest Alaska.* University of Alaska Press, 2023.

Andrews, Clarence L. *The Eskimo and His Reindeer in Alaska.* Caxton Printers, 1939.

Beach, Rex. *The Spoilers.* Harper & Brothers, 1905.

Bockstoce, John R. *Whales, Ice, and Men: The History of Whaling in the Western Arctic.* University of Washington Press, 1986.

Bown, Stephen R. *The Last Viking: The Life of Roald Amundsen.* Da Capo Press, 2013.

Burch, Ernest S., Jr. *Iñupiaq Ethnohistory: Selected Essays.* University of Alaska Press, 2013.

Carrighar, Sally. *Icebound Summer.* Knopf, 1956.

——. *Wild Voice of the North: The Chronicle of an Eskimo Dog.* Doubleday & Company, 1959.

——. *Moonlight at Midday.* Knopf, 1958.

Cherry, Jessica and Frank Soos, editors. *Wheels on Ice: Stories of Cycling in Alaska.* University of Nebraska Press, 2022.

Cole, Terrence, editor. *Nome: City of the Golden Beaches.* Alaska Geographic, 1984.

Cox, Lynne. *Swimming to Antarctica: Tales of a Long-Distance Swimmer.* Mariner Books, 2005.

Demuth, Batsheba. *Floating Coast: An Environmental History of the Bering Strait.* W. W. Norton & Company, 2020.

Dolitsky, Aleksander B. *Pipeline to Russia: The Alaska Siberia Air Route in World War 2.* National Park Service, 2016.

Egan, Timothy. *Short Nights of the Shadow Catcher: The Epic Life and Immortal Photographs of Edward Curtis.* Mariner Books, 2013.

Fienup-Riordan, Ann. *Freeze Frame: Alaska's Eskimos in the Movies.* University of Washington Press, 1995.

Fitzhugh, William W. and Aron Crowell, editors. *Crossroads of Continents: Cultures of Siberia and Alaska.* Smithsonian Institution Scholarly Press, 1988.

Ford, Corey. *Where the Sea Breaks Its Back: The Epic Story of the Early Naturalist Georg Steller and the Russian Exploration of Alaska.* Alaska Northwest Books, 2003.

Graybill, Coleen and John. *Edward S. Curtis: Unpublished Alaska.* Vedere Press, 2021.

Guise, Holly Miowak. *Alaska Native Resilience: Voices from World War II.* University of Washington Press, 2024.

Guthrie, Dale. *Dry Creek: Archaeology and Paleoecology of a Late Pleistocene Alaskan Hunting Camp.* Texas A&M University Press, 2017.

Harrison, Edward Sanford. *Nome and Seward Peninsula: History, Description, Biographies and Stories.* The Metropolitan Press, 1905.

Hensley, William L. Iggiagruk. *Fifty Miles from Tomorrow: A Memoir of Alaska and the Real People.* Picador 2010.

Hunt, William R. *North of 53°: The Wild Days of the Alaska-Yukon Mining Frontier 1870-1914.* University of Alaska Press, 2009.

Issenman-Kobayashi, Betty. *Sinews of Survival: The Living Legacy of Inuit Clothing.* UBC Press, 1998.

Jones, Anore. *The Plants We Eat: Nauriat Nigiñaqtaut—From the Traditional Wisdom of the Iñupiat Elders of Northwest Alaska.* University of Alaska Press, 2010.

Jones, Suzi. *Eskimo Drawings.* Anchorage Museum of History and Art, 2008.

Levy, Buddy. *Empire of Ice and Stone: The Disastrous and Heroic Voyage of the Karluk.* St. Martin's Press, 2022.

Lister, Adrian and Paul Bahn. *Mammoths: Giants of the Ice Age.* University of California Press, 2009.

Lomen, Carl J. *Fifty Years in Alaska.* McKay Company, 1954.

Lopp-Smith, Kathleen and Verbeck Smith, editors. *Ice Window: Letters From a Bering Strait Village, 1892–1902.* University of Alaska Press, 2002.

Marston, Muktuk. *Men of the Tundra: Alaska Eskimos at War.* October House, 1969.

Matthiessen, Peter. *Oomingmak: The Expedition to the Musk Ox Island in the Bering Sea.* Hastings House, 1967.

McCartney, Allen, editor. *Indigenous Ways to the Present: Native Whaling in the Western Arctic.* University of Alberta Press, 2003.

Nelson, Edward William. *The Eskimo about Bering Strait.* Government Printing Office, 1900.

Niven, Jennifer. *Ada Blackjack: A True Story of Survival in the Arctic.* Hachette Books, 2004.

O'Neill, Dan. *The Firecracker Boys: H-Bombs, Inupiat Eskimos, and the Roots of the Environmental Movement.* Basic Books, 2007.

——. *The Last Giant of Beringia: The Mystery of the Bering Land Bridge.* Basic Books, 2005.

Oquilluk, William A. *People of Kauwerak: Legends of the Northern Eskimo.* Alaska Pacific University Press, 1981.

Paulsen, Gary. *Winterdance: The Fine Madness of Running the Iditarod.* Harvest Books, 1995.

Pinson, Elizabeth. *Alaska's Daughter: An Eskimo Memoir of the Early Twentieth Century.* Utah State University Press, 2004.

Ray, Dorothy Jean. *Artists of the Tundra and the Sea.* University of Washington Press, 1961.

——. *The Eskimos of the Bering Strait, 1650–1898.* University of Washington Press, 1975.

——. *Freeze Frame: Alaska Eskimos in the Movies.* University of Washington Press, 1995.

Salisbury, Gay and Laney. *The Cruelest Miles: The Heroic Story of Dogs and Men in a Race Against an Epidemic.* W. W. Norton & Company, 2005.

Schaaf, Jeanne and Thetus Smith, editors. *Ublasaun, First Light: Inupiaq Hunters and Herders in the Early Twentieth Century, Northern Seward Peninsula, Alaska.* National Park Service, 2004.

Senungetuk, Joseph E. *Give or Take a Century: An Eskimo Chronicle.* Indian Historian Press, 1971.

Smith, Blake W. *Warplanes to Alaska.* Hancock House, 1998.

Smith-Josephy, Susan. *Lillian Alling: The Journey Home.* Caitlin Press, 2011.

Vorren, Ornulv. *Saami, Reindeer and Gold in Alaska: The Emigration of Saami from Norway to Alaska.* Waveland Press, 1994.

Wilder, Edna. *Secrets of Eskimo Skin Sewing.* Alaska Northwest Books, 1976.

Acknowledgments

I have at last arrived at the end of this long journey and would like to thank the following people for helping this book become what it is: Shoshi Bieler, John Graybill, Amy Guy, Thomas Guy, Diana Haecker, Kirk Hallman, David Holthouse, David James, Lawrence Kaplan, Igor Krupnik, David Lauterborn, Angela Linn, Doreen Martens, Lawrence Millman, Kenneth Pratt, Jeff Rasic, Stuart Rosebrook, Ned Rozell, Angela Schmidt, Susan Sommer, Alex Strickland, Cheryl Thompson, Carl Vonwodtke, Julie Raymond-Yakoubian, and David Reamer. But foremost: Melissa Guy, who always gets sucked into the vortex of my endeavors, against better knowledge.

Articles for the following publications formed the core of some of these chapters: *Adventure Cyclist*, *Adventure Journal*, *Alaska*, *Aviation History*, *First Alaskans*, *Forum Magazine*, *True West*, *Wild West*.

Trained as an anthropologist with a degree from the University of Alaska Fairbanks, Michael Engelhard worked for twenty-five years as a wilderness guide and as an outdoor instructor in youth programs. The editor of four anthologies and author of *Ice Bear*, a cultural history of the polar bear, he has won three Alaska Press Club Awards, a Rasmuson Individual Artist Award, and a Foreword INDIES gold medal in the Adventure and Recreation category. His recent books include the National Outdoor Book Award-winning memoir *Arctic Traverse* as well as the essay collections *No Walk in the Park* and *What the River Knows*. His writing has also appeared in publications like *Outside*, *Sierra*, *Backpacker*, *National Parks*, *Audubon*, *Utne Reader*, and *Times Literary Supplement*, with more than a hundred articles in *Alaska* magazine.

www.ingramcontent.com/pod-product-compliance
Lightning Source LLC
Chambersburg PA
CBHW060759120626
46557CB00001B/33